MAC
McGRAW-HILL

Science

Lucy H. Daniel
Jay Hackett
Richard H. Moyer
JoAnne Vasquez

About the Cover

Chameleons are known as the masters of camouflage. They have the ability to change their skin color and patterns. Chameleons are slow-moving animals so they rely on protective coloration for defense. For protection, a chameleon might show bright colors, which often means "bad-tasting" or "poison" to predators. If this doesn't work, they may shift to a dull color and play dead.

INQUIRY **What else would you like to know about chameleons? Write your own question or questions to answer.**

Macmillan McGraw-Hill

Program Authors

Dr. Lucy H. Daniel
Teacher, Consultant
Rutherford County Schools, North Carolina

Dr. Jay Hackett
Professor Emeritus of Earth Sciences
University of Northern Colorado

Dr. Richard H. Moyer
Professor of Science Education
University of Michigan-Dearborn

Dr. JoAnne Vasquez
Elementary Science Education Consultant
Mesa Public Schools, Arizona
NSTA Past President

Contributing Authors

Lucille Villegas Barrera, M.E.d.
Elementary Science Supervisor
Houston Independent School District
Houston, Texas

Mulugheta Teferi, M.A.
St. Louis Public Schools
St. Louis, Missouri

Dinah Zike, M.Ed.
Dinah Might Adventures LP
San Antonio, Texas

The features in this textbook entitled "Amazing Stories," as well as the unit openers, were developed in collaboration with the National Geographic Society's School Publishing Division.

The McGraw-Hill Companies

Macmillan McGraw-Hill

Published by Macmillan/McGraw-Hill, of McGraw-Hill Education, a division of The McGraw-Hill Companies, Inc., Two Penn Plaza, New York, New York 10121.

Printed in the United States of America

ISBN 0-02-282605-X

11 QVR/LEH 11

Teacher Reviewers

Michelle Dunning
Birmingham, Alabama

Donna Bullock
Chandler, Arizona

Debra Allen
Davie, Florida

Lora Meade
Plantation, Florida

Roxanne Laird
Miami, Florida

Karen Gaudy
Satellite Beach, Florida

Stephanie Sirianni
Margate, Florida

Heidi Stephens
South Daytona, Florida

Rosanne Phillips
Miami, Florida

Brenda Crow
Miami, Florida

Kari Pingel
Pella, Iowa

Christie Jones
Springfield, Illinois

Diane Songer
Wabash, Indiana

Lee Arwood
Wabash, Indiana

Margarite Hart
Indianapolis, Indiana

Charlotte Bennett
Newburgh, Indiana

Donna Halverson
Evansville, Indiana

Stephanie Tanke
Crown Point, Indiana

Mindey LeMoine
Marquette, Michigan

Billie Bell
Grand View, Missouri

Charlotte Sharp
Greenville, North Carolina

Pat Shane
Chapel Hill, North Carolina

Karen Daniel
Chapel Hill, North Carolina

Linda Dow
Concord, North Carolina

Life Science | Earth Science | Physical Science

Life Science Consultants

Dr. Carol Baskin
University of Kentucky
Lexington, KY

Dr. Joe W. Crim
University of Georgia
Athens, GA

Dr. Pradeep M. Dass
Appalachian State University
Boone, NC

Dr. Marie DiBerardino
Allegheny University of Health Sciences
Philadelphia, PA

Dr. R. E. Duhrkopf
Baylor University
Waco, TX

Dr. Dennis L. Nelson
Montana State University
Bozeman, MT

Dr. Fred Sack
Ohio State University
Columbus, OH

Dr. Martin VanDyke
Denver, CO

Dr. E. Peter Volpe
Mercer University
Macon, GA

Earth Science Consultants

Dr. Clarke Alexander
Skidaway Institute of Oceanography
Savannah, GA

Dr. Suellen Cabe
Pembroke State University
Pembroke, NC

Dr. Thomas A. Davies
Texas A & M University
College Station, TX

Dr. Ed Geary
Geological Society of America
Boulder, CO

Dr. David C. Kopaska-Merkel
Geological Survey of Alabama
Tuscaloosa, AL

Physical Science Consultants

Dr. Bonnie Buratti
Jet Propulsion Lab
Pasadena, CA

Dr. Shawn Carlson
Society of Amateur Scientists
San Diego, CA

Dr. Karen Kwitter
Williams College
Williamstown, MA

Dr. Steven Souza
Williamstown, MA

Dr. Joseph P. Straley
University of Kentucky
Lexington, KY

Dr. Thomas Troland
University of Kentucky
Lexington, KY

Dr. Josephine Davis Wallace
University of North Carolina
Charlotte, NC

Consultant for Primary Grades

Donna Harrell Lubcker
East Texas Baptist University
Marshall, TX

Teacher Reviewers (continued)

Beth Lewis
Wilmington, North Carolina

Cindy Hatchell
Wilmington, North Carolina

Cindy Kahler
Carrboro, North Carolina

Diane Leusky
Chapel Hill, North Carolina

Heather Sutton
Wilmington, North Carolina

Crystal Stephens
Valdese, North Carolina

Meg Millard
Chapel Hill, North Carolina

Patricia Underwood
Randleman, North Carolina

E. Joy Mermin
Chapel Hill, North Carolina

Yolanda Evans
Wilmington, North Carolina

Tim Gilbride
Pennsauken, New Jersey

Helene Reifowitz
Nesconset, New York

Tina Craig
Tulsa, Oklahoma

Deborah Harwell
Lawton, Oklahoma

Kathleen Conn
West Chester, Pennsylvania

Heath Renninger Zerbe
Tremont, Pennsylvania

Patricia Armillei
Holland, Pennsylvania

Sue Workman
Cedar City, Utah

Peg Jensen
Hartford, Wisconsin

UNIT A

Life Science

Characteristics of Living Things PAGE A1

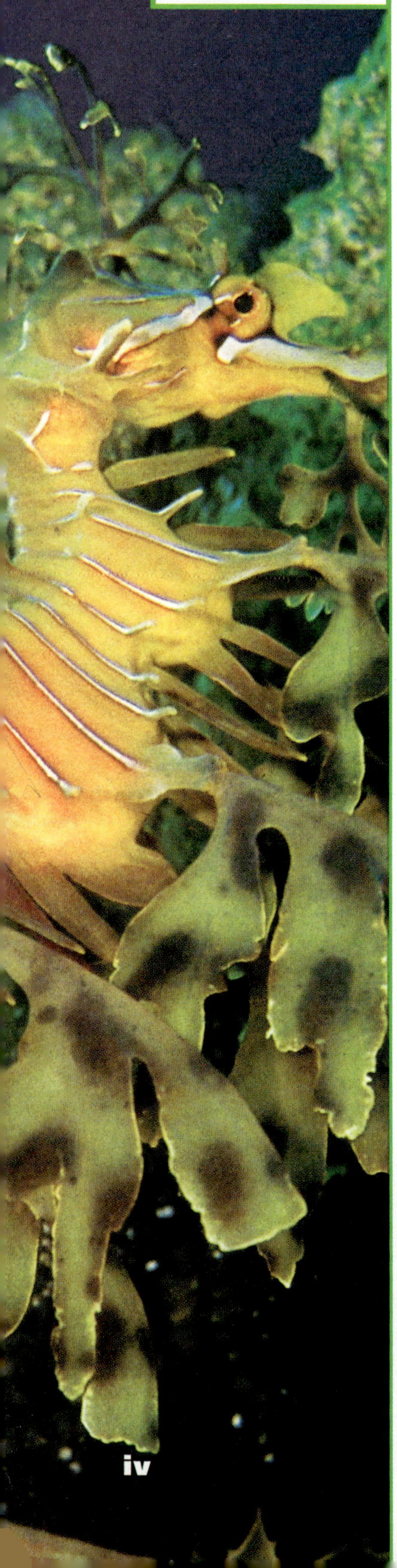

For Your Reference

Science Handbook

Health Handbook

Activities

Unit A

Explore Activities

Quick Labs with FOLDABLES™

Inquiry Skill Builders

UNIT A

Characteristics of Living Things

LOOK!

Is it a plant? Is it an animal? The leafy sea dragon is actually a fish that looks like seaweed! How do you think this helps it to survive?

Characteristics of Living Things

CHAPTER

1

Classifying Living Things

Did You Ever Wonder?

How many living things do you see in this picture? There are some living things, smaller than the smallest flea, you won't be able to see. But we know they are there. People have estimated that today there are more than 10 million different kinds of living things on Earth. We have only identified 1.5 million of them.

INQUIRY SKILL **Define based on observations** What makes something a living thing? Think about how you recognized the living things in this picture.

LESSON 1

The Basic Unit of Life

Vocabulary

organism, A6
cell, A6
chlorophyll, A6
tissue, A9
organ, A9
organ system, A9

Get Ready

Next time you go outside, look at all the things around you. You will see that living things are everywhere. Shrubs, trees, mushrooms, butterflies, and cats are all living things. Even though they seem different, they have many things in common. What are some characteristics all living things share?

Inquiry Skill

You define based on observation when you put together a description that is based on observations and experience.

Explore Activity

What Is the Basic Unit of Life?

Procedure

1. Your group will need to get a plant and a prepared slide of human blood from your teacher.
2. Make a wet-mount slide of your plant by placing a leaf in a drop of water in the center of the slide and carefully putting a coverslip on top.
3. **Observe** View the slide under low power. Then observe the prepared slide of human blood.
4. **Communicate** Draw what you see.

Drawing Conclusions

1. **Communicate** What common traits did you observe using the microscope?
2. **Communicate** What do the organisms the cells come from have in common?
3. **Define** From what you observed, come up with your own definition of a living thing.
4. **FURTHER INQUIRY** **Hypothesize** Examine the drawings you made and think about the organisms that they come from. Do you see any differences? Why do you think cells vary from one organism to another?

Materials

- *Elodea*, moss, fern, or any flowering plant
- prepared slide of human blood
- microscope
- microscope slide
- coverslip
- dropper
- water

Read to Learn

Main Idea **All living things are made of cells, the basic unit of life.**

What Is the Basic Unit of Life?

Do you know what all living things have in common? From the smallest **organism**, or living thing, to the largest, we are all made of cells. A **cell** is the smallest unit of an organism that is capable of life.

Since the cell is the smallest unit of living matter, the processes of life must be carried out by the cells. To do this, cells have structures that work together to maintain the life of the cell. Some of these structures make food, some release energy for the cell to use, and some transport materials.

The cells of different organisms are different. For example, plant cells are different from animal cells. Plants have needs that animals don't have and cell parts that meet these needs.

You don't need a microscope to discover that plants are green. That's because their cells contain a green chemical called **chlorophyll** (KLAWR·uh·fil). It allows plants to use the Sun's energy to make their

Plant Cell

Plant cells have rigid walls and contain chlorophyll.

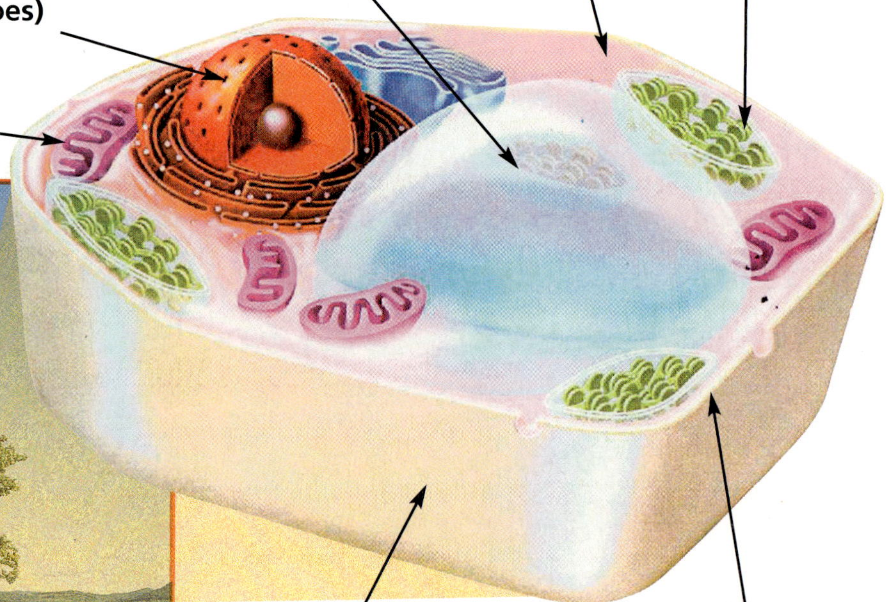

own food. This chemical is found in chloroplasts (KLAWR·uh·plasts).

Plant cells also have a cell wall. Let's look at a tree to find out why plants need cell walls. A tree rises up from the ground. Its rigid trunk supports all its weight. The tree must be made of rigid building blocks—rigid cells that support it. The cell walls of the plant cells keep the tree from collapsing.

Animal cells don't have chloroplasts or a cell wall. However, plant and animal cells share many characteristics because they have many of the same needs. For example, plant and animal cells have a nucleus, cytoplasm, mitochondria, and a cell membrane.

The nucleus of plant and animal cells directs everything the cells do. The cytoplasm is a fluid where all parts of the cell float. The mitochondria release energy the cell needs. Plant vacuoles are used for storing food, water and wastes. The cell membrane holds the cell together.

READING **Draw Conclusions**
What is one of the things plant and animal cells have in common?

Animal Cell

Animal cells do not have a cell wall or chlorophyll.

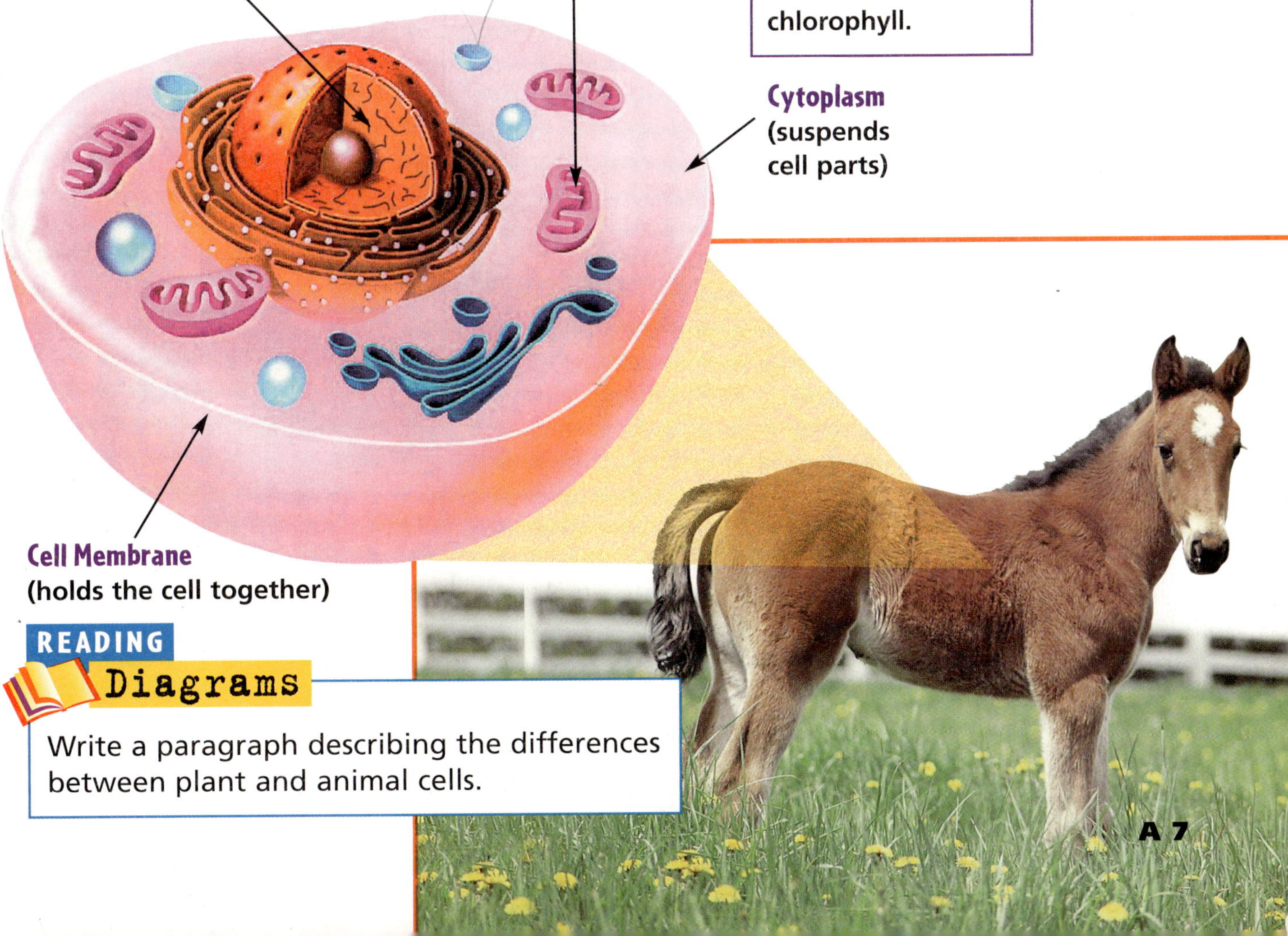

READING **Diagrams**

Write a paragraph describing the differences between plant and animal cells.

What Are Living Things Made Of?

Some organisms, such as bacteria and some fungi, are made of just one cell. Other organisms, such as some algae, are made of many similar cells that benefit from cooperating. They do this by forming colonies of hundreds of cells that move and find food together.

Many-celled living things, such as complex plants and animals, are made of different kinds of cells. The cells of a many-celled organism work together to keep the organism alive. Different kinds of cells do different kinds of jobs. Each cell contributes to the health and survival of the organism in a different way.

For example, in a tree, cells in leaves make the plant's food. Cells in roots, trunk, stems, and branches form tubes through which the food or water is moved, or transported (trans·PAWRT·uhd). Other cells form flowers, fruits, and seeds that allow the tree to reproduce.

Similarly, the cells of animals, including humans, have different functions. Skin cells are flat and wide to protect the cells beneath them, muscle cells are long threadlike cells that allow body movement, nerve cells are long because they transport messages from one part of the body to another.

Similar cells that have the same job or function come together to make a **tissue** (TISH·ew). The "strings" in celery stalks are examples of plant tissues. These tissues carry water and

READING Charts

Give an example of each level organization in many-celled organisms.

Levels of Organization

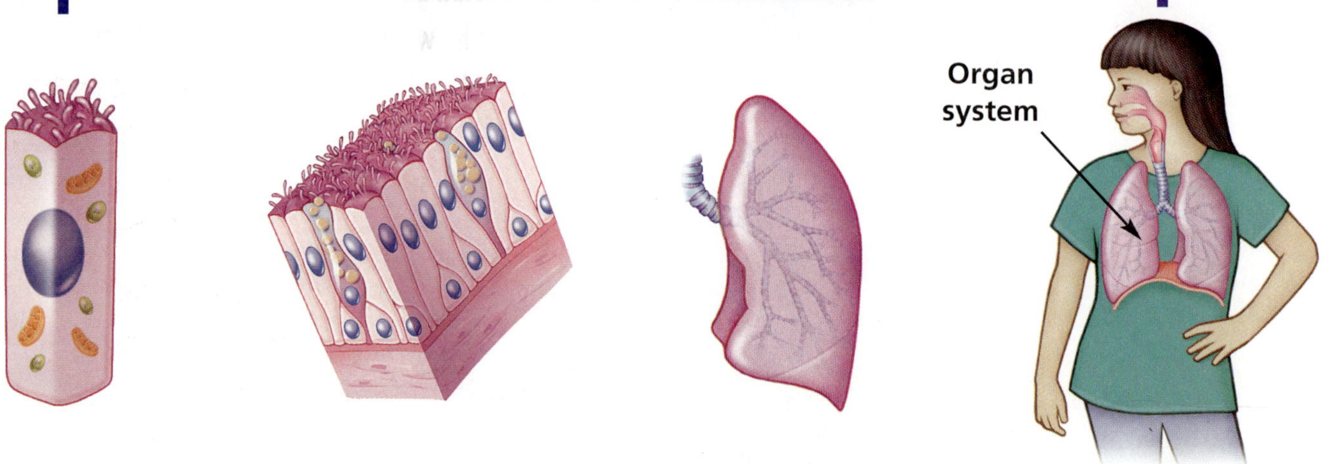

Cell

Tissue

Organ

Organism

minerals from the roots to the leaves of the plant. Another example of a plant tissue is the flesh of fruits. This tissue's function is to protect the plant's seeds.

Examples of animal tissue are the muscles that allow you to move your arms or to walk. The muscles in your body are tissue made of muscle cells. Different kinds of tissue in an animal's body include muscle, bone, skin, nerve, and blood.

Tissues of different kinds come together to make an **organ**. Stems and fruits are examples of plant organs. The heart, the lungs, and the brain are examples of animal organs.

Finally, a group of organs that work together to do a certain job makes up an **organ system**. For example, a fox's digestive system includes its mouth, stomach, and intestines. The roots of a plant are the main organ in the root system of a plant. The stems and leaves are organs of the shoot system.

Organs systems work together so that life processes like breathing and digestion can be carried out. These are the processes that keep many-celled organisms, like you, healthy and alive.

What are the levels of organization of many-celled organisms?

QUICK LAB

Plant Parts

FOLDABLES™ Make a Shutter Fold. (See p. R 42.) Label the tabs as shown.

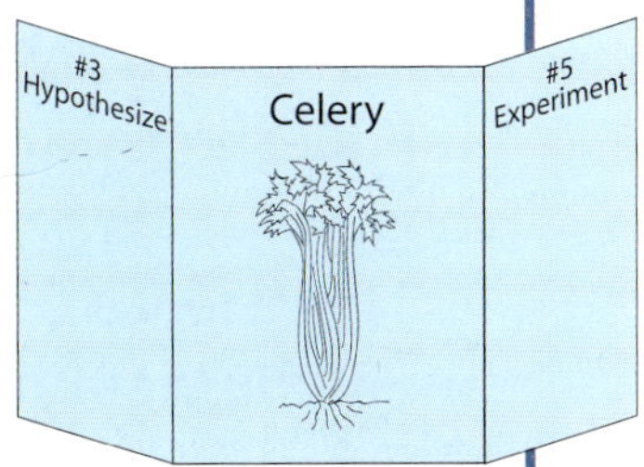

1. **Observe** Use a hand lens to observe the parts of a celery plant.
2. Draw what you see in your Shutter Fold.
3. **Hypothesize** Make a guess about the function of the stem of the celery plant. Write your hypothesis in the left shutter of your Shutter Fold.
4. Label the plant organs you see on your drawing. What levels of organization does your drawing show? Record your answer below your diagram in your Shutter Fold.
5. **Experiment** Add water to a bottle so the water is about 1 inch deep. Add a few drops of food coloring to the water. Cut a piece of stalk and place it in the colored water. Observe it after a few minutes. Record what you see on the right shutter of your Shutter Fold.
6. **Communicate** Explain to the class why your observation supports or doesn't support your guess.

What Traits Are Used to Classify Organisms?

People have always tried to make sense of their surroundings. One way to do this is to look for patterns. For example, if we find patterns among plants we can answer some very important questions, such as: What plants are good to eat? What plants are poisonous?

The science of finding patterns among living things is called *classification* (klas·uh·fi·KAY·shuhn). Cells are used in classification because cells from different organisms are different. Whether an animal grows hair or feathers depends on the kinds of cells it has.

Ancient scientists came up with very simple classification systems. These were based on characteristics that anyone could see. In 350 B.C. the Greek scientist Aristotle classified plants into three large groups—herbs (little plants), shrubs (bigger plants), and trees (the biggest plants).

This made sense at the time. However, as scientists learned more about plants, they realized that size was not the best way to classify them. For example, today we know that a tiny blade of grass is more like a stalk of corn than a dandelion that grows close to the ground.

When it comes to classifying organisms, cells, tissues, organs, and systems all have to be compared carefully. For example, bats and birds have wings and fly. However, if you were to take a close look at the wing of a bat, you would find that it is more like the front leg of a cat than like the wing of an eagle.

So bats and cats are in fact more alike than bats and eagles.

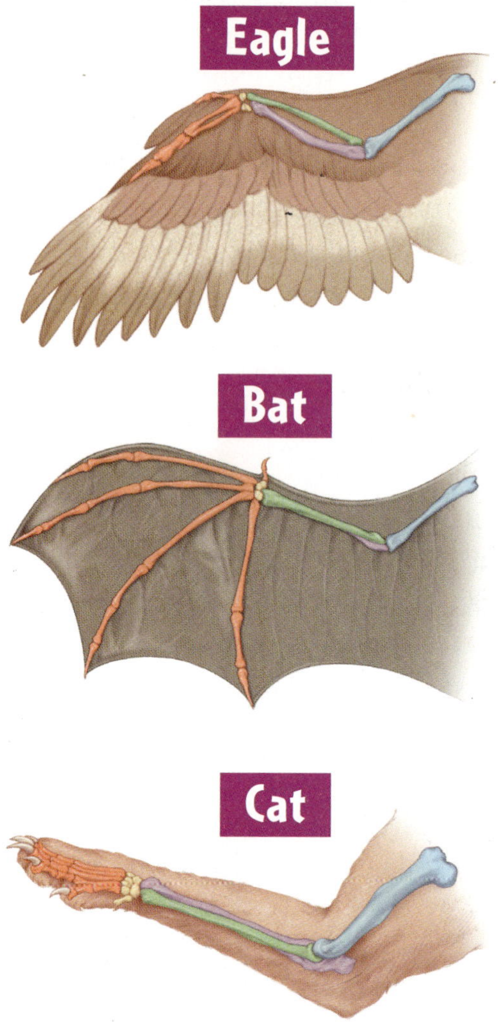

The bones in the diagram above have been color-coded to show similar bones in each animal.

READING Diagrams

How are the bat's wing and the cat's front leg alike?

What parts should be analyzed when classifying an organism?

Lesson Review

Why It Matters

All living things are made of cells. The cell is the basic unit of life because it can carry out all life processes. Some organisms are made of one cell and some are many-celled. Many-celled organisms are organized internally from cells to tissues to organs to organ systems.

Similarities among organisms are found in cells, tissues, organs, and organ systems. All these levels of organization are used to classify organisms.

e-Journal Visit our Web site **www.science.mmhschool.com** to do a research project on the levels of organization of a many-celled organism of your choice.

Think and Write

1. What do all living things have in common?
2. What does the cell wall in plant cells do for plants?
3. What are some examples of animal tissue?
4. What are the two main organ systems in plants?
5. **Critical Thinking** How can cell classification be useful in identifying organisms?

L·I·N·K·S

WRITING LINK

Writing That Compares How are plant and animal cells similar? How are they different? Use a Venn diagram to organize your ideas. Write an essay to present your findings.

MATH LINK

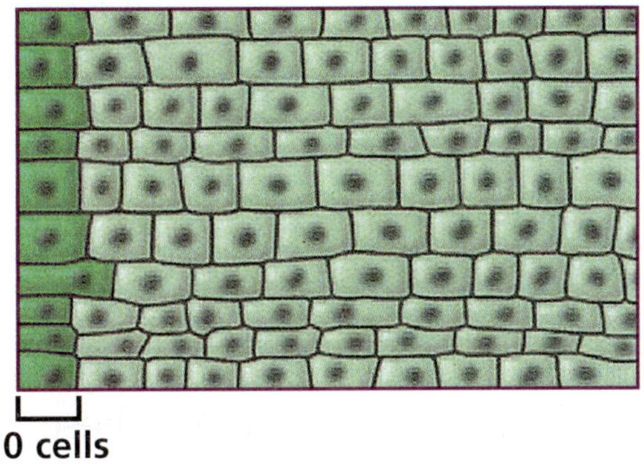

Solve this problem. Use a benchmark number to estimate the number of cells in the slide.

ART LINK

Make a poster. Choose a plant and an animal. Make a poster using drawings and/or photographs to show the levels of organization in the plant and the animal you selected. Research the structure of these organisms so you can complete your poster accurately.

TECHNOLOGY LINK

LOG ON Visit **www.science.mmhschool.com** for more links.

LESSON 2

The Kingdoms of Life

Vocabulary

vascular, A15
nonvascular, A15
invertebrate, A16
vertebrate, A16
fungus, A17
protist, A18
bacteria, A19

Get Ready

There may be millions of living things in the world that we know nothing about. If you discovered a living thing, what would you name it? How could you tell people about it? How would you keep track of all living things? In this lesson, you'll learn what questions scientists ask to group or classify organisms.

Inquiry Skill

You make a model when you make something to represent an object or event.

Explore Activity

What Traits Are Used to Classify Plants?

Materials

- lettuce leaf
- liverwort plant
- stalk of celery
- hand lens

Procedure

1. **Observe** Use the hand lens to observe the lettuce leaf and the liverwort.
2. **Communicate** As you observe each plant, draw and describe the plant.
3. **Observe** Break the piece of celery. Pull apart the two pieces. Remove a 1-cm piece of the string from the celery. Observe the string with the hand lens.
4. **Communicate** Draw and describe the string from the celery.

Drawing Conclusions

1. **Communicate** How are the lettuce, liverwort, and celery similar?
2. **Communicate** How are the plants different?
3. **Infer** What is the purpose of the tubelike parts in the lettuce and the celery?
4. **Infer** How can liverworts live and grow without tubelike parts?
5. FURTHER INQUIRY **Make a Model** Design a model to show how both kinds of plants get water and minerals from the soil.

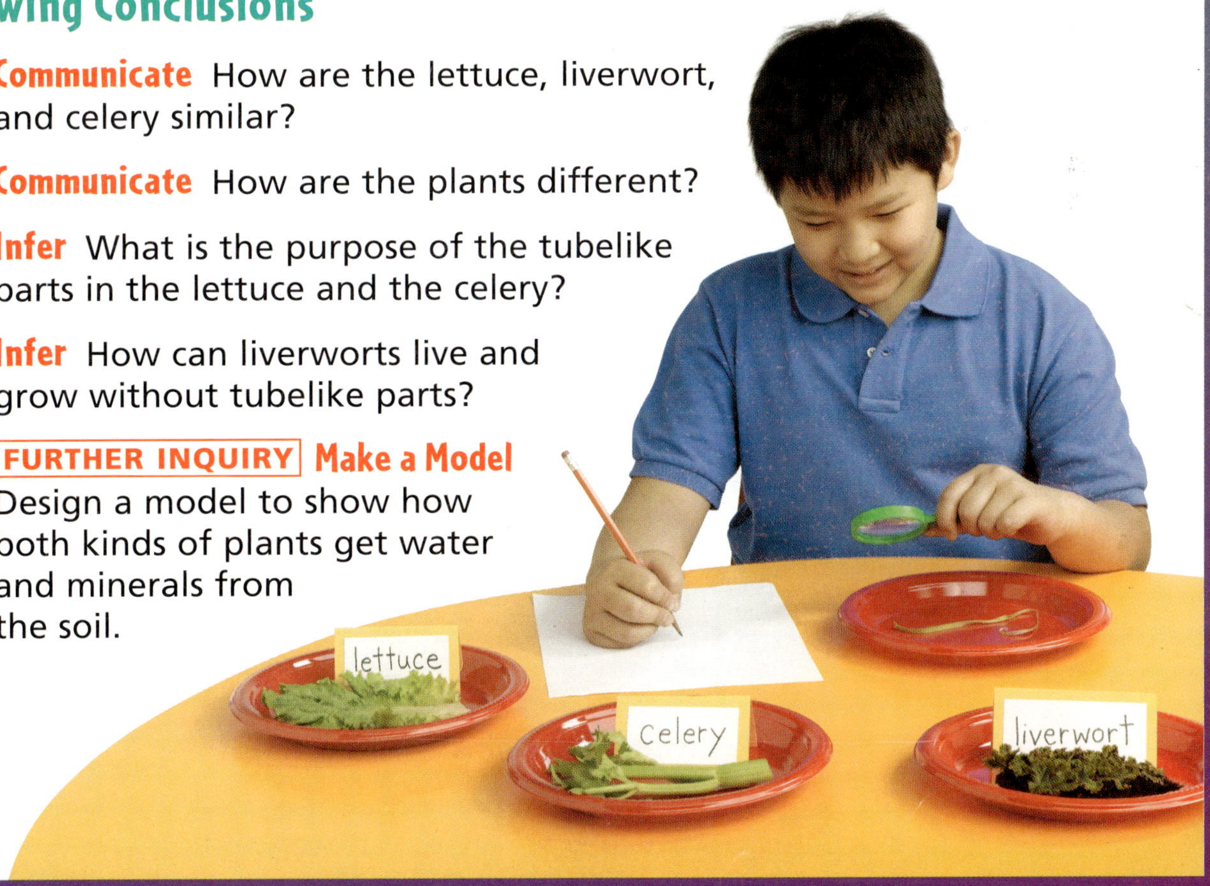

Read to Learn

Main Idea Living things are classified into kingdoms.

What Traits Are Used to Classify Plants?

As you've discovered, all plants have certain characteristics in common. Every living thing that has these characteristics belongs to the plant kingdom. A kingdom is the largest subdivision of living things.

While all plants have certain characteristics in common, they have their differences, too.

Vascular and Nonvascular Plants

By getting a look at what goes on inside plants—not what they look like on the outside—scientists have been able to divide them into two large groups.

If you look closely at a moss you'll see lots of cells packed together like pieces in a jigsaw puzzle. The cells look very much like one another. Water from the outside is passing directly into the cells.

Now, if you do the same thing with the stem of a corn plant you'll see something very different. Lengths of tubelike cells tunnel up and down the

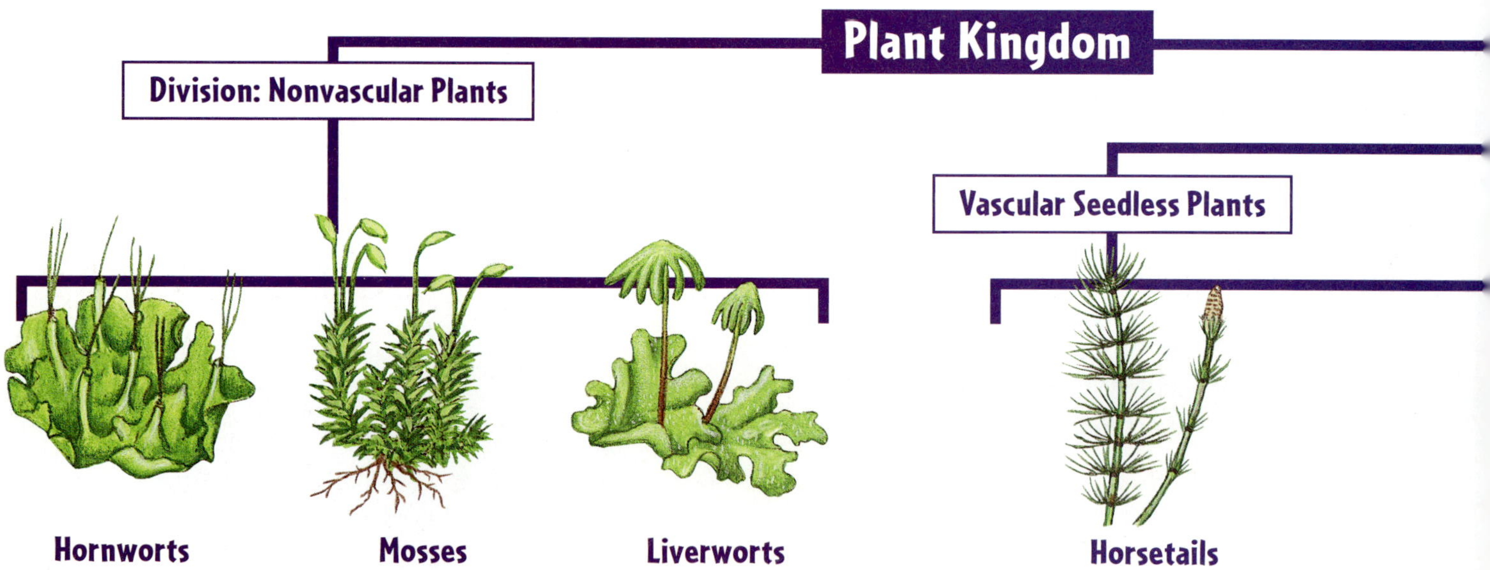

READING Charts

1. Name two plants you are familiar with and the division you think each belongs to.
2. Look at the two plant divisions in the chart. List two ways they are alike. List two ways they are different.

stem. Water taken in by the plant's roots is moving up one set of tubes toward the plant's leaves, flowers, and other parts. At the same time, foods made in the leaves are moving down the other set of tubes, which lead to all the plant's parts. These tubes are called *vascular tissue.*

Scientists call plants that have this kind of tissue—such as trees and flowering plants—**vascular** (VAS·kyuh·luhr) plants. Vascular means "composed of or containing vessels." Scientists call plants that don't have this kind of tissue—such as mosses and other simple plants—**nonvascular** plants. All plants fall into one of these two groups. Each of these groups is called a *division.*

Plants within each of these two divisions are far from identical. This observation prompted scientists to divide these groups even further. They divided vascular plants into seedless plants and plants with seeds. Then they divided seed plants into flowering and nonflowering plants.

The smallest groups have plants most like one another. The larger groups have plants least like one another. This means that the smaller the group, the more closely related its members are.

What are some examples of plants belonging to each division of the plant kingdom?

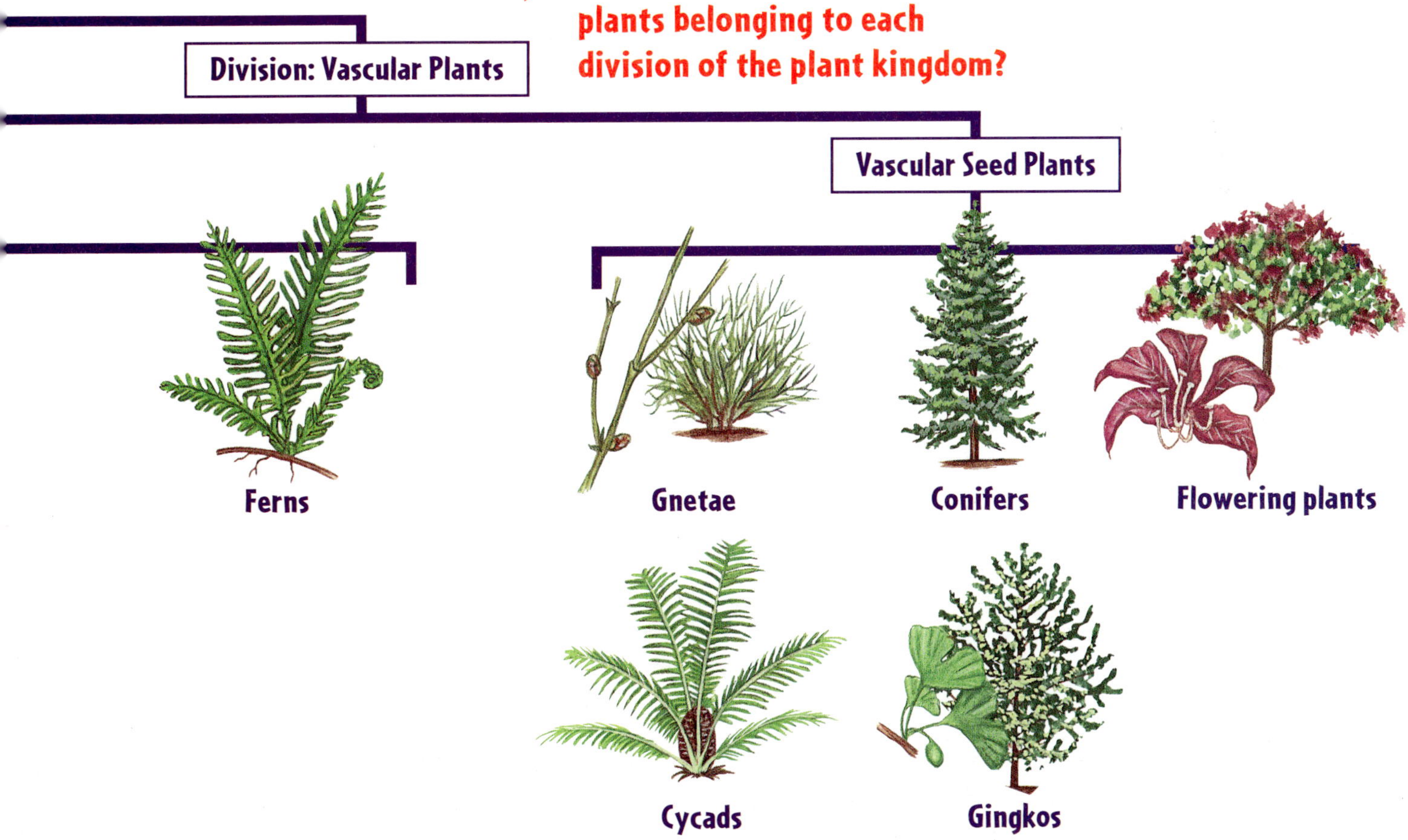

What Makes Animals Different from Plants?

Unlike plants, animals cannot make their own food. Animals also differ from plants because most animals can move from one place to another during some parts of their lives.

All animals are grouped into one kingdom, known as the animal kingdom. The animal kingdom is divided into two large groups. One group is made up of animals that have backbones. The members of this group are called **vertebrates**. The members of the other group do not have backbones. They are called **invertebrates**.

Invertebrates are divided into *phyla* (FIGH·luh) (singular, *phylum*). Some examples are shown on the left. The vertebrates are in the Phylum *Chordata*. Phyla are divided in smaller divisions called *classes*. Some classes of vertebrates are shown on the right.

How are animals different from plants?

Animal Kingdom

Phyla in the animal kingdom are like divisions in the plant kingdom. On the left are members of four phyla without backbones. On the right are five classes of the phylum with backbones. Not all the phyla are shown.

Phyla Without Backbone

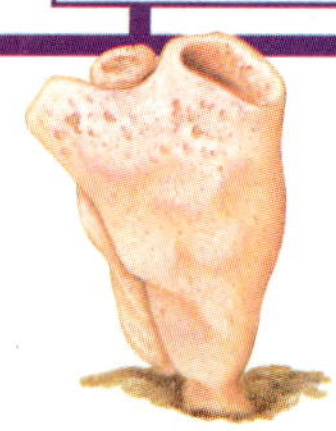

Porifera
Sponges

Platyhelminthes
Flatworms

Cnidaria
Sea Anemones

Arthropoda
Crustaceans

Classes of the Phylum *Chordata* with Backbone

Fish

Birds

Reptiles

Amphibians

Mammals

READING Charts

List the five phyla shown.

What Is a Fungus?

It may be one celled or many celled. It doesn't make its own food as plants do or eat food as animals do. Instead it simply absorbs (takes in) food from decaying dead organisms and wastes in its environment. What is it? It's a **fungus** (FUNG·guhs).

Fungi (FUN·jigh) is the plural of *fungus*. Fungi can be very useful living things. Some of them have great flavors. Others contain chemicals that fight diseases. Still others help bread to rise or turn cheeses sharp and tangy. Fungi in soil break down decaying plants and animals so that their chemicals can be used by living things. You might say that such fungi clean up our environment.

Unfortunately, the fungus kingdom also contains organisms that cause problems for people. Some fungi are poisonous. Some fungi give people itchy diseases, like athlete's foot. Some fungi can spoil food and make you sick. Some fungi coat bathroom tiles and basement walls with smelly black or white fuzz. In the autumn of 1997, one kind of fungus was even responsible for the closing of a library in Staten Island, a part of New York City. The fungus, which grows in damp places like the library's basement, caused people to cough and sneeze as if they had the flu.

The chart on this page shows the groups of the fungus kingdom.

How are members of the fungus kingdom different from plants?

Fungus Kingdom

Yeasts, morels, mildews

Molds

Mushrooms, smuts, rusts

READING Charts

1. Give examples of the three main groups of fungi.
2. Make a chart listing things useful fungi can do.

What Is a Protist?

What do you see when you look into a lake, pond, river, or ocean? Sometimes it looks like clear water. However, that "clear" water is home to millions of microscopic living things that belong to the **protist** (PROH·tist) kingdom. This kingdom isn't made up of just microscopic living things. It also includes living things you can see without a microscope, such as seaweed and green pond scum, called algae. Protists are very important because they provide food for many marine and freshwater animals. Although most protists live in water, some inhabit the land.

Some protists are single cells that swim in the water in search of smaller living things to eat. Others, like seaweeds, are made up of groups of the same cells that are linked together. Protists such as algae don't have to hunt for food. They contain chlorophyll. All they have to do is float on water in the sunlight, soak up the Sun's rays, and make their own food. Still other kinds of protists are one celled, swim around, and contain chlorophyll.

Members of the protist kingdom certainly seem very different. However, if scientists put them in the same kingdom, they must have something in common. You would discover that "something" if you peered at the cells of protists under a microscope. You'd notice a dense, dark structure, called a *nucleus* (NEW·klee·uhs) inside each cell. If you looked very carefully, you'd see that the nucleus was surrounded by a thin envelope. Scientists call this envelope a *membrane* (MEM·brayn). The chart shows some of the groups of the protist kingdom.

How are some protists like plants?

Protist Kingdom

Slime molds

Diatoms

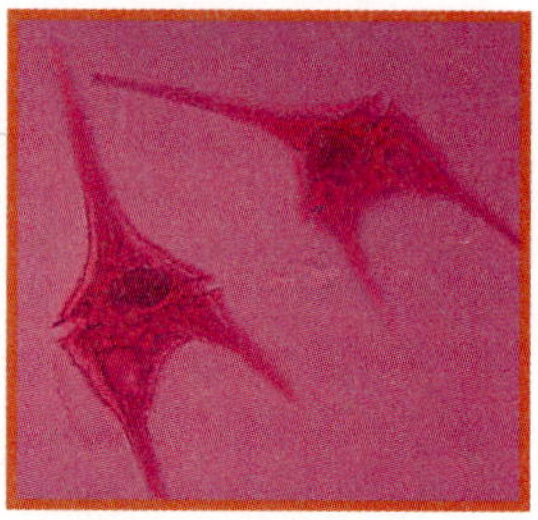
Dinoflagellates

Green algae

Euglenas

What Are Bacteria?

Bacteria (bak·TEER·ee·uh) are the tiniest living things. They are also very simple. Some can cause a great deal of trouble, like infections. Others are necessary for animals and plants to survive.

Some kinds of bacteria group together in clusters or chains. Other kinds don't. You can only see bacteria under a microscope. Each *bacterium* (bak·TEER·ee·uhm) is a single cell without a nucleus.

Bacteria were once classified in a single kingdom called Monera. However, many scientists today recognize two separate kingdoms; the "ancient" bacteria kingdom and the "true" bacteria kingdom. The "ancient" bacteria kingdom includes some fascinating organisms. One type lives in the digestive system of cows. It helps the cow by digesting cellulose, the main substance in grass, which the cow eats but can't digest. Still another kind of "ancient" bacterium lives deep in the ocean, where lava seeps through cracks in the ocean floor. The red-hot lava heats the water up to 105°C. That's hotter than the temperature of boiling water!

The "true" bacteria kingdom also contains some unusual members. Have you ever seen a blue-green lake? This color is due to the presence of *cyanobacteria* (sigh·uh·noh·bak·TEER·ee·uh). These bacteria release oxygen to the air.

Some true bacteria cause diseases in plants and animals. A "strep" throat is caused by a true bacterium. If your stomach aches after eating spoiled food, the culprit is likely to be another true bacterium. More serious diseases like tuberculosis and certain kinds of pneumonia are also caused by true bacteria.

How are bacteria different from plants and other organisms?

Bacteria Kingdoms

"Ancient" Bacteria

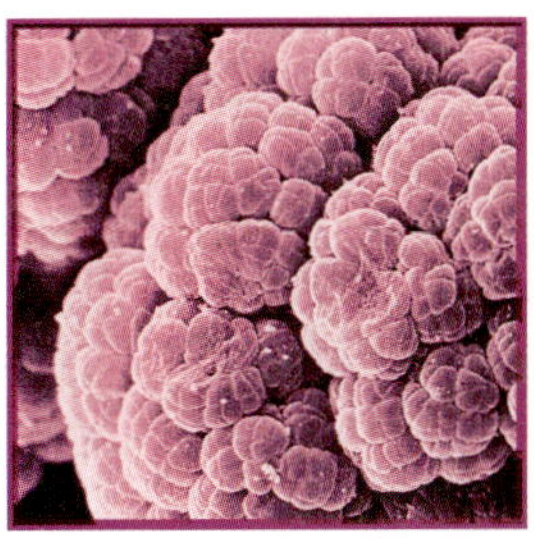

These bacteria are methanogens. They use carbon dioxide and produce methane (natural gas).

"True" Bacteria

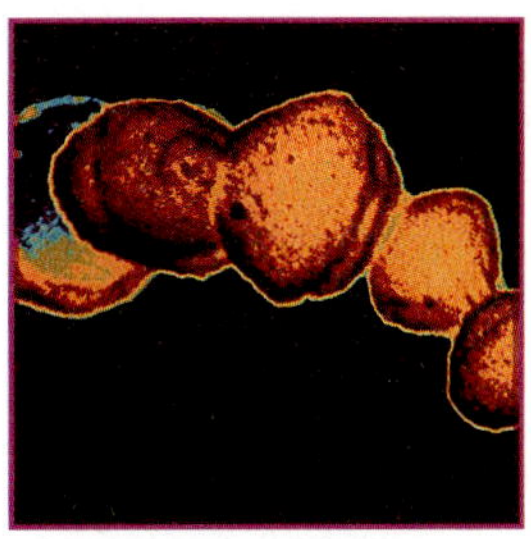

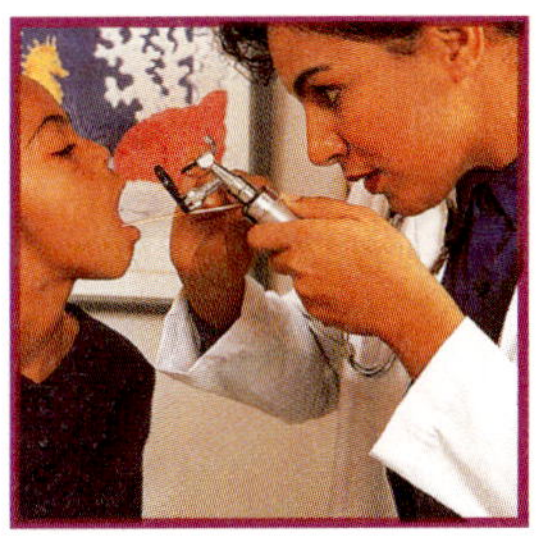

These bacteria are streptococci—the ones that can give you a strep throat.

Inquiry Skill BUILDER

SKILL **Classify**

Using a Key

How should a living thing be classified? Into what group should it be placed?

One way to classify organisms is by using a *classification key*. A classification key lists choices describing characteristics of organisms. It is a series of pairs of statements with directions to follow. These directions will eventually lead you to the identity of the organism you have chosen.

Key to Birds

1. Webbed feet........Go to 3.
No webbed feet...Go to 2.

2. Hooked bill......Red-tailed hawk
No hooked bill...Cardinal

3. Flat bill.....Mallard duck
No flat bill....Go to 4.

4. Pouch...
Brown pelican
No pouch...
Red-faced cormorant

Procedure

1 **Observe** Use the classification key, above right, to identify the birds shown. Starting with the first pair of statements, choose the one that applies to the bird you picked.

2 **Interpret Data** Follow the statement's direction. It will lead you to another pair of statements.

3 Keep following the directions until you come to the identity of the bird you chose.

Drawing Conclusions

Do you think this key would be helpful in identifying birds in your neighborhood? Explain.

Why It Matters

Nature holds many secrets and presents many mysteries. It is the job of scientists to discover the secrets and solve the mysteries. Classifying helps do this. Among other things, it shows which organisms are most closely related to one another. It can also show the order in which they appeared on Earth. Classification can be thought of as a kind of calendar of life on Earth.

e-Journal Visit our Web site **www.science.mmhschool.com** to do a research project on the history of classification.

Think and Write

1. What is the main difference between an invertebrate and a vertebrate?
2. How are plants similar to animals, protists, fungi, and bacteria? How are plants different?
3. How are vascular plants different from nonvascular plants?
4. INQUIRY SKILL **Classify** Name a trait you would use to classify a fish as belonging to either the Phylum *Chordata* or the Phylum *Arthropoda*.
5. **Critical Thinking** How does classification simplify the study of living things?

L·I·N·K·S

WRITING LINK

Expository Writing Write a paragraph to explain why the smallest classification groups have organisms with more similarities than the larger ones. Give facts and examples to support the main idea.

MATH LINK

Solve this problem. Under ideal conditions a bacterium can divide into two bacteria every 20 minutes. Then each of those bacteria can divide into two new ones after another 20 minutes. If you start with one bacterium, how many will you have after one hour? After two hours? After three hours? Five hours? Eight hours?

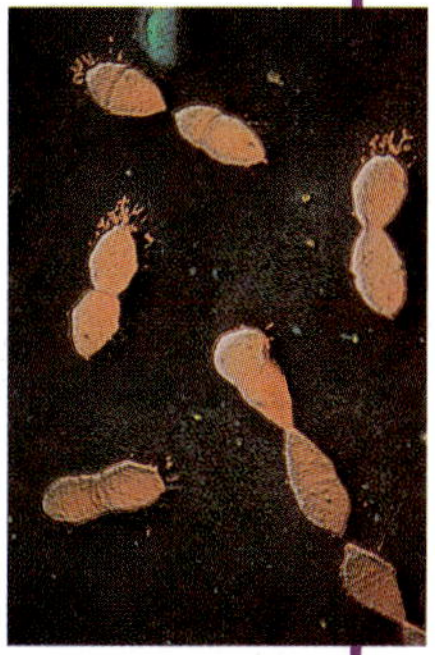

LITERATURE LINK

Read ***The Power of Green***, the story of some of the plants and protists that live in different areas of the world. Think about the plants and protists that live in your area. Try the activities at the end of the book.

TECHNOLOGY LINK

LOG ON Visit **www.science.mmhschool.com** for more links.

Biodiversity

We share Earth with an amazing variety of other living things, from the tallest redwood tree with trillions of cells to the smallest bacterium with just one. We know of more than 1.5 million different species. Millions more in rain forests and oceans are waiting to be discovered.

Why are there so many species? Because each is adapted to a different environment and to a different way of life. Dolphins swim in the oceans, and eagles soar in the skies. Mushrooms digest dead trees, and algae float in sunlit ponds.

This great variety of life is called biodiversity. Each member of each of the kingdoms contributes to our world in its own way. So when a species disappears or becomes extinct, its unique contribution is lost forever.

We depend on other species and the ecosystems they live in. They keep our planet healthy. They provide us with natural resources such as foods, fibers, and medicines. We enjoy them, and we want future generations to be able to enjoy them, too. We have many reasons to protect the many incredible forms of life on our planet.

Plant Kingdom Did you know that the bark of the white willow tree has been used to relieve pain for thousands of years? Aspirin is based on ingredients found in this tree.

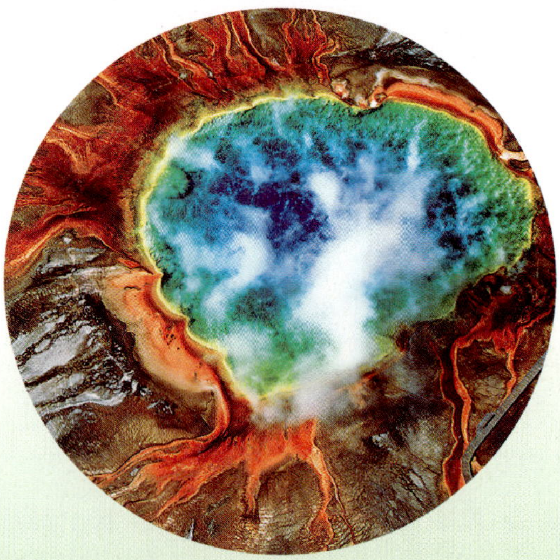

Bacteria Kingdom The *Thermus aquaticus* bacteria live in the hot springs of Yellowstone National Park. These microscopic organisms thrive at a scalding 160 degrees Fahrenheit! Now they are commercially made in laboratories and used in biomedical tests that help diagnose diseases.

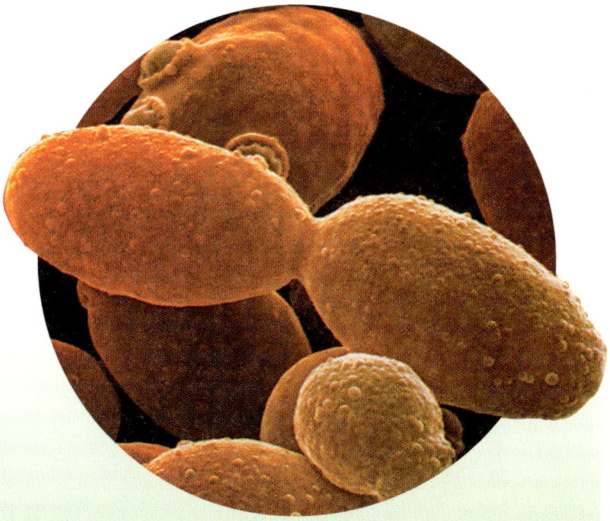

Fungus Kingdom There's more to fungi than mushrooms. *Saccharomyces cerevisiae,* the fungus known as baker's yeast, feeds on sugars in flour dough. This causes carbon dioxide to be released and bread to rise. Bread would be flat without this fungus.

Protist Kingdom From slime molds to mildew, protists may not seem appealing, but you've probably eaten them. Red algae is a seaweed that contains an ingredient used in ice cream, pudding, and chocolate milk!

Animal Kingdom They may be as small as sticks of butter at birth, but each new panda that's born is a big boost to an endangered species.

Write About It

1. Why is it worth protecting endangered animals?
2. Plants can be used as medicines. They also have many other uses. Write about a few.

LOG ON Visit **www.science.mmhschool.com** to learn more about biodiversity.

Chapter 1 Review

Vocabulary

Fill each blank with the best word or words from the list.

chlorophyll, A6
fungus, A17
invertebrate, A16
nonvascular, A15
organ, A9
organ system, A9
protist, A18
tissue, A9
vascular, A15
vertebrate, A16

1. Muscle is an example of a(n) ______.

2. Trees and flowering plants are ______ plants.

3. A group of organs that work together form a(n)______.

4. A(n) ______ is an organism whose nucleus is surrounded by a membrane.

5. A green chemical called ______ allows plants to use the Sun's energy to make their own foods.

6. A mushroom is a(n) ______.

7. An animal that doesn't have a backbone is a(n) ______.

8. A moss is a(n) ______ plant.

9. Tissues of different kinds come together to make a(n) ______.

10. A bird is a(n) ______.

Test Prep

11. Which of the following is a fungus?

A mold
B moss
C fern
D conifer

12. Similar cells that have the same function come together to make a(n) ______.

F organ system
G organ
H tissue
J organism

13. The green "food factories" of plants are ______.

A chloroplasts
B mitochondria
C vacuoles
D cytoplasm

14. The science of finding patterns among living things is called ______.

F mitochondrion
G classification
H organization
J respiration

15. Where do plant cells store food, water and wastes?

- **A** nucleus
- **B** chloroplast
- **C** vacuole
- **D** cell membrane

Concepts and Skills

16. **Reading in Science** Write a paragraph explaining why ferns can grow taller than mosses.

17. **Scientific Methods** How would you determine if a cell is an animal cell or a plant cell? Write up a design for an experiment to find out.

18. **Decision Making** Is there a single correct way to classify an organism? Write a paragraph explaining your answer.

19. INQUIRY SKILL **Experiment** Design an experiment to determine how much mosses, ferns, and grasses depend on water for survival. Write how you would set up the experiment. Write down your hypothesis. Tell what variables you would test.

20. **Critical Thinking** You dig in the ground and find a fossil of a fern. You then dig deeper and find a fossil of a club moss. What reasoning might let you conclude that club mosses existed earlier than ferns? Write a paragraph explaining your reasoning.

Did You Ever Wonder?

INQUIRY SKILL **Communicate** Why are external traits not used to classify living organisms? Explain your answer to your class.

LOG ON Visit www.science.mmhschool.com to boost your test scores.

CHAPTER

2

Plant Structure and Functions

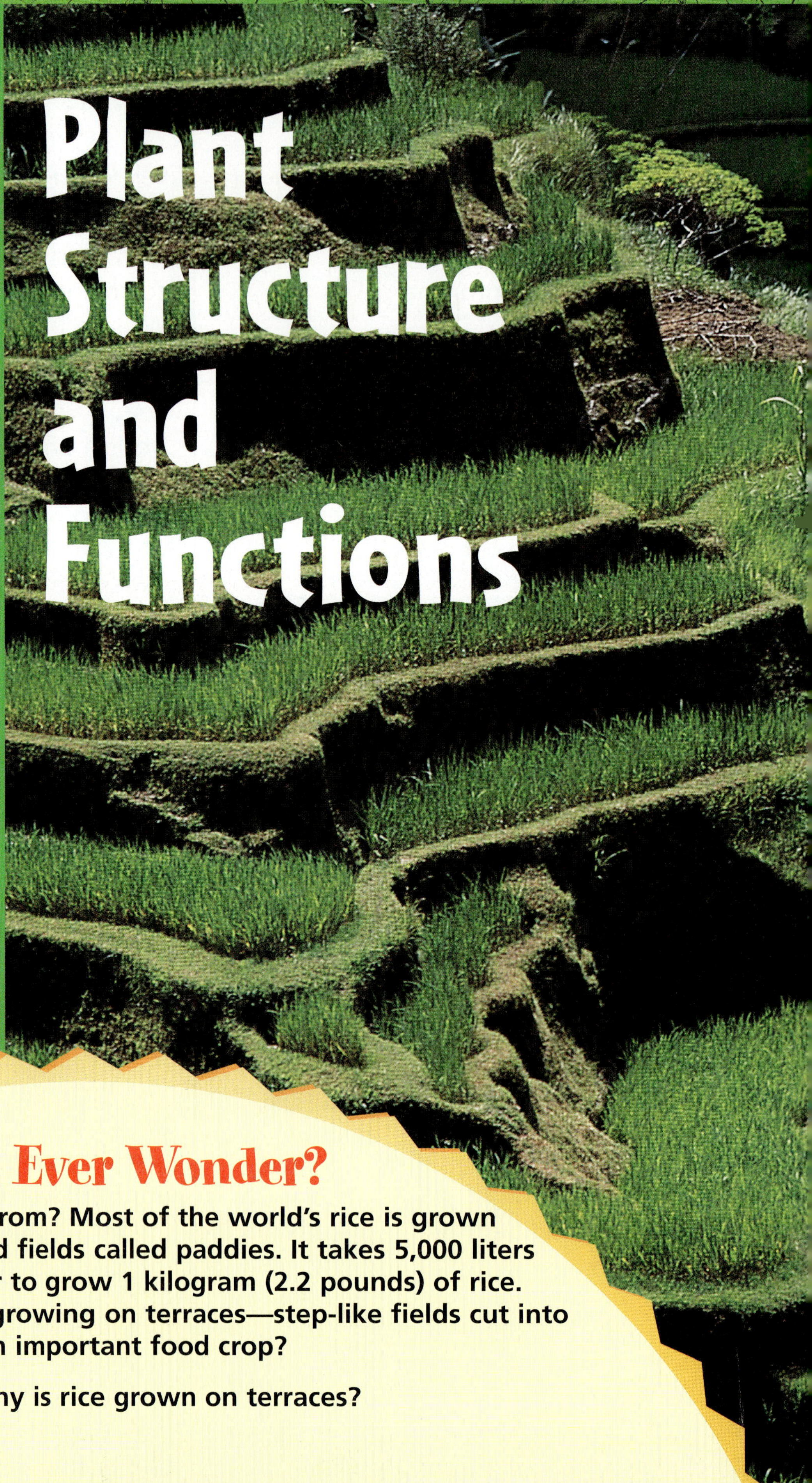

Did You Ever Wonder?

Where does rice come from? Most of the world's rice is grown in Asia, often in flooded fields called paddies. It takes 5,000 liters (1,320 gallons) of water to grow 1 kilogram (2.2 pounds) of rice. These rice paddies are growing on terraces—step-like fields cut into a hillside. Why is rice an important food crop?

INQUIRY SKILL **Infer** Why is rice grown on terraces?

LESSON 3

Roots, Stems, and Leaves

Vocabulary

- **xylem,** A30
- **cortex,** A30
- **epidermis,** A30
- **root cap,** A30
- **root hairs,** A30
- **phloem,** A31
- **cambium,** A31
- **transpiration,** A35
- **photosynthesis,** A36
- **respiration,** A37

Get Ready

What do you have in common with a plant? Would you believe that you and a plant have similar needs? Still, there is a big difference. You can move around to get things. You can change things around you—like your room temperature. Plants stay in one place, yet different kinds of plants can survive in very different places. How? What helps plants survive in their surroundings?

Inquiry Skill

You predict when you state possible results of an event or experiment.

Explore Activity

How Do a Plant's Parts Help It Survive?

Materials

- cactus
- water plant, such as an *Elodea* or a duckweed
- flowering plant, such as a geranium

Procedure

1. **Observe** Look at the physical properties of the leaves of each plant. Note the color, size, and shape of the leaves.
2. **Communicate** List any other plant parts that you see.
3. **Communicate** Observe the physical properties of these parts. Record your observations.

Drawing Conclusions

1. **Interpret Data** How do the parts of a cactus help it survive in a hot, dry desert?
2. **Infer** Would the geranium be able to survive in the desert? Why or why not?
3. **Infer** Could the water plant survive out of water? Why or why not?
4. **FURTHER INQUIRY** **Predict** Could these plants survive outside where you live? Why or why not? For each plant, what conditions would you have to change so that the plant could survive outside where you live?

Read to Learn

Main Idea All plants have certain parts with the same functions.

How Do a Plant's Parts Help It Survive?

Some plant roots help you survive. That's because they are foods. Beets, carrots, sweet potatoes, radishes, and turnips are the roots of different plants. How do roots help a plant survive?

Most plants have roots that hold them in the ground. Some plants, like mosses, don't have true roots. Still, mosses have rootlike structures that anchor them. Roots help keep plants from getting swept away by wind and running water. Roots draw up water and minerals from the soil. Plants must have water and minerals to make their own food. Roots also store food for the plant. That's especially true of sweet potato, sugar beet, and carrot plants.

A root gets its start early in the life of a plant. If you were to look at a lima bean as it sprouted, you would see a tiny piece of the young plant growing straight downward. This is the plant's first root.

This root bores deeper and deeper into the soil. Why don't the rough particles of soil rub away and harm the young root? The tip of the root is protected by a layer of tough cells called the root cap.

Parts of a Root

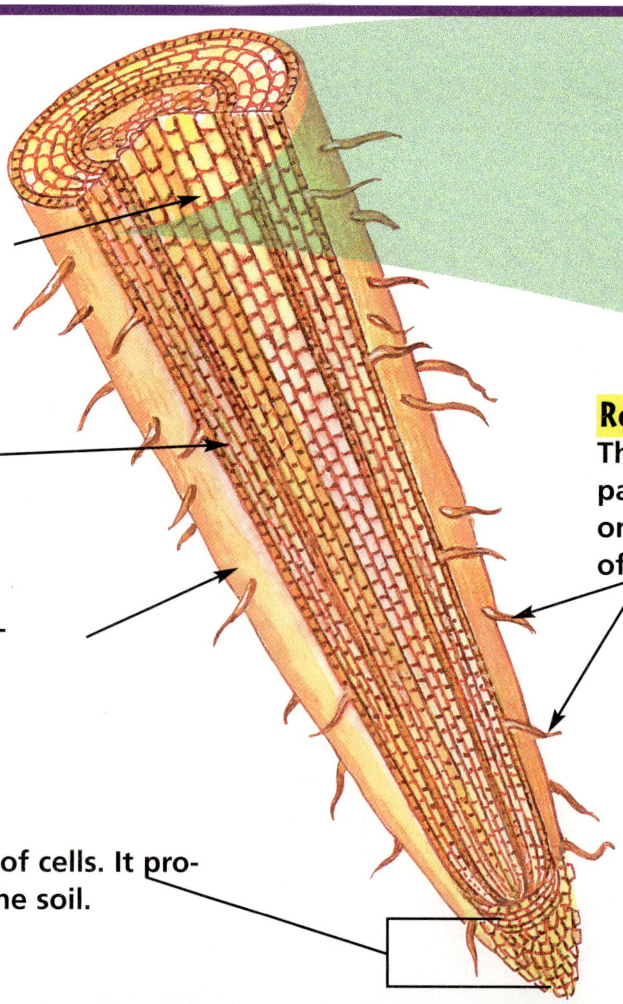

Soon more roots branch out from the sides of the original root. *Taproots* have one large root with a few hairy branching roots. They look like a carrot or a beet. Other roots, like those of grass or rye plants, are made up of only thin hairy branching roots called *fibrous roots*.

Taproots tend to grow deep into the ground and reach water deep down. Fibrous roots spread out near the soil's surface. They collect water where there is little rain that only soaks into the very top layer of soil.

Fibrous roots can make huge networks. The total surface area of the root system of a single rye plant was 639 square meters (6,879 square feet)!

Some plants, like orchids, that grow high in the branches of rain forest trees, have *aerial roots*. These roots never touch the ground. They take in moisture from the air. *Prop roots*, like those of a corn plant, grow like fingers out of the bottom of the stem. These roots help prop up the plant.

The structure of a root helps it absorb water and minerals and send them to other parts of the plant. The diagram shows how this happens.

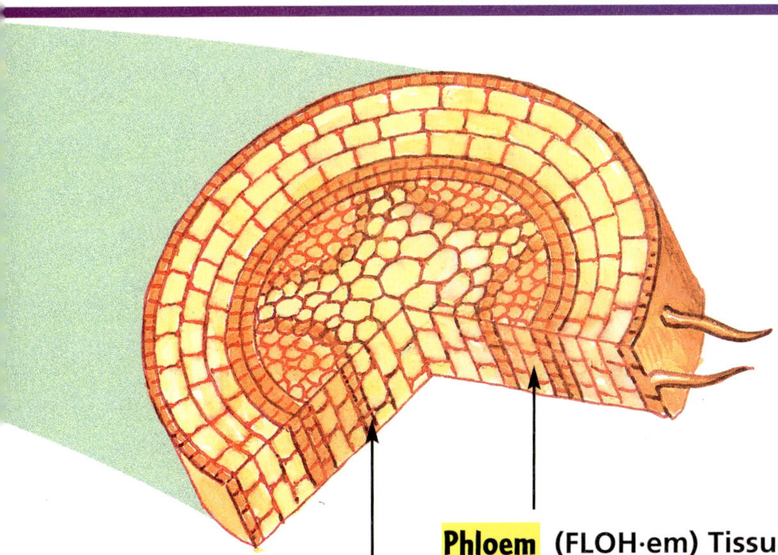

Phloem (FLOH·em) Tissue through which food from the leaves moves down through a plant.

Cambium (KAM·bee·uhm) A layer that separates the xylem from the phloem. The cambium is where new xylem and phloem are produced.

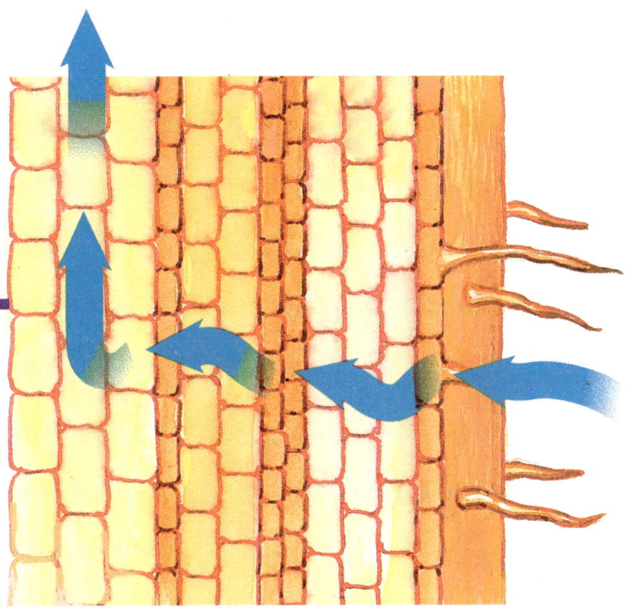

Water and minerals enter the root hairs. They pass through the root's cortex to the xylem. They then move up the xylem, into the plant's stem, and to all parts of the plant.

READING Main Idea

How do roots help a plant survive?

How Are Stems Similar?

Some stems are soft and delicate, like those of a young corn plant. Others are hard and tough, like those of a giant redwood tree. No matter what they look like, all stems have certain things in common.

All stems support leaves. Some also support flowers. Stems help leaves reach open places, where the leaves can be bathed in sunlight.

Stems also hold the transportation system for plants. This system lets water and minerals move from the roots to all parts of the plant, especially its leaves. It moves foods made in leaves to all other parts of the plant.

The *xylem* makes up the part of the transportation system that moves water and minerals up from the roots. The *phloem* moves food from the plant's leaves to its other parts. Many stems also have a *cambium*—a layer of cells—that separates the two. In addition, woody stems are protected by a tough outer layer of tissue, called bark.

Parts of a Stem

Soft and woody stems have the same basic parts for transporting water, minerals, and food to all parts of a plant.

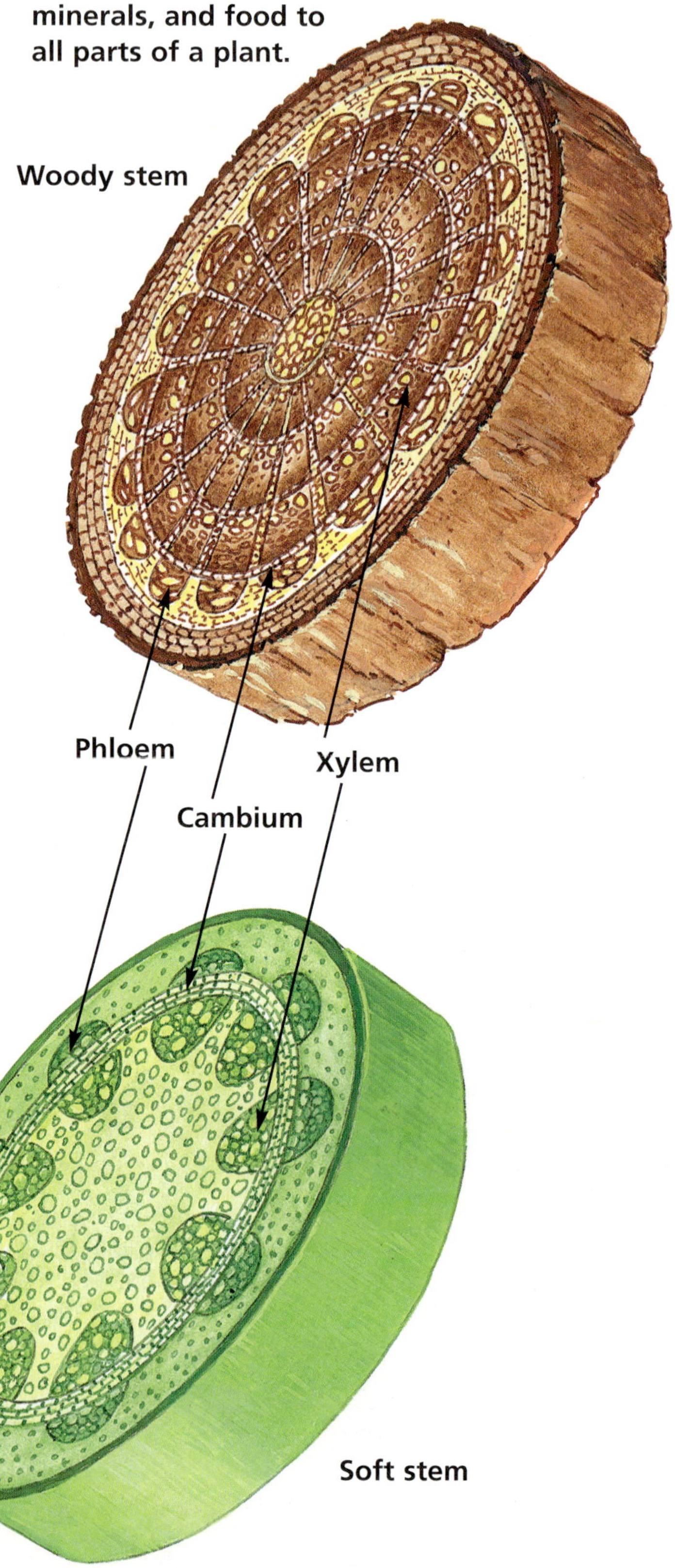

READING Diagrams

How are the xylem, phloem, and cambium arranged differently in a woody stem and in a soft stem?

Strawberry stems, called runners, grow along the ground.

A potato is an underground stem.

Some stems do more than support a plant and give it a transportation system. For example, the stems of plants like potatoes and sugarcane store food for the plants to use later. The potatoes and sugarcane you eat actually are stems. The stems of cactus plants store water, which the plants use during long dry periods in the desert. Still other stems, like those of asparagus, help make the plant's food.

Not all stems grow up into the air. Those of strawberries grow along the ground. That's how a strawberry patch spreads and grows.

What are two ways in which all stems are similar?

The stem of the cactus stores water.

Parts of Leaves

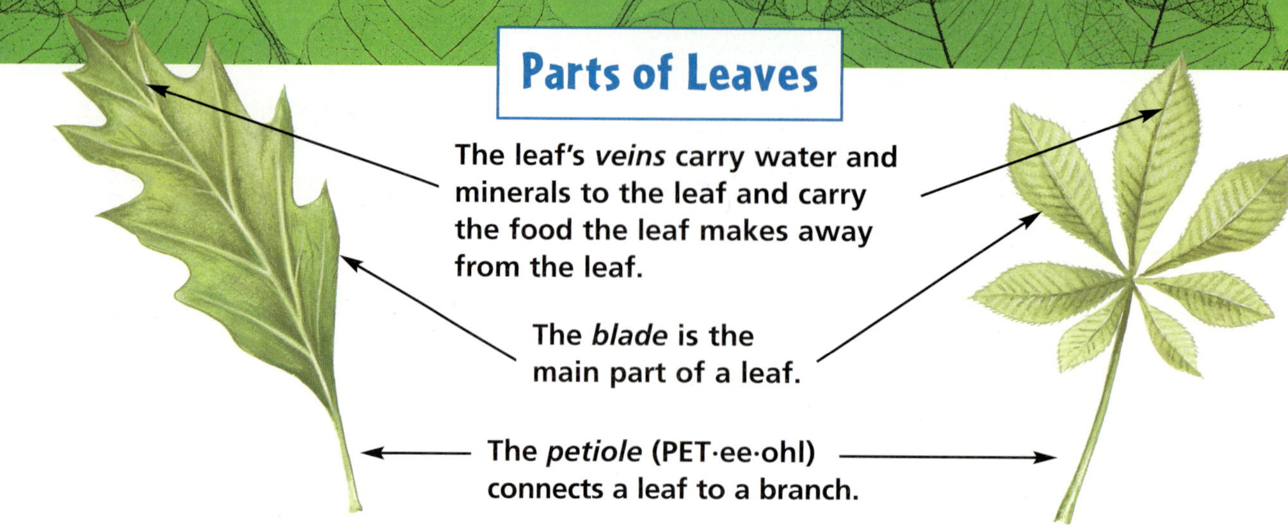

READING Diagrams

1. What holds a leaf to a branch?
2. Write a paragraph about what a leaf needs in order to make food for the plant.

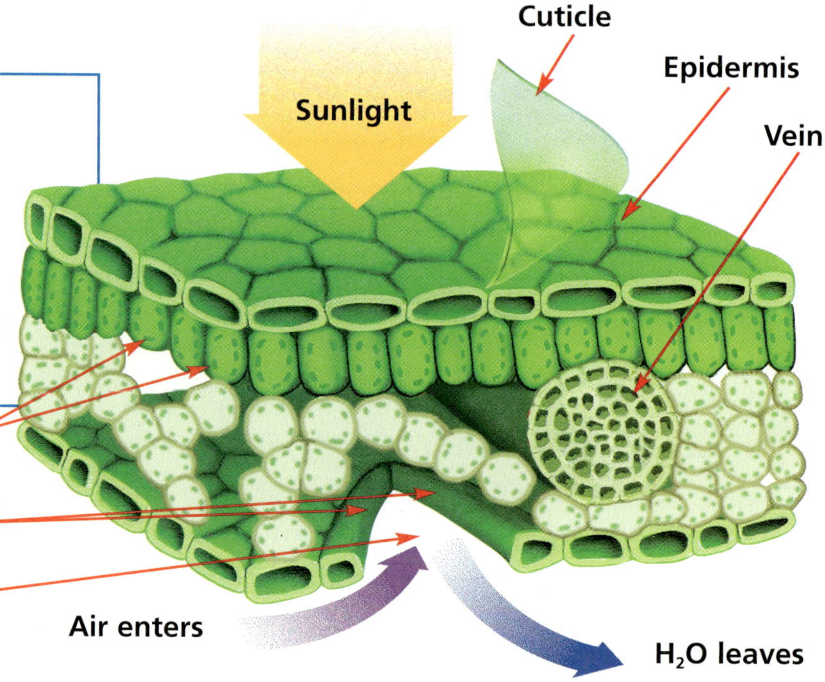

What Are Leaves?

Leaves come in all shapes and sizes. Most of the leaves you see hang from their plants as single leaves or in groups. Maple and oak trees have single leaves. They're called *simple* leaves.

Horse chestnut and locust leaves come in clusters. These are called *compound* leaves.

The parts of a leaf work together to help keep the plant alive.

The outermost layer of a leaf is its *epidermis*. Cells of the epidermis secrete a waxy coating, called a *cuticle* (KYEW·ti·kuhl). The cuticle helps keep water from leaving the leaf.

The leaf makes food in cells between the layers of the epidermis. These cells contain chloroplasts, the green food factories of plants. In addition to sunlight, these factories need water, minerals, and the carbon dioxide in air to make food.

The air comes through tiny pores in the bottom of the leaves called *stomata* (STOH·muh·tuh) (singular, *stoma*). When the stomata are open to let in air, water can also evaporate from the leaf. The job of opening and closing each stoma is performed by two *guard cells* that surround it.

When the plant has plenty of water, the guard cells swell and pull open the stoma. When the plant has too little water, the guard cells shrink and close the stoma.

Importance of Leaves

Many leaves have green, broad, flat surfaces that help "capture" the sunlight the plant needs to make its food. Other leaves have different shapes for different purposes. The spines on a cactus reduce the leaf's surface area, cutting down water loss. The needles of a pine tree are covered with a wax that keeps the tree from losing too much water. The layers of an onion store food. The leaves of the garden pea plant wind around objects to give the plant added support.

The leaves of the Venus's-flytrap are colorful insect traps. They snap shut when an insect flies inside.

Leaves are often far from roots, yet they help roots take in water from soil. When water evaporates from the leaves, more water moves up through the plant to replace the lost water. This process is called **transpiration** (tran·spuh·RAY·shuhn).

People eat all parts of plants, including leaves such as lettuce, cabbage, parsley, and spinach. Why are leaves important to you?

What do leaves do for a plant?

QUICK LAB

Leaves

FOLDABLES™ Make a Pocket Book. (See p. R 42.) Label the pockets as shown.

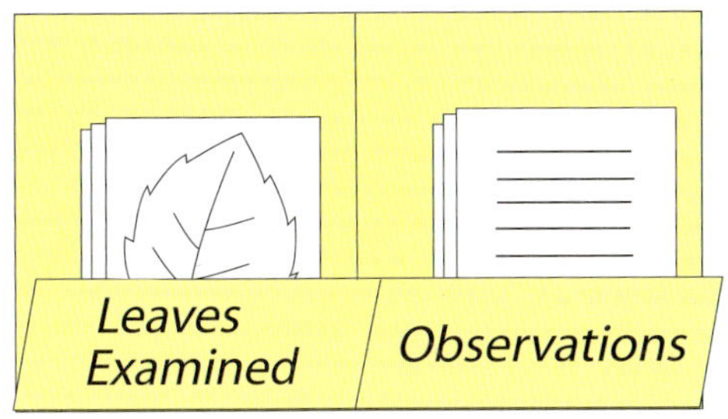

1. Collect a variety of different leaves that you eat as food.
2. **Observe** Examine them with a hand lens.
3. Make a sketch of at least 12 leaves, including their veins, on quarter sheets of photocopy paper.
4. **Classify** Into how many kinds of vein patterns can you group your sketches? Use quarter sheets of notebook paper to explain the similarities and differences you used to classify the leaves. Store your sketches and explanations in your Pocket Book.

What Is Photosynthesis?

When you walk to a grocery store to buy food, you are really doing two things. You are using energy to get to the store, and you are buying energy at the store. Walking uses energy. Food provides you with energy.

All living things need energy to survive. Where do they get energy? Animals eat food to get energy. Plants make their own food. Where does the plant get energy to make food? It comes from light, especially sunlight.

Light is a form of energy that plants use to make their food. Plants capture the energy of light and trap it in the foods they make. Later, when they need this energy, they get it back from the food. The food-making process is called **photosynthesis** (foh·tuh·SIN·thuh·sis). This term comes from Greek words that mean "putting together by light." The process is very complex, but basically here's how it happens.

First, sunlight strikes a green part of a plant, such as a leaf. The leaf is green because it has a green chemical called chlorophyll. The chlorophyll is found in plant parts called chloroplasts. The chloroplasts act like tiny chemical factories. Inside them water and carbon dioxide from the air combine to make sugar and oxygen. However, this reaction could not happen without the help of light energy. Sugar molecules are only made in the presence of sunlight.

The sugars that the leaf makes go into the leaf's veins and then to all parts of the plant. The oxygen the

Photosynthesis

$$\text{Carbon dioxide} + \text{Water} \xrightarrow[\text{Chlorophyll}]{\text{Light}} \text{Sugar} + \text{Oxygen}$$

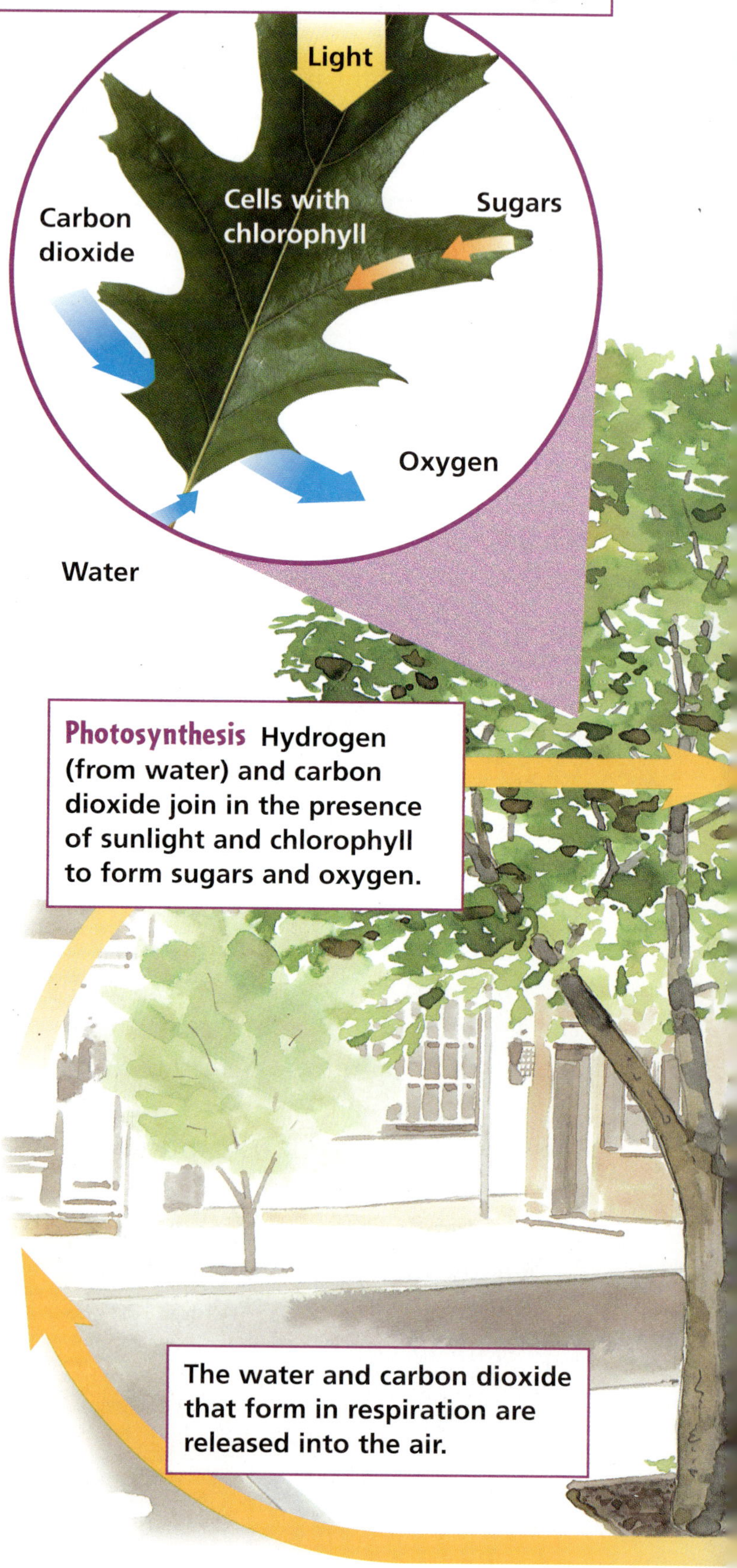

Photosynthesis Hydrogen (from water) and carbon dioxide join in the presence of sunlight and chlorophyll to form sugars and oxygen.

The water and carbon dioxide that form in respiration are released into the air.

plant makes goes into the air. All animals must breathe in oxygen to stay alive. At the same time, they breathe out carbon dioxide, which the plants need.

Now that the Sun's energy is trapped in the sugars that the plant made, how does the plant get the energy back out? Its cells use oxygen to break apart the sugar. When the sugar breaks apart, it releases energy that the plant uses. This process is called **respiration** (res·puh·RAY·shuhn). This is the same process that releases energy in animals.

About 21 percent of the air you breathe is oxygen. You use this oxygen to release energy from the foods that you eat. The results of the process of respiration are carbon dioxide, water, and energy.

How is photosynthesis different from respiration?

READING Diagrams

In what process is carbon dioxide released?

Respiration In respiration, which occurs in plants and animals, sugars and oxygen join to produce water, carbon dioxide, and energy.

How Does Water Get from Roots to Leaves?

If you were to dry 1,000 g (2.2 lb) of leaves, you would end up with between 50 and 300 g (1.8–11 oz) of crumbly matter. That's because plants are made up of 70–95 percent water.

Cells in all parts of a plant need water to live and grow. They need water to carry out many vital chemical reactions, including photosynthesis. They also need water to stay firm and not wilt.

Plants constantly lose water through transpiration. Over its lifetime an average plant in a mild climate area will lose more than 100 times its weight in water!

It is very important for a plant to efficiently move water from its roots to all its other parts. The diagram on page A39 shows how this is done.

Tropical rain forests pump great amounts of water into the air.

Why is it important for a plant to move water from its roots?

If a normal plant (left) gets too little water, it will lose firmness and wilt (right).

How Water Is Moved Through a Plant

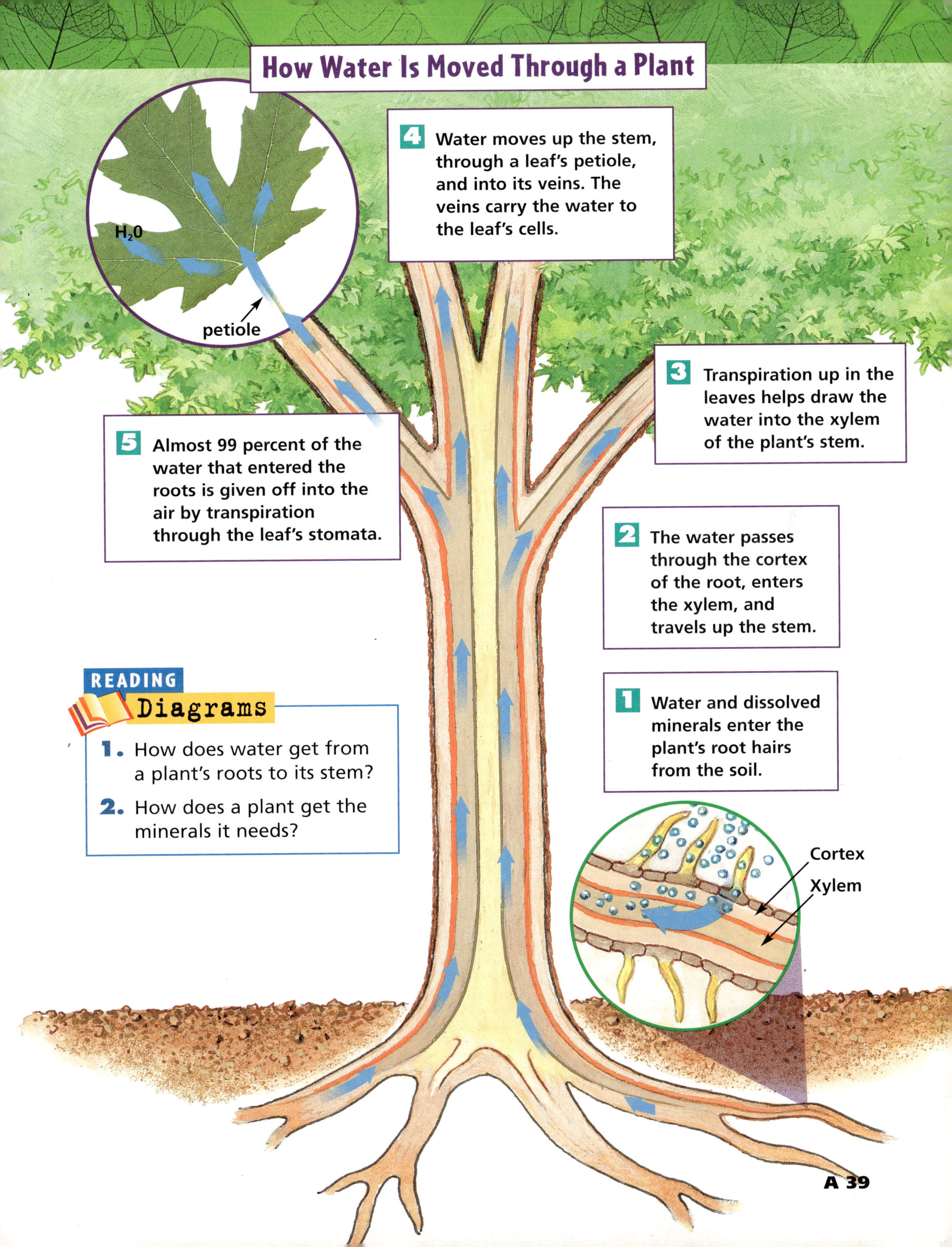

READING Diagrams

1. How does water get from a plant's roots to its stem?
2. How does a plant get the minerals it needs?

What Parts of Plants Do You Eat?

There probably isn't a part of a plant that you haven't eaten at one time or another. Whether you know it or not, you've eaten roots, stems, leaves, seeds, fruits, flowers, and even the bark and sap of plants. If you don't believe this is true, look at the chart on this page. Which of these plant parts have you eaten?

What are five examples of plant parts that people use for food?

READING Charts

What part of a plant is a tomato? A peanut?

Plant Parts and Their Foods

Root	Stem	Leaf	Fruit	Seed	Flower	Bark	Sap
beet	 celery	basil	apple	barley	 broccoli	 cinnamon	 maple syrup
carrot	ginger	cabbage	eggplant	bean	caper		
horse-radish	potato	lettuce	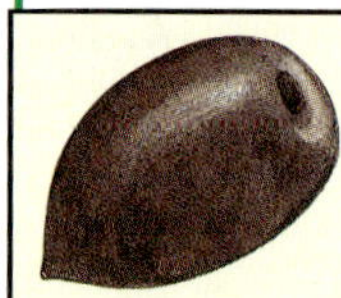 olive	chocolate	cauliflower		
parsnip	sugar	onion	orange	corn	clove		
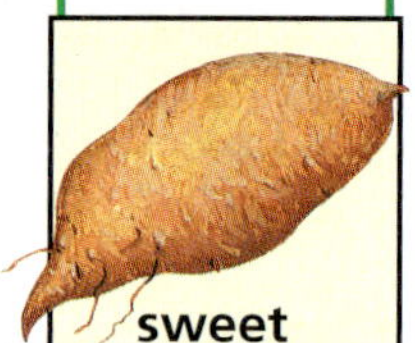 sweet potato		oregano	pepper	mustard			
		 parsley	tomato	oats			
		spinach	vanilla	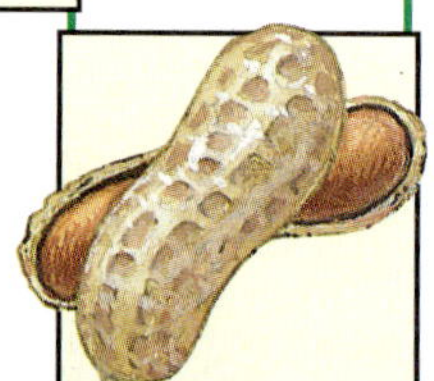 peanut			
		tea		rice			
				rye			
				soybean			
				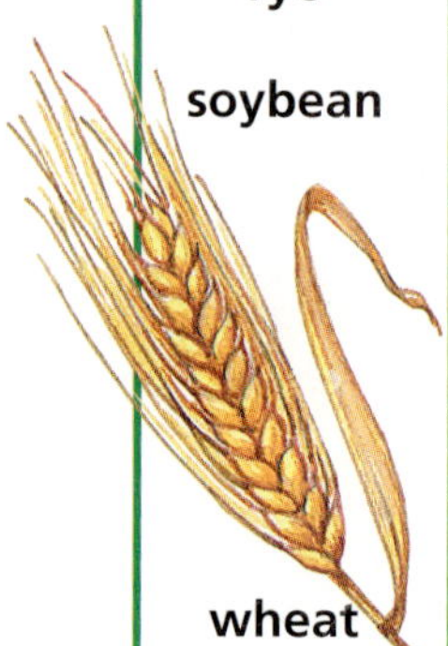 wheat			

Lesson Review

Why It Matters

We depend on plants for many things. Among them are food, clothing, and shelter. Since plants are needed by all living things, it is important to know what they need to survive. Part of a plant's ability to survive depends on how well its parts work together to move water and minerals in one direction and food in the other direction. The parts that do this are roots, stems, and leaves.

e-Journal Visit our Web site **www.science.mmhschool.com** to do a research project on the importance of plants.

Think and Write

1. List three things plants need in order to live and grow.
2. How do roots, stems, and leaves help a plant survive?
3. Describe the process of photosynthesis.
4. Describe the process of respiration in plants.
5. **Critical Thinking** If there were no plants, would animals be able to survive? Explain.

L·I·N·K·S

ART LINK

Make a poster. Trace the path of water from the soil, through a plant, and into the air. Make a poster using drawings to show this path.

WRITING LINK

Expository Writing The giant leaves of the royal lily pad are strong enough to hold up the weight of a small child. Search for information about this Amazon plant. Write a research report to present your findings.

MATH LINK

Solve this problem. Find the total surface area of the leaves of a single tree. Use graph paper to estimate the surface area of a single leaf. Then estimate the number of leaves on a single branch. (Find the average of several branches.) Estimate the number of branches on the tree. Find the total number of leaves, then find their total surface area.

TECHNOLOGY LINK

LOG ON Visit **www.science.mmhschool.com** for more links.

LESSON 4

Plant Responses and Adaptations

Vocabulary

response, A44
stimulus, A44
tropism, A44
adaptation, A46

Get Ready

What happens when you jump up? Why don't you just fly up and away from Earth's surface? There is a pull between Earth and everything on it. This pull is called gravity.

Mangrove roots have developed many adaptations to survive in a harsh environment. They filter salt from sea water. They have developed prop roots that arch out from the tree to the soil to help the plant withstand coastal waves. How do these roots respond to gravity?

Inquiry Skill

You predict when you state possible results of an event or experiment.

Explore Activity

How Do Roots Grow?

Materials
- petri dish (plastic)
- 2 paper towels
- marking pen
- tape
- 4 bean seeds that have been soaked in water overnight

Procedure

1. Soak two paper towels. Wrinkle the paper towels, and place them in the bottom half of the petri dish.
2. Place the four seeds on top of the wet paper towels as shown in diagram 1. Place the seeds so that the curved part is turned toward the center of the dish.
3. Place the top on the petri dish. The top will hold the seeds in the wet paper towels. Seal the top with transparent tape. Draw an arrow on the petri dish with the marking pen as shown in diagram 2. This will show which direction is down. Write the number or name of your group on the petri dish.
4. In a place your teacher provides, stand the petri dish on its edge so the arrow is pointing downward. Tape the petri dish so that it will remain standing. Do not lay the dish down flat.
5. **Predict** Make and record a prediction about the direction you think the roots will grow.
6. **Communicate** Examine the seeds for the next four days. Record the direction of root growth.

1

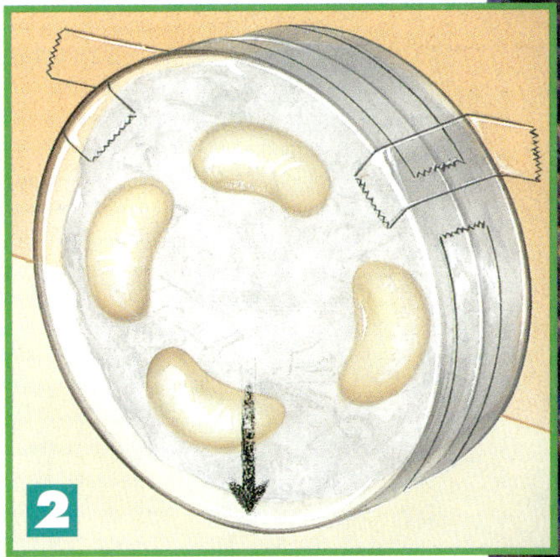
2

Drawing Conclusions

1. **Observe** In what direction were the roots growing on day 1 of germination? On day 4?
2. **Interpret Data** Is your prediction supported by your data?
3. **FURTHER INQUIRY** **Predict** What would happen if a seedling were not able to grow its roots down into the soil? Design an experiment to test your prediction. Try it and report your results.

Read to Learn

Main Idea **Tropisms and other responses and adaptations help plants survive.**

What Are Tropisms?

If the flash of a camera goes off near your eyes, you are likely to respond to the bright light by blinking. The flash of light stimulated your blinking. Anything in the environment—light, heat, gravity, and more—that produces such a **response** is called a **stimulus** (STIM·yuh·luhs).

Plants also respond to a stimulus, but they tend to respond more slowly than animals do. Plants slowly bend or curve toward or away from a stimulus. Scientists call this kind of response a **tropism** (TROH·piz·uhm). Tropisms help a plant survive in its environment. For example, as seeds sprout, their roots grow downward. Why do you think the seeds' roots grow downward?

There are several major kinds of tropisms. One of these is *gravitropism*. A plant's roots respond to the stimulus of gravity and grow downward.

The roots of a plant show positive gravitropism. No matter how the plant is tilted, its roots will always grow downward into the soil. The roots grow in the direction Earth's gravity is pulling them. Stems show negative gravitropism. They grow away from the force of gravity. They grow into the air, where their leaves can get the most sunlight.

Light, of course, is very important to plants' survival. Plants respond to changes in light. These responses are called *phototropisms*. (*Photo* comes from a Greek word meaning "light.") If a plant is exposed to light coming from only one direction, its stem will bend in that direction. That is positive phototropism.

If a plant bends toward a stimulus, its change is called a positive tropism. If it bends away, the change is called a negative tropism.

If you examine the roots of a willow tree growing near a stream, you will discover *hydrotropism*. *Hydro* means "water." The willow's roots show positive hydrotropism. They grow toward a source of water.

Some plants, like squash and grape plants, show a response to touch. Grape vines grow around posts farmers stick in the ground. The vines send out threadlike tendrils that coil toward whatever they touch.

The tendrils of this plant respond to touch as they coil around other objects.

People long knew about plant tropisms. However, they didn't always know the process inside a plant that made a plant's parts move. The first clue was discovered by Charles Darwin and his son Francis in the 1870s. Charles Darwin cut off the tips of some very young plant shoots. He left other plants alone. The plants with tips bent toward light. The plants without tips did not. Darwin concluded that something in the tips was causing the bending, but what?

Charles Darwin showed that when the tip of a plant shoot is cut off, the plant will not bend toward light.

The second clue was found in the 1920s by Dutch scientist Frits Went. Went guessed that a chemical made only in the shoot's tip was responsible for the bending. He separated many chemicals from shoot tips. One by one he placed them on the cutoff tops of plant shoots. Finally, he found the chemical that let the cut shoots bend toward light.

The chemical is called an *auxin*. Auxins are chemicals that stimulate plant growth. Auxins work on all parts of the plant and cause tropisms of all kinds. How do auxins cause plant parts to bend? When one side of a stem is exposed to light, for example, auxins move to the other side and down. Auxins cause more cells to grow—and some to grow more in length—on the dark side, but not on the side facing the light. This unequal growth causes the stem to bend toward the light.

What are examples of a positive tropism and a negative tropism?

How Do Plants Survive?

Plants survive in deserts, rain forests, and the Arctic. They survive in all these places because they have adapted to their environment. An **adaptation** (ad·uhp·TAY·shuhn) helps an organism survive in its environment.

Desert plants have adaptations for collecting, storing, and saving water. Cactus plants have roots that absorb water very quickly. The water is stored in the center of the plant. A thick, waterproof, waxy coating helps stop water loss. Finally, the plant's stomata open only at night, when temperatures are cooler. Less water is lost through transpiration.

Carnivorous (meat-eating) plants can't get enough nutrients from the soil. These plants trap and digest insects to get some of the nutrients they need.

Plants like spinach, lettuce, and wheat bloom in late spring and early summer. They are called *long-day* plants. That's because when they bloom, there is much more daylight than darkness. By contrast, *short-day* plants, like strawberries, soybeans, and ragweed, bloom in early spring or in the fall. Short-day plants bloom when there is more darkness and less daylight. This flowering response is called *photoperiodism*.

What adaptations help plants survive water shortages?

Short-Day, Long-Day Plants

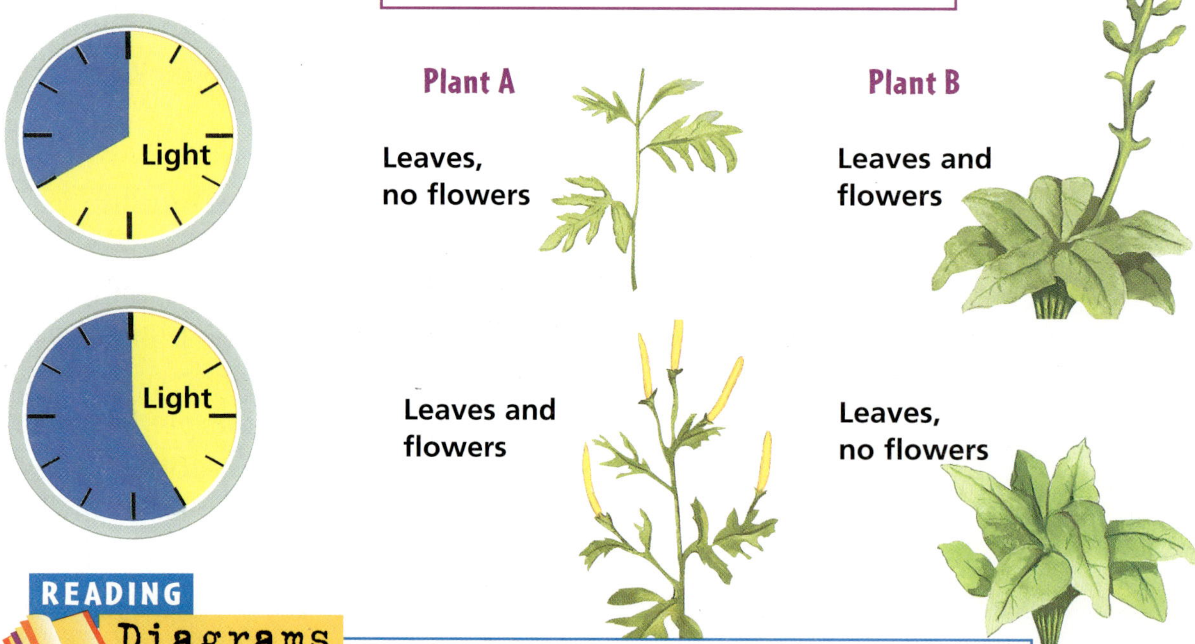

READING Diagrams

1. Which plant is a long-day plant? Which is a short-day plant?
2. In what season would plant A bloom?

Unlike the plant below, which is being eaten by an insect, plants such as the poison ivy, above, produce chemicals that keep insects away or make them sick.

Why Do Plants Compete?

Like all organisms, plants compete with one another for what they need to survive and grow—sunlight, water, and nutrients.

Each plant has its own strategy for winning its battle with other plants. Vines, like ivy and honeysuckle, climb the trunks of trees to get a greater share of sunlight. The trees themselves rise to great heights. They spread their branches to form leafy canopies above the forest. That's why in a forest, trees like oaks and maples have more leaves at their tops.

Have you ever been in a forest full of giant redwoods or other conifers? These trees preserve the nutrients and water in the soil for themselves. They do this by blocking sunlight from reaching the ground. Without sunlight few plants can grow in the soil and soak up nutrients and water near great trees.

Some plants use another strategy for keeping other plants at a distance. They produce chemicals that are poisons to other plants. Creosote bushes, which live in dry areas, release such a poison from their roots. The poison keeps the seeds of other plants from germinating. It may even kill other plants that are already growing.

Plants also make chemicals that discourage insects and other animals from feeding on or infecting them. The most powerful insect-fighting plant chemical is made by the neem tree of Africa and Asia. This chemical is so strong that if you dissolved a teaspoon of it in a medium-sized swimming pool and sprayed the water on a plant, insects would not feed on it. Some plants, like the water hemlock, even make poisons that can kill a person.

How do plants compete with each other?

Inquiry Skill BUILDER

SKILL Experiment

Why Leaves Change Color

To find out why leaves change color in autumn, the first thing you might do is figure out what changes occur in the fall that might cause leaves to change color. Scientists call such changes *variables*. You might identify two of these variables as the amount of daylight and the temperature, both of which go down in the fall.

Next you would make a guess that seems to make sense about which variable causes leaves to change color. This guess is called a *hypothesis*. It is often made in the form of an "*if . . . then . . .*" statement. For example, "*If* the plant doesn't get water, *then* it won't grow." To see if your hypothesis is a good idea, you would perform an experiment. That experiment has to be set up so that it gives a clear answer.

A

B

C

Procedure

1. Look at the drawings. They show three experiments—A, B, C. Study the setups.
2. **Observe** What variable or variables are being tested in the first experiment? Record your answer. What variable or variables are being tested in the other two experiments?

Drawing Conclusions

1. **Infer** Which experiment is testing to see whether light causes leaves to change color? Explain.
2. **Infer** Which experiment is testing to see whether temperature causes leaves to change color? Explain why.
3. **Infer** Which experiment will not give a clear answer? Explain why not.

Lesson Review

Why It Matters

Plants respond to changes in their environment. They have to be able to adapt to changes in light, water, and temperature. These adaptations help them survive. Other equally important adaptations help plants reproduce successfully and fight off enemies such as insect pests.

e-Journal Visit our Web site **www.science.mmhschool.com** to do a research project on how plants adapt to changing seasons.

Think and Write

1. What are tropisms? Give an example of one.
2. How do auxins help plants grow toward the light?
3. Compare the way vines and trees compete for sunlight.
4. INQUIRY SKILL **Experiment** How would you design an experiment to see if the changing temperature or the changing amount of daylight plays a bigger part in why leaves change color in autumn?
5. **Critical Thinking** What do you think might happen if all plants bloomed at the same time?

L·I·N·K·S

MATH LINK

Solve this problem. How big does a giant *sequoia* (si·KWOY·uh) grow? Research giant sequoias to find how tall they grow, how big around they get, and how much they weigh. Which weighs more—a giant sequoia or a blue whale?

WRITING LINK

Explanatory Writing Research how a scientist uses a tree's rings to tell about weather conditions. Write an essay that explains the steps in the process. Use time-order words to tell what the scientist does first, next, and last.

ART LINK

Make a poster. Find pictures illustrating several plant tropisms, and use them to help you design a poster. Include a description of each tropism you illustrate.

TECHNOLOGY LINK

Science Newsroom CD-ROM Choose *Color My World* to learn more about how leaves change color.

LOG ON Visit **www.science.mmhschool.com** for more links.

Cleaning Pollution with Plants

Plants help us in many different ways. They produce oxygen for us to breathe. They provide food for us to eat. We build homes with wood from trees. Lifesaving medicines are made from some plants. Now research shows plants have another amazing use—they help us clean up pollution!

Every year millions of gallons of oil leak into the soil from pipelines, storage tanks, and industrial sites. The usual method of cleanup is to dig up the polluted soil and dispose of it elsewhere. This method is very expensive and disturbs the soil structure.

Researchers Katherine Banks and Paul Schwab have discovered that certain plants—along with tiny soil microbes—will clean up the soil pollutants. The microbes in the soil break down the oil and use it for food. The plants speed up the microbes' activity by getting more oxygen into the soil.

Banks and Schwab have found that certain grasses clean pollution well. Clover and alfalfa plants also are effective because they increase microbe growth. Finding the right plant, however, can be tricky. Since oil spills occur in different parts of the world, scientists need to use plants that will survive in different climates.

Plants can be used to clean up other kinds of soil pollution, too. Some plants can absorb heavy metals and radioactive material from soil. The plants store the substances in their tissues. Then the plants become toxic and must be destroyed. Mustard plants, for example, can soak up metals, such as lead. In Ukraine, mustard plants were used to remove radiation pollution from the soil around a nuclear plant that exploded.

There are many reasons why using plants may one day be the best way to clean up soil pollution. The method is cheaper, prettier, and powered by an unlimited source of energy—the Sun!

Researchers Katherine Banks and Paul Schwab of Purdue University discovered that grasses with large root surfaces work well at cleaning up polluted soil.

Mustard plants can soak up heavy metals, such as lead. The plants are then burned or dried to recycle the metals.

Sunflowers can be used to clean up radioactive wastes from water.

What Did I Learn?

1. In Ukraine, mustard plants were used to

- **A** remove pesticides from the soil.
- **B** clean up oil spills in lakes.
- **C** remove radiation pollution from soil.
- **D** clean up oil in parking lots.

2. Plants help clean up oil spills by

- **F** speeding up the "oil-eating" microbes' activity.
- **G** using the oil as plant food.
- **H** absorbing the oil like a paper towel.
- **J** getting more carbon dioxide into the soil.

LOG ON Visit **www.science.mmhschool.com** for more information on plants.

Chapter 2 Review

Vocabulary

Fill each blank with the best word or words from the list.

adaptation, A46
cambium, A31
cortex, A30
epidermis, A30
phloem, A31
root cap, A30
stimulus, A44
transpiration, A35
tropism, A44
xylem, A30

1. The outer layer of a root is the _____.

2. Water and minerals flow up through the _____.

3. Foods flow down from the leaves through the _____.

4. Water and minerals pass through the root's _____ to the xylem.

5. A characteristic that helps an organism survive in its environment is a(n)_____.

6. Bending toward or away from a stimulus is a(n)_____.

7. Something in the environment that produces a response in an organism is a(n) _____.

8. The layer of tough cells that protects the root is called the _____.

9. The process by which water goes out of leaves is _____.

10. The _____ separates xylem from phloem.

Test Prep

11. Tropism is the process of _____.

A movement of a plant toward or away from a stimulus
B making sugar from sunlight
C transporting water along a stem
D adaptation to a hot climate

12. In the process of making food, plants give off _____.

F sugar
G carbon dioxide
H oxygen
J chloroplasts

13. What causes sunflowers to bend toward the sunlight?

A positive tropism
B transporation
C pollination
D negative tropism

14. Leaves help roots take in water through a process called _____.

F photosynthesis
G transpiration
H respiration
J perspiration

15. When plants use stored sugar for energy, they go through a process called _____.

A photosynthesis

B transpiration

C respiration

D perspiration

Concepts and Skills

16. Reading in Science Write a paragraph explaining why light is a stimulus.

17. Scientific Methods How would you determine the length of time a geranium plant needs to be exposed to light daily in order to survive? Write up a design for an experiment that would test this.

18. Decision Making What advice would you give to a friend who is opening a plant store in your neighborhood? What kinds of decisions would your friend need to make regarding the features and the location of the store?

19. INQUIRY SKILL **Experiment** Design an experiment to determine two ways that adaptations can help plants survive. Write how you would set up the experiment. Write down your hypothesis.

20. Critical Thinking If you were lost in the woods in the United States, had no compass, and could not see the sky, how might plants help you infer direction? Write a paragraph explaining your answer.

Did You Ever Wonder?

INQUIRY SKILL **Use Variables** Find two window plants about the same size. Keep all the variables the same except one—give one plant fertilizer. Record your observations every three days for a month.

LOG ON Visit **www.science.mmhschool.com** to boost your test scores.

CHAPTER

3

Plant Diversity

Did You Ever Wonder?

Where do orchids grow? Of the thousands of different kinds of orchids, many grow in tropical rain forests. However, about 100 kinds of orchids grow in Europe, Asia, and North America. What do orchids have in common with other flowering plants?

INQUIRY SKILL **Form a hypothesis** **Why are most orchids found in tropical rain forests?**

LESSON 5

Plants Without Seeds

Vocabulary

- **rhizoid,** A58
- **spore,** A58
- **frond,** A61
- **rhizome,** A61
- **asexual reproduction,** A62
- **fertilization,** A62
- **sexual reproduction,** A62

Get Ready

Have you ever seen plants like these? If so, there were probably none as tall as these. You are looking at ferns in Costa Rica's Monteverde rain forest, one of Earth's dampest places. These ferns grow taller than a six-story building. Their leaves are more than three times longer than you are tall.

Ferns do best in warm, wet places. So do mosses, but mosses grow low to the ground. Why do ferns grow tall while mosses don't? How do the parts of mosses help them live where they do?

Inquiry Skill

You predict when you state possible results of an event or experiment.

Explore Activity

What Are the Parts of Mosses?

Procedure

1. **Observe** Place a moss on a paper towel. Use a hand lens to find its rootlike, stemlike, and leaflike parts. Record your observations.
2. **Measure** Use the forceps to remove a leaflike part. Make a wet-mount slide of the part. Observe its cells using the microscope on low power. Determine how thick the leaflike part is by moving the focus up and down.
3. **Observe** Find a capsule-shaped object at the end of the brownish stalk. Observe it with the hand lens. Place the capsule on a slide. Add a drop of water. Place a second slide on top of the capsule. Press down on the top slide with your thumb, and crush the capsule. Carefully remove the top slide and place a coverslip over the crushed capsule. Examine the released structures under low power. Draw what you see.

Drawing Conclusions

1. **Observe** Which parts of the moss are green? Explain why they are green.
2. **Observe** How many cell layers did you see in the leaflike structure?
3. **Interpret Data** What structures anchor the moss plant? What was the capsule?
4. FURTHER INQUIRY **Predict** What do you think the objects inside the capsule do? How would you test your prediction?

Materials

- hand lens
- forceps
- dropper
- 3 microscope slides
- coverslip
- microscope
- moss plant

Read to Learn

Main Idea Seedless nonvascular plants and seedless vascular plants have different structures but similar life cycles.

What Are Mosses?

Mosses and their close relatives the liverworts are nonvascular plants. They don't have the long tubelike structures vascular plants have. They cling to damp soil, sheltered rocks, and the shady side of trees. Mosses and liverworts are tiny plants, only 2 to 5 centimeters (about 1 to 2 inches) tall. Mosses' leaves are only one or two cells thick.

Mosses and liverworts don't have roots. However, they stay anchored in one place. That's because they have hairlike fibers that do a job much like roots. The fibers are called **rhizoids** (RIGH·zoydz). Rhizoids, like other parts of mosses and liverworts, can take in water from their surroundings. The water then travels directly from one cell to the next.

Most of the plants you see every day grow from seeds. However, mosses and liverworts are seedless plants. They grow from **spores**. Spores are cells that can develop into new organisms.

Nonvascular

Mosses

Liverworts

Mosses and liverworts grow in damp places. Most are tiny plants, growing only 2 to 5 centimeters (about 1 to 2 inches) tall.

Club mosses

Club mosses produce spores at the ends of stems in structures that look like tiny pine cones.

Spores are tiny structures found inside a capsule called a *spore capsule*.

Many mosses look like green, fuzzy pillows. Many liverworts look more like flat leaves. Ancient people thought that the shape of these plants resembled a liver. That's how they got their name.

Seedless Vascular Plants

True mosses and liverworts are seedless plants. So are their more distant relatives club mosses, spike mosses, horsetails, and ferns. All of them use spores to reproduce. However, mosses and liverworts are different from the other four in a very important way. Mosses and liverworts don't have a vascular system. Club mosses, spike mosses, horsetails, and ferns do.

The vascular tissue in these plants is made up of long tubelike cells. These cells let water and food move easily over long distances. That is why vascular plants can grow very tall and thick. That is also why nonvascular plants like true mosses and liverworts are so short and delicate. The trunks of the largest ferns can be as thick as your body.

What are mosses like?

Vascular

Horsetails

The stems of horsetails are hollow, have a ring of vascular tissue and joints, and contain a gritty, sandy substance called silica.

Ferns

Ferns come in all sizes and shapes and live in different kinds of climates.

Spike mosses

Spike mosses, such as this "resurrection plant," live in the desert. Resurrection plants can dry out when there is no rain, but they do not die. They revive when water becomes available again.

QUICK LAB

Ferns

FOLDABLES™ Make a Folded Table. (See p. R 42.) Label it as shown.

Fern	Form	Function
stem		
leaves		
spores		

1. Use the Folded Table to record your observations.
2. **Observe** Carefully examine a fern plant. Look at the stem. Observe how the leaves grow from the stem. Find the veins in the leaves.
3. **Observe** Find a leaf whose bottom is covered with brownish spots. These are spore cases.
4. **Experiment** Place a drop of water on a clean slide. Use a toothpick to scrape one of the spore cases into the drop of water.
5. **Observe** Examine the spore case under the low power of a microscope. What does the spore case contain?
6. **Infer** Describe what ferns and mosses have in common on the back of your Folded Table.

What Are Ferns?

Ferns once formed huge forests on Earth. You can still find them today in many wooded areas. Many people also grow ferns at home. What are ferns like?

Finding spore cases on the bottom of a fern leaf

Preparing a slide for viewing one spore case

Ferns have leaves that are called **fronds** (FRAHNDZ). They grow above the ground from an underground stem called a **rhizome** (RIGH·zohm). Roots, which anchor the plant to the soil or to a tree, branch out from the rhizome.

The bottom sides of some fronds are covered with rows of brownish or rust-colored spore cases that contain spores. Under the right conditions, the spore cases pop open and spray spores as far away as a few meters. If the spores land in a place where conditions are right for fern growth, the spores will develop into the first stage in a new fern's life cycle.

READING **Compare and Contrast**
How do mosses and ferns get water?

Spore cases arranged on the bottom of a fern frond will pop open, spraying spores all around. If conditions are right where the spores fall, the spores will produce new fern plants.

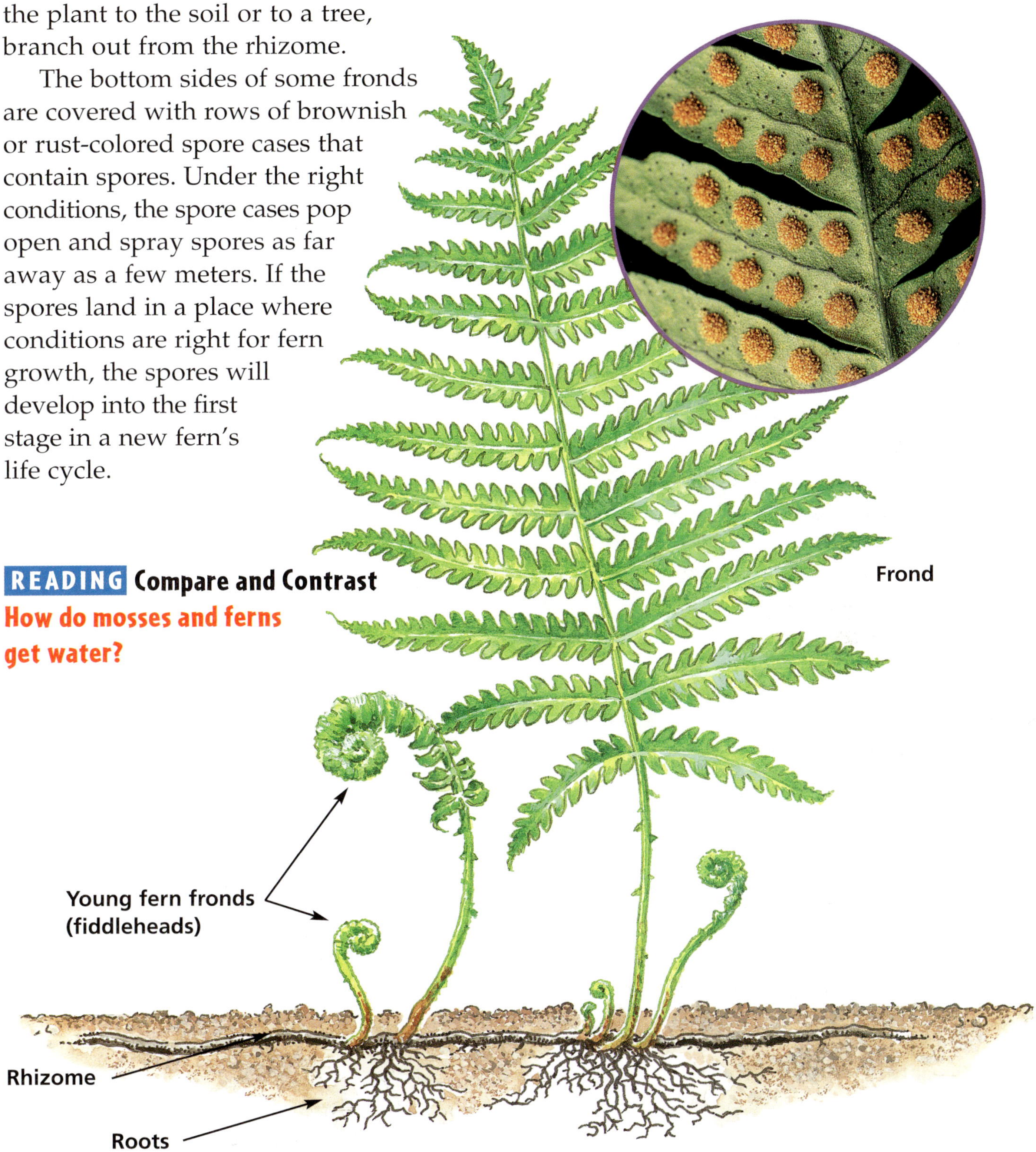

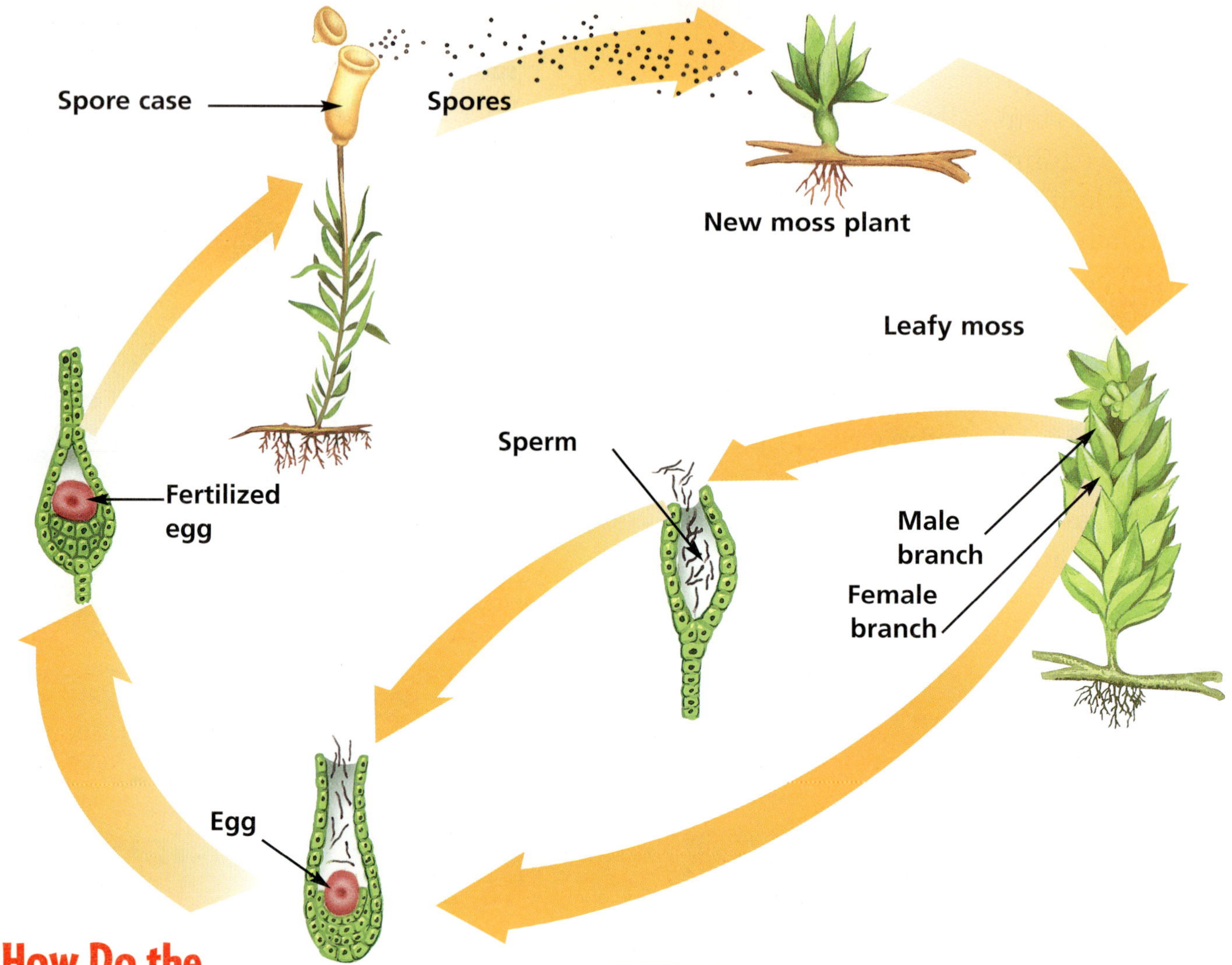

How Do the Life Cycles of Mosses and Ferns Differ?

Since mosses and ferns use spores to *reproduce* (ree·pruh·DEWS)—make new plants—you might guess that their life cycles are similar. That guess would be correct, but there are differences, too.

The diagrams on these two pages will help you compare and contrast the life cycles of mosses and ferns.

Both mosses and ferns have two separate stages to their life cycles. One stage is when they produce spores. This stage in the life cycle is called **asexual reproduction** (ay·SEK·shew·uhl ree·pruh·DUK·shuhn). That's because the plant needs only one type of cell—the spore—in order to reproduce.

Moss spores grow into leafy moss plants that have male branches and female branches. The male branches produce *sperm*—male sex cells. The female branches produce eggs—female sex cells. When a male sex cell meets a female sex cell, the two may join together. This is called **fertilization** (fur·tuh·luh·ZAY·shuhn).

This stage in the cycle is called **sexual reproduction** (SEK·shew·uhl ree·pruh·DUK·shuhn). That's because

Life Cycle of a Fern

READING Diagrams

Where are a fern's spores produced?

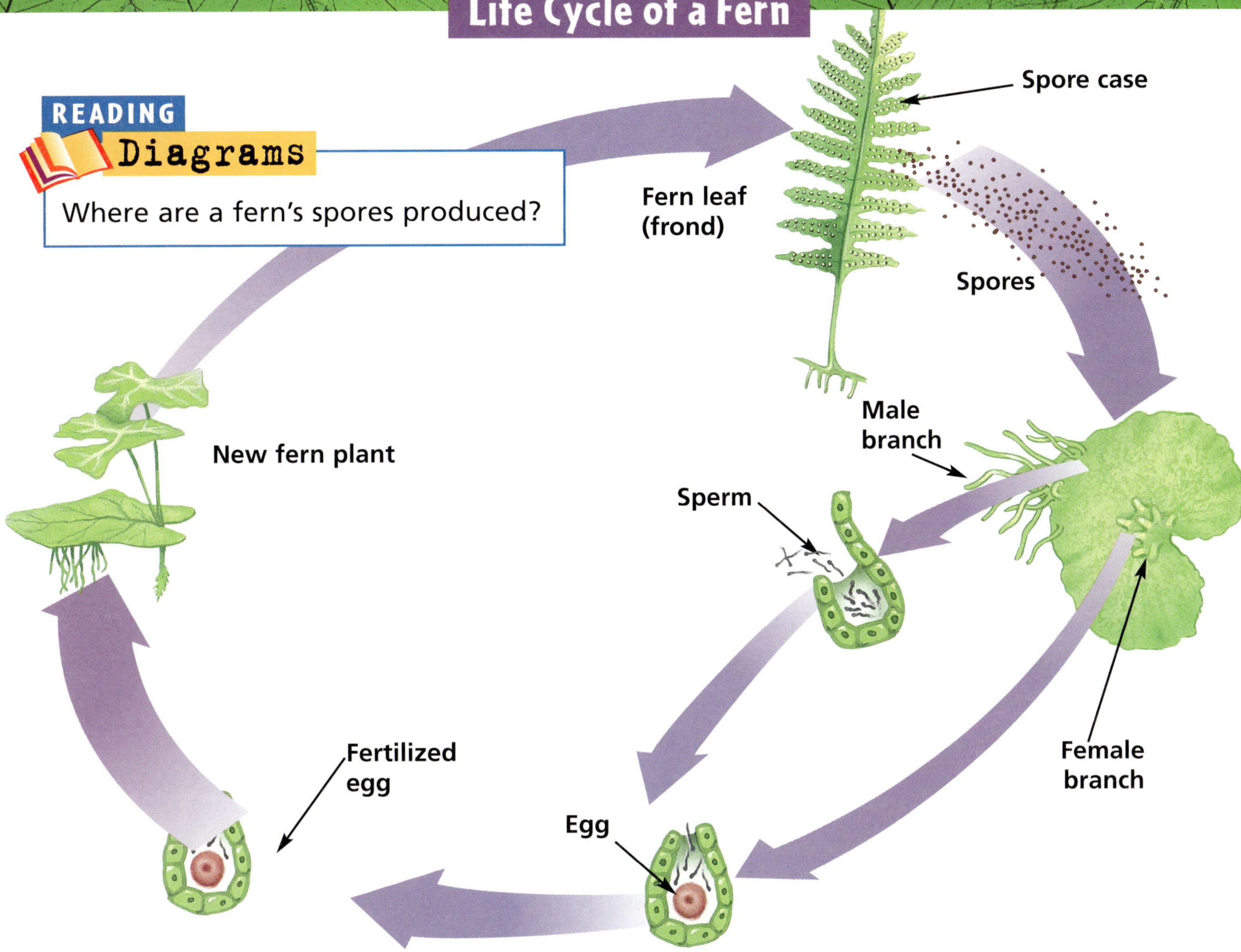

the plant needs both male sex cells and female sex cells in order to reproduce.

The fertilized egg eventually becomes a thin stalk with a spore case on top. When the spore case opens, the spores are released. Spores that land on damp ground may grow into new moss plants, and the cycle begins again.

This process of going from sexual reproduction to asexual reproduction to sexual reproduction again is called *alternation of generations*.

Ferns also reproduce by alternation of generations. Leafy fern plants produce spores on the undersides of their fronds.

Spores landing in shady, moist soil are most likely to grow. The spores grow into small, heart-shaped plants. These plants produce male and female sex cells.

If a male sex cell fertilizes a female sex cell, the fertilized egg starts to form a new plant. The new plant develops into a leafy fern plant. Spore cases on the fern's fronds produce spores, and the cycle begins again.

In what ways are the life cycles of mosses and ferns alike?

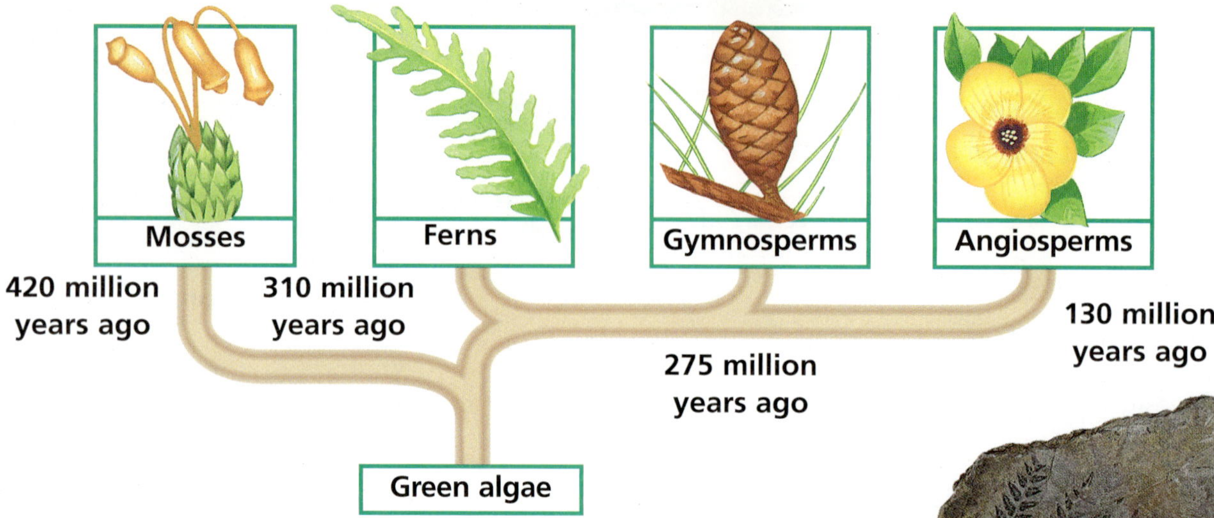

What Were the Ancestors of Plants?

The first land plants developed from living things that lived in the water. Which living things were the ancestors of land plants?

Scientists searched for clues linking organisms that lived in water to those that first grew on land. A good place to start was with photosynthetic organisms. These were living things that made their own food.

To narrow the search, the scientific detectives compared the chlorophyll of various simple organisms living today with that of plants. They found the closest match was with green algae.

Scientists found other clues. The cell walls of both green algae and plants contain cellulose. Cellulose can help plants survive on land, since a strong cell wall helps plants stay upright.

There was another clue. Both green algae and plants store food as starch.

Next, scientists hunted for fossils—the preserved remains of living things.

This fernlike plant was found in rock that is over 340 million years old.

Fossils are found mostly in rocks. Scientists have ways of finding out how old different rocks are. If you know the age of a rock, you also know the age of the fossil in it.

Putting all the pieces of this puzzle together, scientists concluded that the first land plants to evolve, or develop, from algae were probably nonvascular plants similar to mosses. These early land plants first appeared about 420 million years ago. Vascular plants appeared more recently. The earliest vascular plants, the ferns, were seedless. The first plants with seeds were gymnosperms, followed by angiosperms, or flowering plants.

How did scientists find the ancestors of plants?

Why It Matters

Mosses and ferns were among the first plants to live on land. Today mosses are often the first plants to return to an area where plant life has been destroyed. Mosses help break down rocks into soil. Mosses also help hold on to the soil, making it easier for other plants to survive in the area. Without mosses, perhaps your favorite plants would never have had a chance to grow where they do.

e-Journal Visit our Web site **www.science.mmhschool.com** to do a research project on mosses and ferns.

Think and Write

1. Why do mosses grow close to the ground?
2. Why do people sometimes add moss to a garden?
3. How do mosses change rocky areas so other plants can grow?
4. List two differences between mosses and ferns.
5. **Critical Thinking** How do cell walls help plants survive on land?

L·I·N·K·S

ART LINK

Make a poster. Find pictures of different kinds of ferns, and make a chart. Label each fern, and write a brief description of where each one can be found. Try to include at least one of the following: interrupted fern, leather fern, strap fern, vine fern, shoestring fern, ostrich fern. How do you think these ferns got their names?

WRITING LINK

Expository Writing Write a guidebook about the kinds of ferns found in your area. Use facts and descriptive details. On each page, place a photograph or drawing of one of the ferns. Include a caption that describes the fern as well as information about where it can be found.

MATH LINK

Solve this problem. Study the time line on page A64. About how long after early land plants first appeared did gymnosperms appear? About how long after gymnosperms did angiosperms appear?

TECHNOLOGY LINK

LOG ON Visit **www.science.mmhschool.com** for more links.

LESSON 6

Plants with Seeds

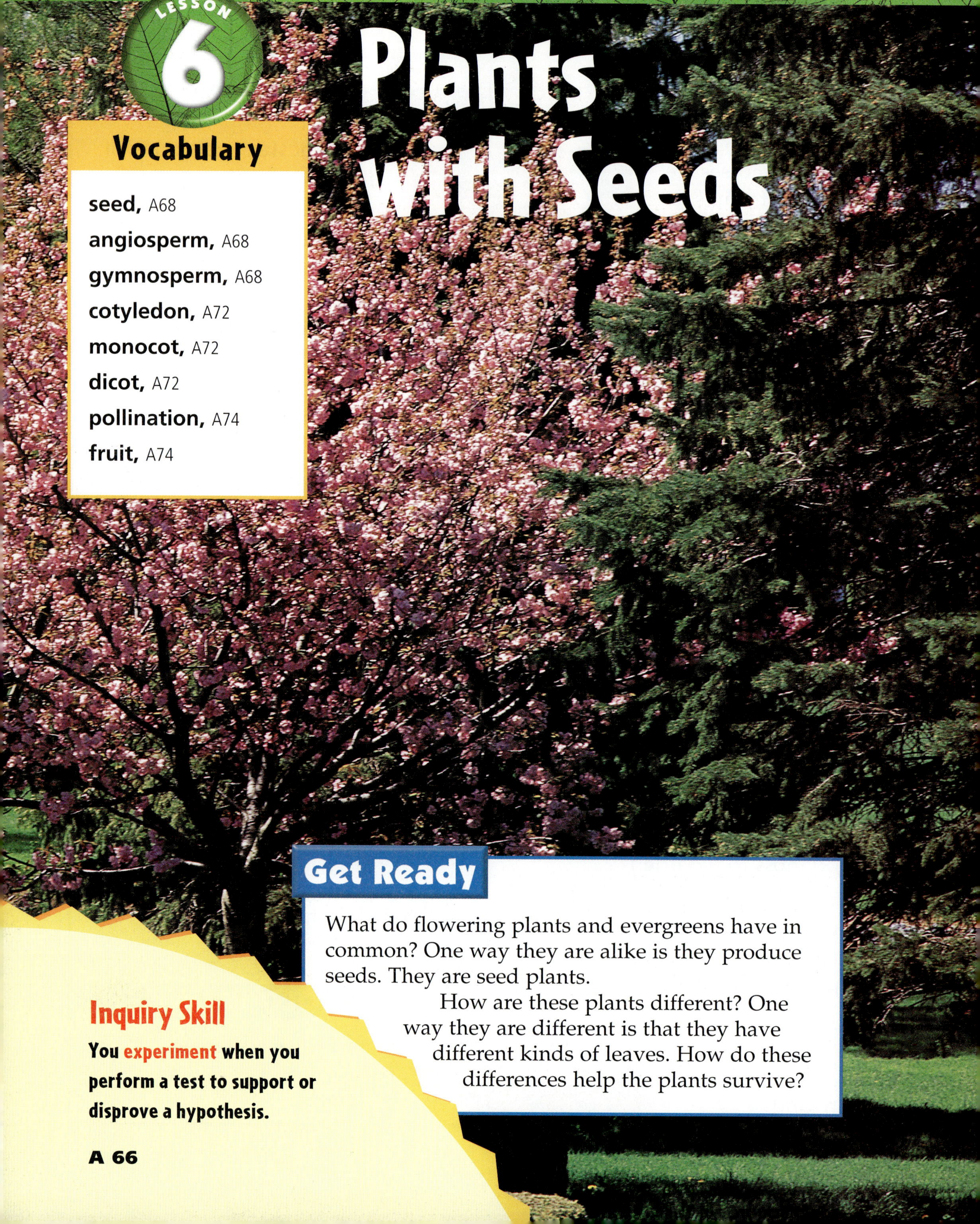

Vocabulary

seed, A68
angiosperm, A68
gymnosperm, A68
cotyledon, A72
monocot, A72
dicot, A72
pollination, A74
fruit, A74

Get Ready

What do flowering plants and evergreens have in common? One way they are alike is they produce seeds. They are seed plants.

How are these plants different? One way they are different is that they have different kinds of leaves. How do these differences help the plants survive?

Inquiry Skill

You experiment when you perform a test to support or disprove a hypothesis.

Explore Activity

How Do Seed Plants Differ?

Procedure

1. **Observe** Examine each plant. Use the hand lens to examine a leaf from each one. Draw each leaf, and label it with the name of the plant it came from.
2. **Observe** Remove a part of the lower epidermis from the grass leaf. Make a wet-mount slide. Examine the slide under low power.
3. **Communicate** Draw what you observe.
4. **Observe** Repeat step 2 with a pine needle and a houseplant leaf (such as a geranium). Draw what you observe.

Materials

- small pine seedling or other conifer
- grass plant
- garden plant or houseplant, such as a geranium
- hand lens
- microscope slide
- coverslip
- microscope

Drawing Conclusions

1. **Interpret Data** How are the leaves of the three plants alike? How are the leaves of the three plants different from one another?
2. **Infer** Which one of the plants do you think is least like the other two? Explain your reasoning.
3. **FURTHER INQUIRY** **Experiment** Of the plants you examined, predict which could survive best in a dry environment. How do you think the plant's leaves would help it do this? Design an experiment that would test your prediction.

Read to Learn

Main Idea **One group of seed plants produces seeds on cones, the other group produces seeds inside fruits.**

How Do Seed Plants Differ?

How are the leaves of a grass plant, a pine tree, and a geranium different? Two of these plants come from one major group of seed plants, while the other comes from a different group.

Both groups are vascular plants. Both groups reproduce from **seeds**. A seed contains an undeveloped plant and stored food for the young plant.

Most of the plants that you see every day are seed plants. They include grasses, trees, shrubs, and bushes. They all have roots, stems, and leaves. Some, called **angiosperms** (AN·jee·uh·spurmz), produce flowers. The others, called **gymnosperms** (JIM·nuh·spurmz), do not produce flowers. These are the two major groups of seed plants.

The gymnosperms are the oldest seed plants. They include such evergreen trees as pine, fir, cedar, juniper, yew, larch, and spruce.

Gymnosperms first appeared on Earth about 250 million years ago. One hundred million years would pass before the first angiosperms appeared.

The fruits, vegetables, grains, and almost all of the nuts you eat are produced by angiosperms. However, one tasty nut—the pine nut, or pignoli—is a gymnosperm seed. It is the seed of certain pine trees.

Gymnosperms

Gymnosperms include some of the largest and oldest living things.

Conifers are found mostly in the northern parts of the world.

The seed for this bristlecone pine sprouted about 5,000 years ago.

The giant redwood (left) can grow as tall as a 30-story building.

The gymnosperms are divided into four divisions. They are the *conifers* (KAHN·uh·furz), *cycads* (SIGH·kadz), *ginkgoes* (GING·kohz), and *gnetophytes* (NE·toh·fights). Look at the photographs on these pages. You'll notice that these plants look different. However, they all have certain things in common.

Their seeds are produced on the scales of female cones. The seeds are not surrounded by a fruit. The leaves of most gymnosperms look like needles or scales. Most gymnosperms are *evergreens*. Evergreens lose only a few leaves at a time and constantly replace the leaves they have lost.

Some conifers, such as the larch, dawn redwood, and bald cypress, lose their leaves each fall. Plants that do this are called *deciduous* (di·SIJ·ew·uhs).

When gymnosperms evolved, most of Earth was cold and dry. These plants are well adapted to cold, dry climates. For example, the needles of conifers have a very small surface area and are covered with a thick cuticle. They lose less water than the wider leaves of flowering plants.

READING Compare and Contrast
How are angiosperms and gymnosperms different?

Cycads (left) live in warm climates. The red strawberry-shaped structures are not fruits but female cones.

The maidenhair tree (right) is the only member of the ginkgo division. It has fan-shaped leaves and round green fruit.

Gnetophytes (right) are more closely related to flowering plants than any other gymnosperm.

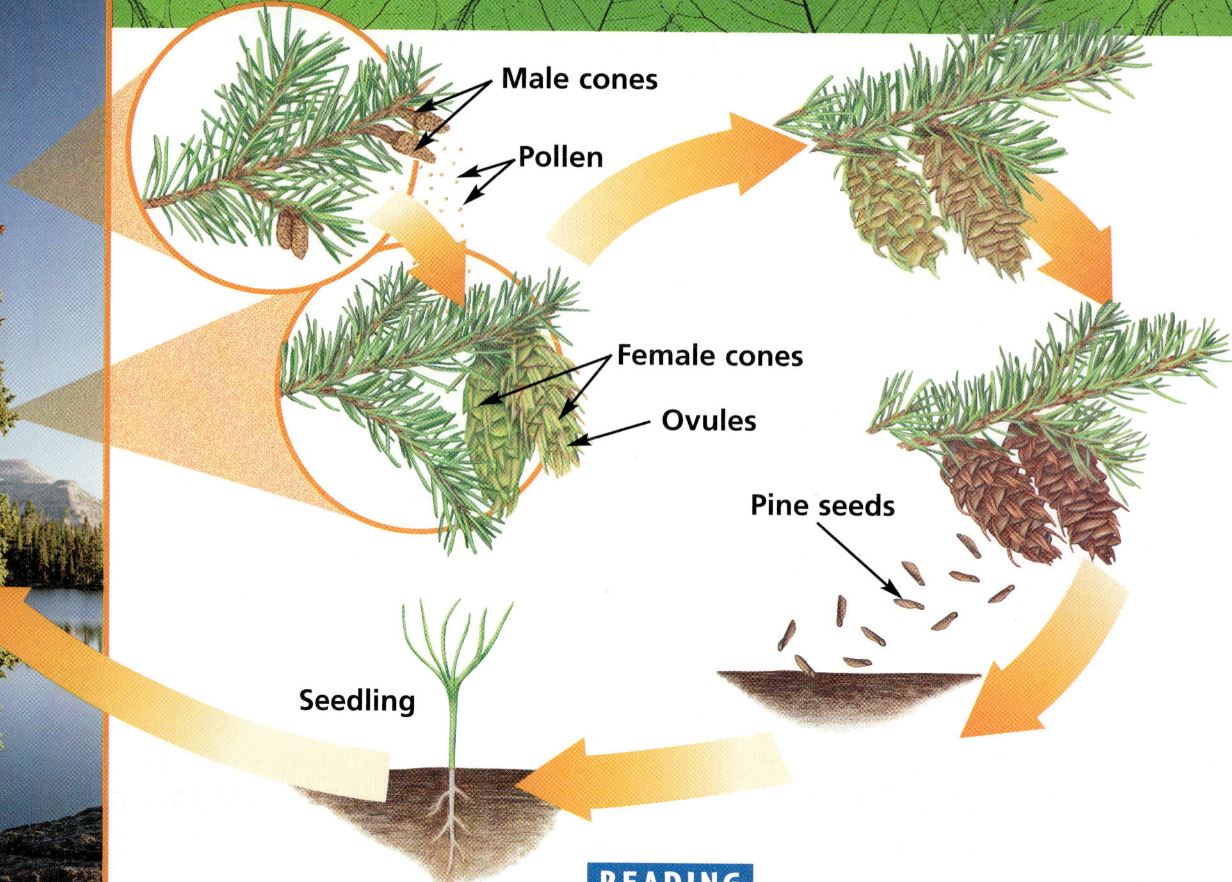

READING Diagrams

What are the steps in the life cycle of a conifer?

What Is the Life Cycle of a Conifer?

Since gymnosperms don't produce flowers or fruits, their life cycle is not the same as the life cycle of angiosperms. However, there are similarities. As you look at the diagram on this page, and later at the life cycle of angiosperms, think of their similarities and differences.

Let's examine the life cycle of a pine tree. A pine tree belongs to a group of gymnosperms called conifers. Pines produce male and female cones on a mature tree. The scales that form the cones carry spore cases that produce the plant's sperm and egg cells. Male cones produce pollen grains, which contain sperm cells.

When pollen grains fall away from a male cone, the wind carries them through the air. If a pollen grain happens to land on a female cone, a sperm cell from the pollen may fertilize an egg cell in the female cone.

The fertilized cell eventually becomes a seed. As autumn and winter come, the female pine cones fall from the trees. Their seeds scatter on the ground. Sometimes wind or water will carry the seeds far from the tree. If they end up in a place where conditions are right for germination, the seeds will sprout, and a new pine tree will start growing.

Where are conifer seeds found?

What Are Angiosperms?

Angiosperms are the most recently evolved and best-adapted division of seed plants. There are about 235,000 different kinds of angiosperms, which makes them the largest division in the plant kingdom.

The world's largest flower belongs to this parasitic plant, Rafflesia, which lives in Southeast Asia.

Some, like duckweed, float on water and are about the size of a large bee's eye. Duckweed is the smallest flowering plant. The largest flowering plant is the giant eucalyptus tree, which can be 100 m (330 ft) tall and 20 m (66 ft) in circumference.

Angiosperms live in all climates and in all parts of the world. The saguaro cactus lives in the hot, dry desert. Duckweed and water lilies grow only in the water. Some orchids live high in the air attached to trees in hot, damp rain forests. Other angiosperms flower near the Arctic Circle. Oddly, a few angiosperms cannot live on their own. They have little or no chlorophyll and are *parasites*. That is, they live off other plants. The plant with the largest flower is this kind of parasitic angiosperm. The flower can be a meter across, as thick as your thumb, and weigh as much as a small dog.

How can you tell an angiosperm from a gymnosperm? Angiosperms produce flowers; gymnosperms do not. The seeds of angiosperms are inside a fruit. Gymnosperms do not produce fruits.

Flowering trees produce the fruits you eat.

What are two locations where angiosperms live?

What Are Cotyledons?

Scientists divide the angiosperms into two classes. As you might guess, scientists are able to do this because of some particular characteristic that sets the two classes apart. That characteristic turns out to be the number of an angiosperm's **cotyledons** (kaht·uh·LEE·duhnz). A cotyledon, also called a seed leaf, is a tiny leaflike structure inside a seed.

Some angiosperm seeds contain only one cotyledon. Plants whose seeds contain only one cotyledon are called *monocotyledons*, or **monocots** (MAHN·uh·kahts) for short. (The prefix *mono-* comes from a Greek word meaning "one.") There are over 60,000 different kinds of monocots. Corn, rice, wheat, grasses, orchids, and coconut palms are examples of monocots.

Angiosperms whose seeds contain two cotyledons are called *dicotyledons*, or **dicots** (DIGH·kahts) for short. (The prefix *di-* comes from a Greek word meaning "two.") There are over 170,000 kinds of dicots. Bean plants, maple trees, rose plants, and cactuses are some of the dicots.

What are three differences between monocots and dicots?

Characteristics of Monocots and Dicots

Characteristics	Monocots	Dicots
Cotyledons	 One	Two 
Leaf veins	Parallel 	 Branched
Flower parts	 Multiples of three	Multiples of four or five 
Vascular system	Scattered in bundles 	 In rings

Inquiry Skill BUILDER

SKILL Observe

Flowering Plants

In this activity you will observe flowering plants in order to try to classify them. That is, you will examine several plants and try to determine whether each is a monocot or a dicot. As you examine each plant sample, refer to the chart on page A72 to help you classify the sample.

Materials

sample leaves and flowers from various angiosperms

Procedure

1. **Observe** Get together with a few of your classmates and go on a leaf- and flower-collecting field trip. (Make sure to avoid poison ivy, poison oak, and poison sumac leaves. Your teacher can tell you how to spot them.)
2. **Observe** Find a number of different angiosperms. Try to get a sample of a leaf and flower from each plant. If you can't get a flower, a leaf will do.
3. **Interpret Data** Look at the chart of Characteristics of Monocots and Dicots. It will give you clues on how to tell if the sample leaves and flowers you chose are monocots or dicots.

Drawing Conclusions

1. **Observe** Examine the plant parts you have chosen. For each sample leaf, describe how the leaf veins look. For each sample flower, tell how many parts the flower has. Record your answers.
2. **Classify** Mount the leaves and flowers on a heavy sheet of cardboard, and indicate whether each came from a monocot or a dicot.

Life Cycle of an Angiosperm

What Is the Life Cycle of An Angiosperm?

The life cycle of an angiosperm is similar to the life cycle of a gymnosperm in many ways. The main difference between the two cycles is that angiosperms produce flowers and fruits.

Let's examine the life cycle of a cherry tree. The cherry is an angiosperm. The flowers of angiosperms usually have both male and female parts. The male parts are the stamens. The stamens produce pollen grains, which contain sperm cells. The female part is the pistil. The pistil contains the ovules, which produce the egg cells.

Pollen grains are transferred from a flower's stamen to its pistil, or to another flower's pistil. Pollen grains contain a nucleus. This transfer is called **pollination** (pahl-uh-NAY-shuhn). Once in the stigma, the male nucleus and the egg cell become a seed. As the seeds develop, the surrounding ovary enlarges and becomes the **fruit**. The fruit protects the seeds inside it. If the fruit reaches a place where conditions are right for germination, the seeds will sprout, and a new cherry tree will start growing.

READING **Compare and Contrast**
How are the life cycles of angiosperms and gymnosperms similar?

Lesson Review

Why It Matters

Plants with seeds provide us with many useful products such as cotton, paper, foods, and construction materials.

Understanding the life cycles of seed plants is important because it enables people to control the growth and reproduction of the plants. People can change the life cycle of plants to fit their needs.

e-Journal Visit our Web site www.science.mmhschool.com to do a research project on the different things plants with seeds provide us.

Think and Write

1. How are the life cycles of gymnosperms and angiosperms different?
2. How are flowers important to a plant?
3. What are the differences between monocots and dicots?
4. INQUIRY SKILL **Observe** List five plants that are angiosperms and five plants that are gymnosperms. Explain what characteristics helped you determine which was which.
5. **Critical Thinking** How have seed plants become adapted to the environment?

L·I·N·K·S

WRITING LINK

Writing a Story Use your imagination to write a story about a special plant. Classify the plant as an angiosperm or a gymnosperm and as a monocot or dicot. Describe the setting, characters, and problem at the beginning of your story. Solve the problem at the end.

ART LINK

Make your own flip books. Illustrate a "year in the life of an angiosperm" by making a flip book. Do the same for a gymnosperm.

MATH LINK

Make a pie chart. Make a list of the 10 vegetables and fruits you eat the most. Research whether each of these foods are monocots or dicots. Make a pie chart to show the percentage of monocots you eat compared with the percentage of dicots.

TECHNOLOGY LINK

LOG ON Visit www.science.mmhschool.com for more links.

LESSON 7

Flowers and Seeds

Vocabulary

ovary, A78

self-pollination, A80

cross-pollination, A80

embryo, A82

seed coat, A82

Get Ready

Have you ever seen bees buzzing around flowers? Don't disturb them. From a distance you might watch as a bee goes from flower to flower. What do you think it is doing?

Insects and other animals, such as butterflies and hummingbirds, also hover around flowers. What do you think they do for the plants? What do plants use their flowers for?

Inquiry Skill

You infer when you form an idea from facts or observations.

Explore Activity

How Do Flowers Differ?

Procedure: Design Your Own

1. Decide how you will compare the flowers you look at. You may choose to look for parts that they seem to have in common. Describe what the parts are and how they differ from plant to plant.
2. Begin by removing the outer leaflike parts. Examine them. Draw what they look like.
3. Remove the petals. Examine them. Draw what they look like.
4. **Observe** Examine the rest of the flower. Draw what you see.
5. **Communicate** Draw the parts you decided to compare in different flowers.

Drawing Conclusions

1. **Communicate** What color is each flower? What do you think the job of the petals is? How would you design an experiment to find out?
2. **Infer** What do you think the flower parts you chose are for? Do you think the same parts of different flowers do the same kinds of jobs for their plants?
3. **FURTHER INQUIRY** **Infer** Why do you think a plant has flowers? Design an experiment to test your hypothesis. Try it and report your results.

Materials

- several large flowers from different plants
- hand lens
- forceps
- dropper
- toothpick

Read to Learn

Main Idea **Fertilized flowers produce seeds that become new plants.**

How Do Flowers Differ?

Not all flowers are alike. Some flowers are *complete flowers*. Complete flowers have sepals, petals, stamens, and pistils. *Incomplete flowers* are missing one of these parts. Some flowers are called perfect. *Perfect flowers* have both female and male parts, that is, both pistils (female parts) and stamens (male parts).

Imperfect flowers have either pistils or stamens, but not both. You might think of these flowers as "female" or "male." Some plants, like corn and oak trees, have separate male and female flowers on the same plant. Other plants,

Parts of a Flower

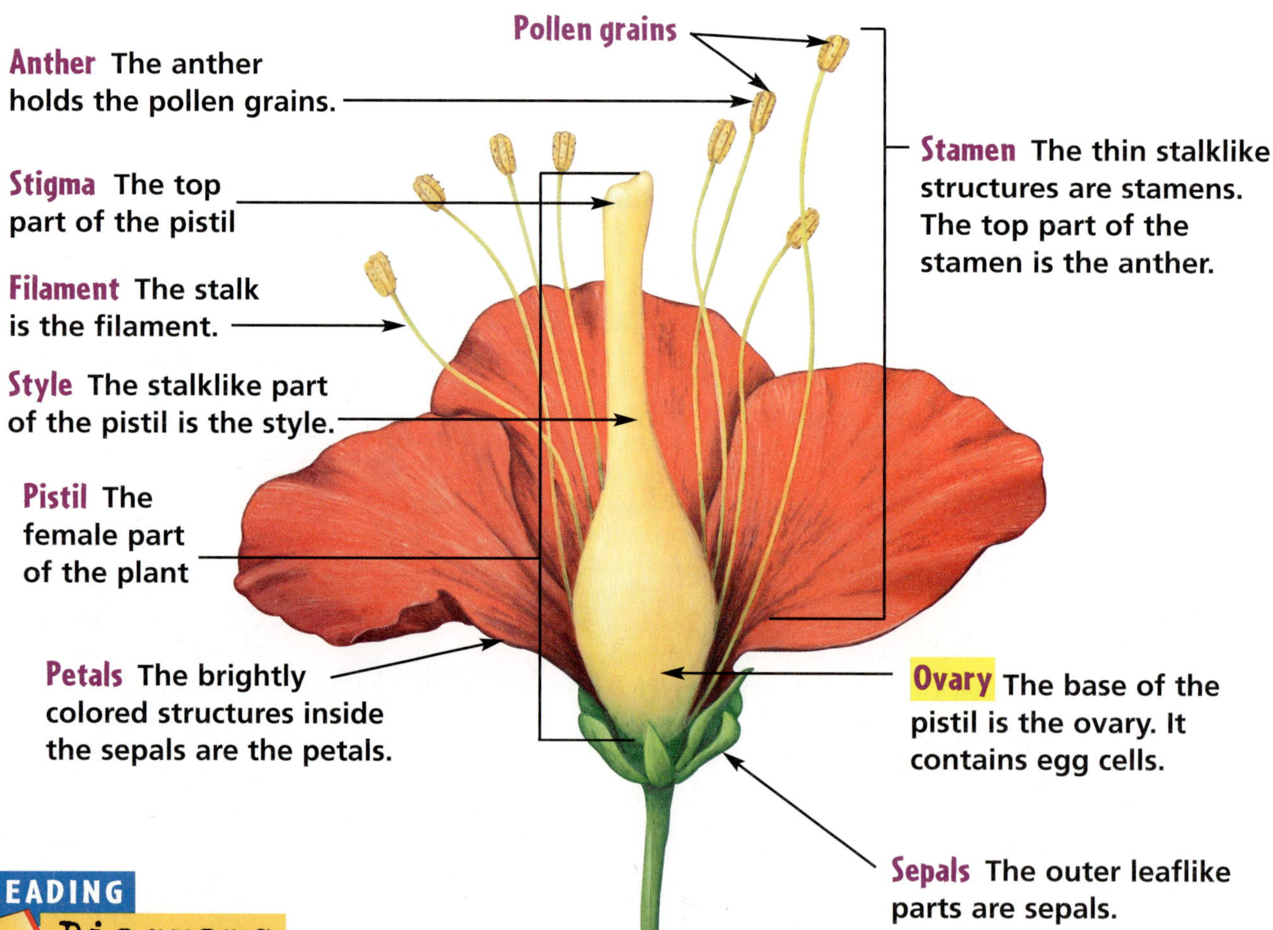

READING Diagrams

Organize the information from this picture into a chart. Include which parts are "male" and which are "female."

Does this holly tree have male flowers or female flowers? How can you tell?

like willow trees and holly trees, have only male flowers or female flowers.

The red holly berries that you see on holly trees in the late fall appear only on holly trees with female flowers. In order to produce the berries (the holly's fruit), the tree with female flowers needs to be fertilized by pollen from a holly tree with male flowers. An oak tree has both male and female flowers on the same tree.

READING Compare and Contrast
How do complete and incomplete flowers differ?

An oak tree has tiny green flowers.

What Are Pollination and Fertilization?

Some seeds are very tiny, whereas others are really large. The largest is produced by the double-coconut tree, whose seeds can be about half your weight. Some of the smallest seeds belong to orchid plants. You could put thousands of them in a teaspoon.

No matter how large or small, all seeds develop the same way. Look at the diagram on this page. It will help you understand the difference between pollination and fertilization.

As you learned in Lesson 6, pollination occurs when a pollen grain is transferred from the anther to the stigma. If the pollen is transferred from an anther to a stigma in the same flower, the process is called **self-pollination**. If the transfer is from one flower to the flower of another plant, the process is called **cross-pollination**.

Pollination

Self-Pollination
Pollination occurs when a pollen grain from an anther reaches the stigma. This flower is pollinating itself because its own pollen is reaching its own stigma.

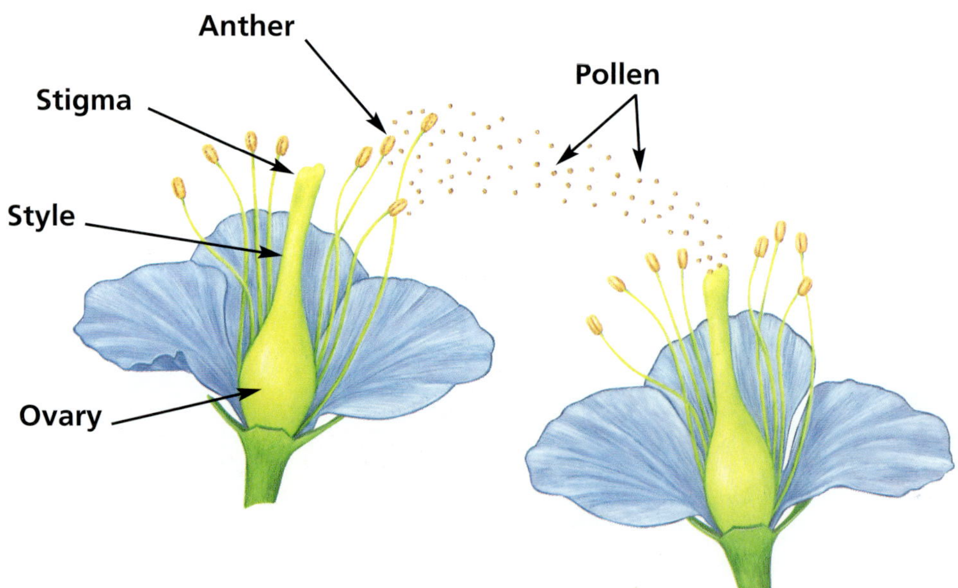

Cross-Pollination
Pollination can occur between two or more flowers on separate plants. Here the pollen of one flower reaches the stigma of another.

READING Diagrams

How are self-pollination and cross-pollination alike? How are they different?

On the stigma a tube forms from the pollen grain. The tube grows down the style and into the flower's ovary. The pollen's nucleus travels down the tube, through the style, and into the ovary. There, it combines with, or fertilizes, an egg cell. This combining is called *fertilization*.

A seed develops from a fertilized egg cell. Under the right conditions, a new plant will develop from the seed. As you have learned, the process of making a new plant from the joining of a sperm and an egg cell is called *sexual reproduction*.

What are the steps involved in cross-pollination and fertilization?

Fertilization

1 Once the pollen has landed on the sticky stigma of a pistil, a pollen tube starts to grow.

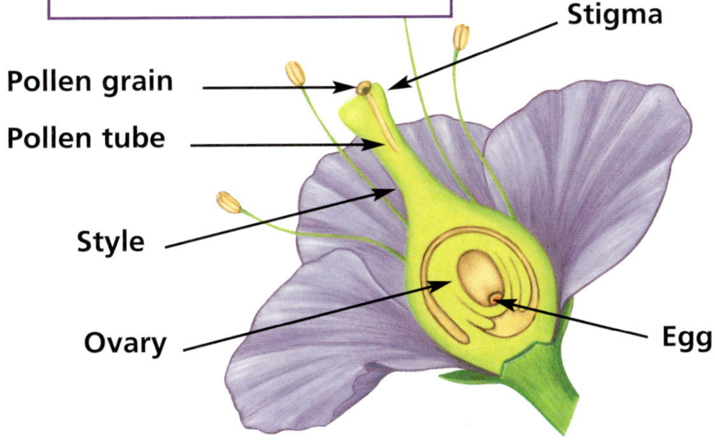

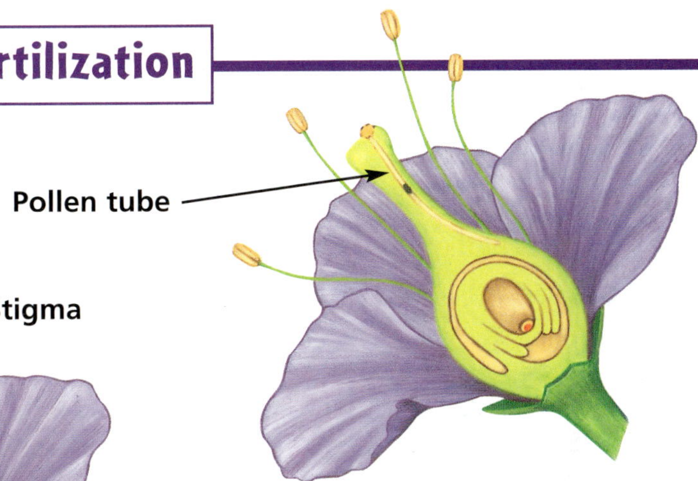

2 The pollen tube grows from the pollen grain down the style. It grows into the ovary until it reaches an egg cell.

Fertilization
Fertilization occurs when a nucleus from a pollen grain travels down the style and combines with an egg in the ovary.

3 The nucleus travels down the pollen tube and fertilizes the egg cell.

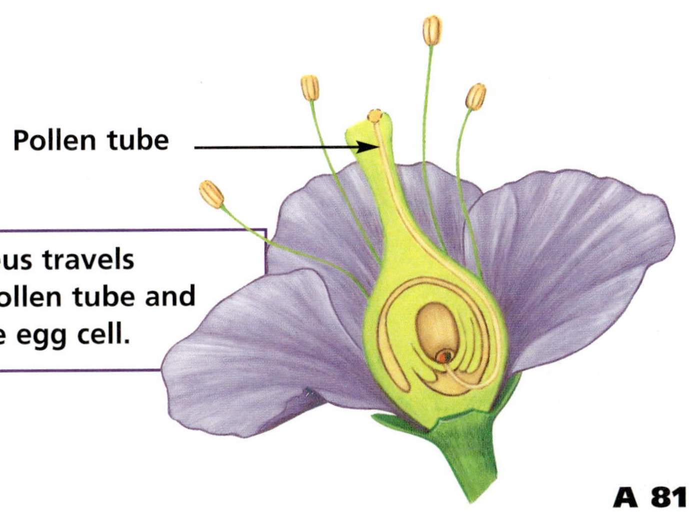

QUICK LAB

Inside a Seed

FOLDABLES™ Make a Two-Tab Book. (See p. R 41.) Label the tabs as shown.

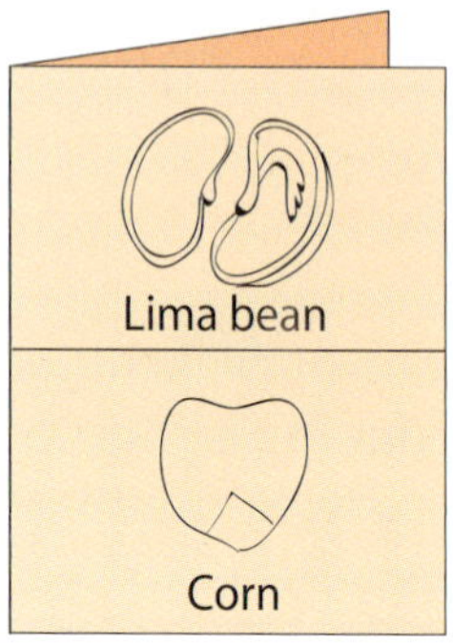

1. Soak a lima bean in water overnight.
2. **Observe** Carefully pull apart the two halves of the lima bean. Examine the halves with a hand lens. Draw what you see.
3. **Infer** Which part is the embryo?
4. On your drawing, label the seed coat and the cotyledon, where food is stored.
5. **Communicate** Compare a corn kernel with a lima bean. Describe how its parts are similar to or different from the lima bean in your Two-Tab Book.
6. **Classify** Which seed is a dicot? Which is a monocot? Explain how you know which is which in your Two-Tab Book.

What Is in a Seed?

A seed contains an **embryo** (EM·bree·oh). An embryo is an immature plant. Often the embryo includes large cotyledons, where food is stored in the form of starch. A seed also has a **seed coat**. The seed coat encases the whole seed in a tough, protective covering.

Parts of a Seed

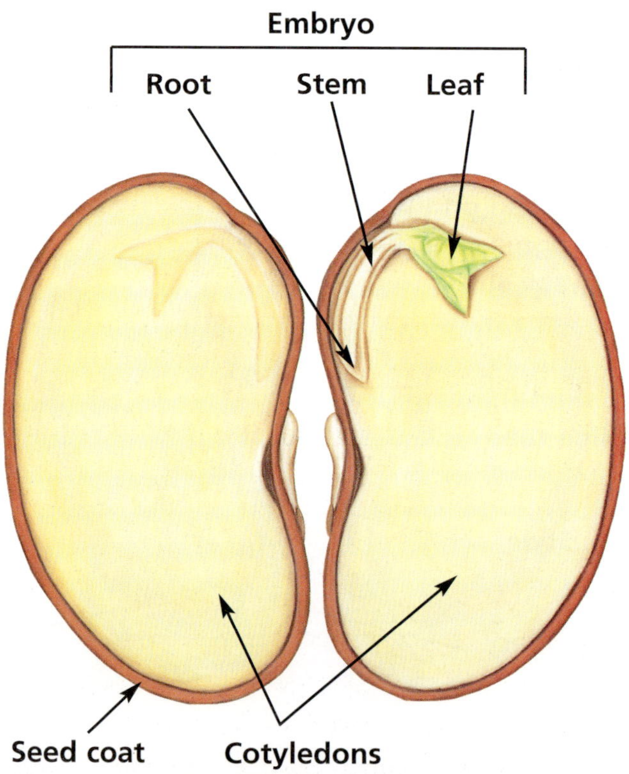

From Seed to Plant

Two things must happen for a seed to produce a new plant. First, the seed must move from the flower to a place where it can sprout. This is called *seed dispersal* (SEED di·SPUR·suhl). Second, the place must provide everything that is needed for sprouting, which is called *germination* (jur·muh·NAY·shuhn). The right temperature and water are the two most important needs for germination. Food is not needed because the seed has its own supply of stored food.

Coconut seeds rely on ocean currents and sea breezes to move them.

The seeds of a cocklebur have tiny hooks that cling to the fur of animals or the clothing of people.

Usually the seed must move a relatively long distance from its parent plant. Why? Competition from its parent, and plants like it, may make the development of a new plant difficult. For example, nearby plants may block sunlight from reaching the young plant. They may soak up the water or minerals from the soil that the new plant needs.

Animals eat fruits and the seeds inside.

Seeds have evolved all sorts of adaptations for dispersal. For example, dandelion fruits and cottonwood seeds have feathery "parachutes." These parachutes can be blown great distances by the wind. Animals also help move plant seeds.

Animals eat fruits. A fruit is a mature ripened ovary of a plant. The animals digest the soft parts of the fruits, but not the hard seeds inside. As the animals move from place to place, they deposit the seeds in their wastes.

How Gymnosperms Spread Seeds

Gymnosperms don't produce fruits. They disperse their seeds in other ways. For example, the cones of the balsam fir tree shatter. When they do this, they release winglike seeds that ride on the wind. Animals move cones from place to place. Heavy rains, floods, and streams can disperse them also.

What do the three main parts of a seed do?

The awful-smelling jack-in-the-pulpit flower attracts insects that help the plant reproduce.

Why Do Flowers Have Aromas?

The characteristics of living things help them survive in their environment. It would make sense to expect that the aromas of flowers do the same for their plants.

To your nose, some of these aromas are very pleasing. That's why flowers, such as roses and jasmines are used in perfumes. However, some flowers, like those of the jack-in-the-pulpit plant, smell awful. Surprisingly, both beautiful and awful aromas attract insects! What is the advantage of this?

When an insect enters the flower, it brushes against a part of the flower that holds tiny grains of dust, called pollen. These grains contain the plant's male sex cells.

The pollen sticks to the insect. As the insect moves around the flower—or moves to another flower on the plant—some of the pollen rubs off on parts of the flower that hold female sex cells. The two sex cells join, and the reproduction of a new plant begins.

Many plants attract one particular kind of insect. The jack-in-the-pulpit attracts dung beetles and flies. These insects generally feed on dead or decaying animals or animal wastes, which smell bad. The insects mistake the aroma of the plant for that of a good meal.

Once inside the flower, the insects discover that its sides are so smooth, they can't climb out. As they rush around inside the flower, they keep transferring pollen to the part of the flower that holds female sex cells.

After about 24 hours, something strange happens. The inside of the flower changes from smooth to wrinkled. Their job done, the insects can now get a foothold, escape, and move on to another flower.

How does a flower's aroma help it survive?

Why It Matters

Almost all of the plants that you eat are flowering plants. Flowering plants also produce food that wild and domesticated animals eat.

Like all plants, flowering plants help keep the balance of gases in the air by using up carbon dioxide and producing oxygen.

Flowering plants also decorate the landscape and homes with beautiful colors. Some produce chemicals that are used in perfumes and other cosmetics.

e-Journal Visit our Web site **www.science.mmhschool.com** to do a research project on flowers and seeds.

Think and Write

1. Identify the different parts of a flower, and tell what each part does.
2. Explain how seeds are produced.
3. Give at least three examples of how seeds are dispersed.
4. Describe the difference between fertilization and germination.
5. **Critical Thinking** How do you think trees having flowers that look like bees can help a plant survive?

L·I·N·K·S

LITERATURE LINK

Read *Jonathan Chapman: The Appleseed Man*, the story of the man who brought apple trees to the Old West. Think about the pros and cons of moving plants. Try the activities at the end of the book.

WRITING LINK

Persuasive Writing If farmers grow only one kind of plant, other plants become extinct. Research the advantages of plant diversification. Write a persuasive letter to the editor of a farmer's newsletter. Use facts.

MATH LINK

Solve this problem. About 1.8 billion metric tons of rice, wheat, and corn are produced every year. A metric ton equals 2,205 pounds. How many pounds of these grains are produced?

TECHNOLOGY LINK

Science Newsroom CD-ROM Choose *Flower Power* to learn more about how flowers attract pollinators.

LOG ON Visit **www.science.mmhschool.com** for more links.

It Takes One to Grow One

What if you could make an exact copy of yourself by removing a part of your body, say a foot, and watching it grow into a new "you"?

It may sound bizarre, but that's actually how some plants make new plants. Reproducing this way is a type of asexual reproduction called vegetative propagation. It's what happens when a part of a plant separates from the main plant, then grows into an exact copy of the plant.

Potatoes are a good example of vegetative propagation. It all starts with the dimples, or "eyes," on a potato. A new plant grows from the potato's eyes, which are actually clusters of tiny buds.

To start their potato crops, farmers cut potatoes into small pieces and plant them. As long as each piece has an eye, a new potato plant can grow. The tiny buds grow roots into the ground and shoots that sprout up through the soil. A new potato plant is born!

Other plants reproduce this way, too. In some species, new plants can grow from the stems, roots, or leaves of a parent plant.

- Strawberry plants send horizontal stems, called runners, that grow along the ground. Shoots and roots grow in places along the runner and develop into new plants.
- When the leaves of African violets are planted, they sprout new African violet plants.

From potatoes to strawberries, this is an amazing way for a part to become a new whole.

Strawberry plants send runners out to form new plants. Young plants that develop this way receive nourishment from the parent plant, so they have a better chance of survival.

A farmer gathers potatoes. With vegetative propagation, plants don't need seeds or partners to reproduce. They can also make many identical plants, helping to ensure the survival of their species.

This potato's "eyes" will grow shoots that can become a new potato. The new plant is genetically identical to its parent.

Write About It

1. What advantages might a farmer identify in vegetative propagation over sexual reproduction?
2. Vegetative propagation produces an exact copy of the parent plant. When could this be a disadvantage to the plant?

LOG ON Visit **www.science.mmhschool.com** to learn more about vegetative propagation.

Chapter 3 Review

Vocabulary

Fill each blank with the best word from the list.

angiosperm, A68
conifer, A69
cotyledon, A72
cross-pollination, A80
fertilization, A62
frond, A61
gymnosperm, A68
rhizoid, A58
self-pollination, A80
spore, A58

1. A plant that has flowers is called a(n) ____.

2. The transfer of a pollen grain from one flower to the stigma of another flower is called ____.

3. Transferring a pollen grain from an anther to a stigma in the same plant is known as ____.

4. A ____ is a gymnosperm.

5. Hairlike fibers that do the same job as roots are ____.

6. A seed plant that does not produce fruits is a(n) ____.

7. A new moss plant is produced by a(n) ____.

8. The leaflike structure of a fern is a(n) ____.

9. A tiny leaflike structure inside a seed is a(n) ____.

10. Male and female cells join together in ____.

Test Prep

11. Unlike other plants angiosperms produce ____.

A seeds
B flowers
C cones
D spores

12. Which of the following are gymnosperms?

F apple trees
G ferns
H fir trees
J grains

13. Bees help flowers reproduce through a process called ____.

A fertilization
B phototropism
C transpiration
D pollination

14. Mosses and liverworts are examples of ____.

F seedless non-vascular plants
G seedless vascular plants
H vascular plants
J gymnosperms

15. The process of making a new plant from the joining of a sperm and an egg cell is known as ______.

A asexual reproduction
B cross-pollination
C sexual reproduction
D self-pollination

Concepts and Skills

16. Reading in Science Write a paragraph explaining the difference between a monocot and a dicot.

Rose

Lily

17. Product Ads Look at the ingredients listed on boxes of breakfast foods. What kinds of plants are most commonly used to make breakfast foods? Write a paragraph explaining why.

18. Scientific Methods What would you do to ensure that a plant does not self-pollinate? Make an illustration to explain your answer.

19. INQUIRY SKILL **Observe** Tell which of these plants are angiosperms and which are gymnosperms—bristlecone pine, rose, wheat, oat, fir, cedar, lily, juniper, yew, larch, violet, tomato, spruce, giant redwood tree. Write a paragraph explaining your answer.

20. Critical Thinking How do you think trees that produce seedless oranges are grown? Write down your prediction. Then do library research to see if your prediction was correct.

Did You Ever Wonder?

INQUIRY SKILL **Communicate** The tiger orchid has some fascinating properties. Research this orchid and communicate your findings to the class.

LOG ON Visit www.science.mmhschool.com to boost your test scores.

CHAPTER 4

Animal Diversity

Did You Ever Wonder?

Where do starfish live? Although starfish live in every ocean on Earth, there are more kinds of starfish in the northern Pacific than anywhere else. Are starfish really fish? What other kinds of animals can you see in this photo?

INQUIRY SKILL **Predict** What happens when a starfish loses an arm?

LESSON 8

Animal Traits

Vocabulary

fish, A95
amphibian, A95
reptile, A95
bird, A95
mammal, A95

Get Ready

What do a tick and a zebra have in common? Animals can be very different from each other. However, all animals have certain traits in common. These traits have been developed as a response to similar needs. Many different kinds of animals visit a watering hole in Africa. What do these animals have in common?

Inquiry Skill

You classify when you place things that share properties together in groups.

Explore Activity

What Are the Traits of Animals?

Materials

- 25 pictures of animals
- 5 sheets of paper
- tape
- scissors

Procedure

BE CAREFUL! Be careful using scissors.

1. Cut out 25 animal pictures from old magazines.
2. **Classify** Think about the kinds of things all of the animals you found need to survive. Then, think about the traits that enable these animals to fulfill those needs.
3. **Communicate** Write why you think these animals are classified as animals.
4. **Classify** Now that you have seen the animals' similarities, look at their differences. What traits would you use to classify the 25 animals you have into different groups? How many groups would you make?

Drawing Conclusions

1. What trait was used most often for grouping the pictures?
2. **Infer** What is the best method for grouping the animals?
3. **FURTHER INQUIRY** **Infer** Why do you think scientists all over the world use a single system for grouping organisms?

Read to Learn

Main Idea **Animals with similar traits are classified in the same group.**

An octopus uses its tentacles to trap a fish.

What Are the Traits of Animals?

You know that a tarantula is an animal. You also know that a donkey is an animal. But do you know what makes an animal an animal?

Animals are many-celled organisms that are made of different kinds of cells. Most animal cells have a nucleus and specialized structures surrounded by a membrane. As you learned in Lesson 1 animal cells are organized to form tissues, organs, and organ systems. Organ systems enable animals to perform different functions such as sensing the environment, getting rid of wastes, and reproducing.

Animals can't make their own food. Some eat plants to supply their energy needs. Some animals eat other animals and some eat both plants and animals.

Most animals can move from place to place. They move to find food, shelter, mates, and to protect themselves from predators. Animals live in different kinds of environments—from the North Pole to the Amazon forest. They have developed organ systems and behaviors that allow them to survive in these different environments.

For example, since different animals eat different foods, they have developed different methods of getting food. Octopuses have tentacles that they use to capture prey, such as oysters, shrimp, or fish. Frogs have a long and sticky tongue so they can snare prey such as flies.

A frog uses its sticky tongue to trap a fly.

There are as many animal adaptations as there are animal species and there are about 10 million species of animals on Earth! So, how do scientists classify all these animals? Animals are divided into two large groups. Vertebrates are a group made up of animals that have backbones. The members of the invertebrate group do not have backbones. Vertebrates and invertebrates are divided into smaller groups. For example, vertebrates are divided into the following classes:

- **Fish** are the most diverse vertebrate group. Fish are vertebrates that live their whole life in water. Most fish have gills to take oxygen directly from the water. Fish are usually covered by scales.
- **Amphibians** are adapted to live part of their life in water and part of their life on land. Most adult amphibians can live on land, but they need water to reproduce. Amphibians have a thin moist skin and most have four legs.
- Snakes, turtles, alligators, and lizards are **reptiles**. Reptiles can reproduce on land. Unlike the thin moist skin of amphibians, reptiles have dry, thick skin covered with scales. Reptiles breathe with lungs.
- **Birds** are different from all other vertebrates in that they have both feathers and wings. Birds also have hollow bones and air sacs that help them to fly.
- **Mammals** are vertebrates whose young drink milk from their mothers' bodies. Humans are mammals, so when you study the traits of mammals, you will learn about yourself too.

On the following pages are some of the groups of invertebrates and vertebrates. They are listed from the simplest to the most complex. Look at each example closely and think about how these different animals carry out different functions.

A bat is a mammal.

A cat is a mammal.

READING **Summarize**
What trait do scientists use to divide all animals into two main groups?

Invertebrates

One of the simplest kinds of animals is a sponge. Sponges belong to a group called *Porifera* (pawr·IF·er·ah). A sponge's body is like a hollow tube with lots of holes in it, called pores. Sponges have different kinds of cells that do different jobs. They have some tissues but no organs. Sponges live in water.

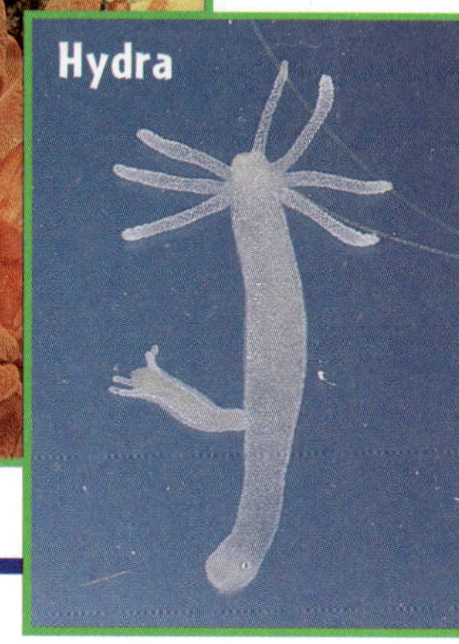

Hydras, sea anemones, and jellyfish are the *Cnidaria* (nigh·DAYR·ee·uh). They do not have heads or tails. They live in water. They have soft bodies and tentacles—long threadlike structures. At the end of each tentacle, they have cells that make poisons. They inject the poisons into small animals they kill to eat.

Flatworms are *Platyhelminthes* (pla·tee·hel·MIN·theez). Their bodies are flat. They have heads and tails. They also have organs cnidarians do not have. Most flatworms do not have true organ systems. Some flatworms live in water. Some live inside other animals.

Roundworms, or *Nematoda* (nee·mah·TOHD·ah), have round bodies, a digestive system, and a simple nervous system. Roundworms live all over Earth, including inside plants and animals.

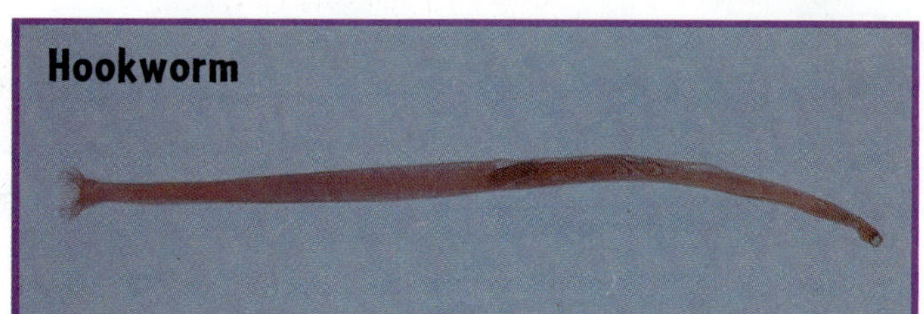

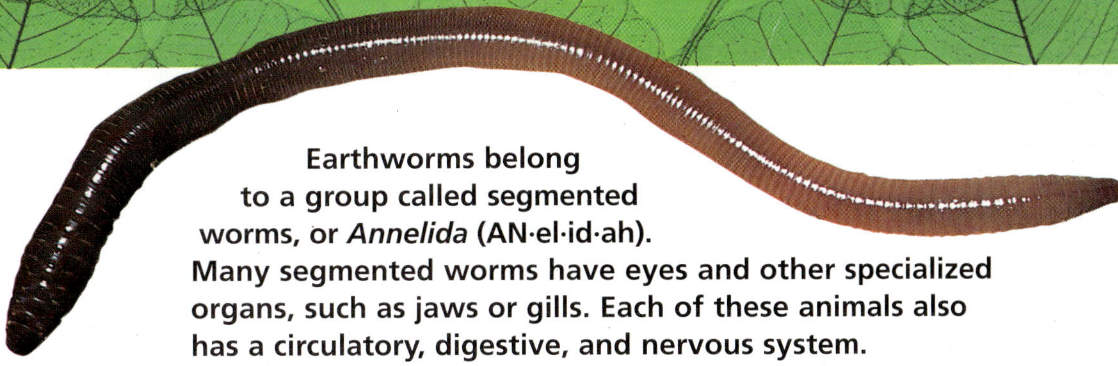

Earthworm

Earthworms belong to a group called segmented worms, or *Annelida* (AN·el·id·ah). Many segmented worms have eyes and other specialized organs, such as jaws or gills. Each of these animals also has a circulatory, digestive, and nervous system.

Octopus

Snails, clams, and octopuses belong to the *Mollusca* (MAHL·us·kah), the mollusks. Almost all mollusks have a shell. The shell may be either inside or outside the mollusk's body. Mollusks have three main body parts, a kind of foot, a tissue covering called a mantle, and a compartment holding internal organs. They have gills for breathing. They have jaws or other organs for capturing food. They each have a circulatory system for moving blood. More complex mollusks, like octopuses, have a well-developed brain.

Tree snail

Grasshopper

Lobster

What has a tough outer skeleton, jointed legs, and a body made up of two, three, or more sections? It is an arthropod—a member of the group *Arthropoda* (AHR·thruh·pohd·ah). There are more arthropods on Earth than any other kind of animal. They include insects, spiders, centipedes, millipedes, lobsters, and crabs.

Spider

Unlike arthropods, the *Echinodermata* (i·KIGH·noh·durm·ah·tah), or echinoderms, have a skeleton inside their bodies. Most also have a spiny skin and tubelike feet with suction cups.

Starfish

Vertebrates

Lamprey

The simplest fish, the *Agnatha* (AG·nah·thuh), do not have jaws or bones. Their skeletons are made of tissue called cartilage. These fish do not have backbones, but each does have a tough nerve cord that runs down its back. They look more like big worms than like fish.

Shark

Reef sting ray

Like those of lampreys and hagfish, the skeletons of sharks and rays are made of cartilage, not bone. However, the cartilage running down their backs is made of a chain of smaller parts called vertebrae. Unlike lampreys and hagfish, sharks and rays have jaws. They also have paired fins. These fish are *Chondrichthyes* (kahn·DRIK·theez).

Tropical fish

Bony fish, or *Osteichthys* (AHS·tee·ik·theez), have bones instead of cartilage. Many have fins that look like fans with spokes in them. These fish have a movable flap over their gills. The movement of this flap lets bony fish breathe while staying still. Unlike sharks, most bony fish have an organ called a swim bladder, or air sac, that allows them to hover at any depth.

Frog

Frogs, toads, and salamanders are *Amphibia* (am·FIB·ee·uh), the amphibians. Most adult amphibians have four legs and skin that is not covered with scales. Adult amphibians breathe with lungs instead of gills. In their early stages of life, amphibians live in water. As adults, most live on land.

Salamander

Crocodile

Turtle

Snake

The first vertebrates to grow and develop out of water were the *Reptilia* (rep·TEE·lee·uh), the reptiles. Reptiles breathe through lungs. Most have waterproof scales on their skin that keep them from drying out on land. Their eggs have a leathery or hard covering that protects the eggs from drying out.

Frigate bird

Ostrich

Not all birds can fly, but all birds belong to the group *Aves* (AY·veez). Birds have feathers, walk on two hind limbs, and have front limbs that are wings. Their bones are strong but very lightweight.

Whale

Shrew

You belong to the group called *Mammalia* (mam·AYL·ee·uh), the mammals. All mammals feed their young milk. At one time or another, all mammals have at least some hair or fur. No other animals have these traits. For their size, most mammals have larger brains than other vertebrates.

Inquiry Skill BUILDER

SKILL Make a Model

Model a Backbone

Vertebrates have an internal skeleton with a backbone. Skeletons are made of bones or cartilage that give the body its overall shape. In this activity, you will learn more about the structure of a backbone as you make a model.

Materials

- pasta wheels
- soft-candy circles
- craft sticks
- hard-candy circles

BE CAREFUL! Do not eat anything in the lab.

Procedure

1. Use pasta wheels, soft-candy circles, and a craft stick to make a model of a backbone.
2. Alternately string the pasta wheels and the soft-candy circles on the craft stick until the row of candy and pasta is about 10 cm long.
3. Fold each end of the craft stick so the pasta wheels and candy do not come off.
4. Slowly bend the model. Does it move easily?
5. How far can you bend the model?
6. Compare your backbone to the model.

Drawing Conclusions

Build a model using hard-candy circles with the pasta wheels. Compare the two models. Which model allows for more flexibility?

Lesson Review

L·I·N·K·S

Why It Matters

Many animal species disappear every year. This is due in part to competition between humans and animals for resources, such as land. Understanding animals and their needs helps us plan our use of resources so that we can coexist with other species.

e-Journal Visit our Web site **www.science.mmhschool.com** to do a research project on endangered animal species.

Think and Write

1. Name three traits you might use to classify an animal.
2. What is the main difference between an invertebrate and a vertebrate?
3. Name a trait you would use to classify a fish as belonging to either the lamprey and hagfish group or the shark and ray group.
4. **INQUIRY SKILL** **Make a Model** How would you design a model of the exoskeleton of an invertebrate?
5. **Critical Thinking** Which do you think are more closely related—whales and goldfish or whales and mice? Explain.

LITERATURE LINK

Read *Operation Migration*, the exciting true story about how scientists taught a group of young whooping cranes in Indiana how to migrate. After you finish reading, think about why it is important to save endangered animals. Then try the activities at the end of the book.

WRITING LINK

Expository Writing Look at the picture of the animal shown here. It swims underwater. It has a ducklike bill and webbed feet. It lays eggs like a bird, yet its eggshells are like those of a reptile. It is a *platypus*. Write an essay to explain how you would classify it.

MATH LINK

Solve this problem. The smallest bat is 4 centimeters long. The blue whale is 3,300 centimeters long. How much longer is the blue whale than the smallest bat?

TECHNOLOGY LINK

LOG ON Visit **www.science.mmhschool.com** for more links.

Animal Life Cycles

What if you saw a tadpole but had never seen a frog? Would people have a hard time convincing you a frog was a grown-up tadpole?

When you see seedlings, you can predict that the fully grown plants will be on stems and have leaves. However, some baby animals look nothing like the adults. They change shape by going through metamorphosis.

Frogs lay eggs in ponds and lakes. The eggs hatch into tadpoles. They must live in water because they have gills, like fish, not lungs.

The tadpoles begin to change. They grow legs. Their tails disappear. They develop lungs and lose their gills. Now they can live on land and in the water!

Insects have two kinds of metamorphosis—complete and incomplete. During complete metamorphosis an egg hatches into a wormlike larva. It eats a lot and grows to become a pupa. This is a resting phase. Many body changes take place. Some larvae spin protective cocoons. Finally, the adult winged insect emerges.

During incomplete metamorphosis the insect changes shape gradually. An egg hatches into a nymph that looks like a small adult without wings. The nymph grows and slowly changes. Finally, it grows wings and becomes an adult.

What Did I Learn?

1. To go from egg to adult, a frog goes through a process called

A childhood.
B adolescence.
C the pupa stage.
D metamorphosis.

2. The stages of complete metamorphosis are:

F egg, larva, pupa, adult
G egg, larva, nymph, pupa, adult
H egg, nymph, pupa, adult
J egg, nymph, adult

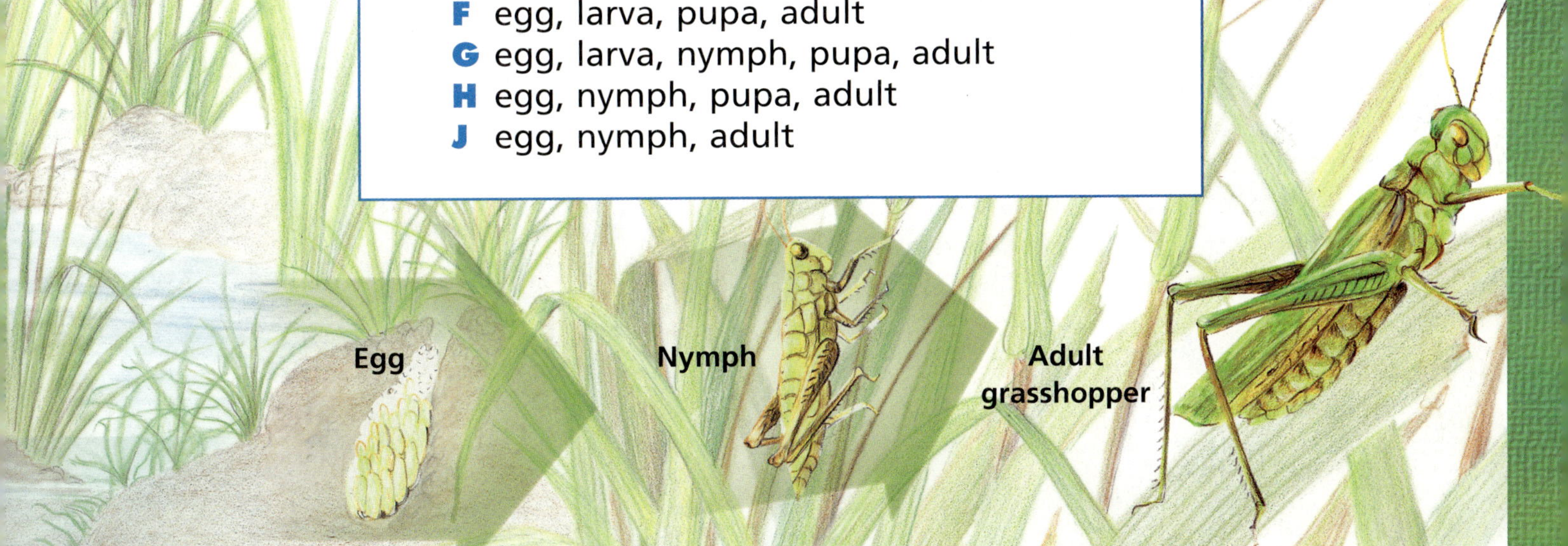

LOG ON Visit **www.science.mmhschool.com** for more links.

LESSON 9

Animal Adaptations

Vocabulary

mimicry, A106

camouflage, A108

protective coloration, A109

heredity, A110

hybrid, A112

crossbreeding, A112

diversity, A114

Get Ready

Alaska is home to many animals, including the snowshoe hare. You might think this hare is a little strange. Its fur changes color from white in the winter to brown in the summer. How does this help the snowshoe hare survive in its environment?

Inquiry Skill

You experiment when you perform a test to support or disprove a hypothesis.

Explore Activity

How Do Sow Bugs Adapt to Their Environment?

Materials
- 10 sow bugs
- tray
- paper towels
- water

Procedure

BE CAREFUL! Handle live animals with care. Wash your hands well when you finish this activity.

1. **Observe** Place a sow bug in the center of the tray, and observe it. What traits does it have that enable it to live in the soil and under decaying wood or leaves? Record your observations.
2. **Observe** Touch the sow bug. How does it react?
3. **Experiment** Place all the sow bugs in the center of the tray. Do the animals tend to stay together?
4. **Experiment** Move the sow bugs to one end of the tray. Dampen three or four paper towels, and place them in the opposite end of the tray. Observe for several minutes. Record your observations. When the animals move, do they tend to move faster in the dry section or wet section of the box?

Drawing Conclusions

1. **Infer** How do sow bugs protect themselves?
2. **Infer** Can the behavior of sow bugs when exposed to moisture be related to their survival? If so, how?
3. **FURTHER INQUIRY** **Experiment** Design an experiment to test the reactions of sow bugs to light. Try it and report your results.

Read to Learn

Main Idea **Animals have certain characteristics, behaviors, and adaptations that help them survive.**

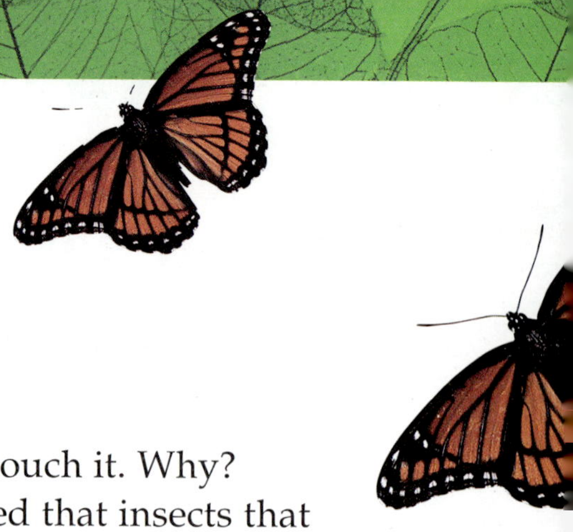

How Do Animals Adapt?

Certain traits animals have help them to survive in their environment. Such traits are called adaptations.

An animal has many adaptations. One important group of adaptations helps the animal keep from getting eaten by a *predator* (an animal that might eat it). How can an animal avoid being eaten?

Through experience, you have learned to avoid certain things. For example, if you see a buzzing black-and-yellow striped insect, you are not likely to try to touch it. Why? You have learned that insects that look like this can give you a painful sting. They are called yellow jackets. Animals that feed on insects have also learned to avoid yellow jackets.

They also avoid a harmless insect called a syrphid (SUHR·fuhd) fly. Why? It looks very much like a yellow jacket. In nature, looking like something else—especially something unpleasant—is called **mimicry**.

Mimicry

One of these insects stings. One does not. To be safe, insect-eating animals avoid both. This helps both the wasp (left) and the harmless syrphid fly (right) to survive. Animals avoid the harmless fly because it mimics a stinging wasp.

When food spoils, it tastes bad. If you don't want to get sick, you quickly dispose of spoiled food. Some birds might like to make a meal out of the good-tasting viceroy butterfly. However, birds often avoid gulping down a viceroy. Why? The viceroy looks like a monarch butterfly, which, birds have learned, tastes awful.

Birds avoid eating the good-tasting viceroy butterfly (top) because it looks like the awful-tasting monarch butterfly (bottom).

You are probably very careful when you meet a cat you don't know. You have learned that its sharp claws can give you a nasty scratch. Certain predators have learned the same thing about thorny plants. The predators stay away from such plants.

This gives thornbugs protection from being eaten. That's because thornbugs look like thorns. When the bugs cluster on the stem of a plant, a predator mistakes them for the thorns on a plant. The predator stays away, and the thorn-bugs live to see another day.

Why is mimicry a good adaptation for an animal to have?

Monarch larvae (caterpillars) feed on milk-weed. Milkweed contains a substance that can make animals ill. Birds that have eaten one monarch butterfly learn to avoid eating both monarchs and look-alike viceroys.

The dark "thorn" on the branch is a thornbug. Because thornbugs look like thorns that can scratch, predators stay away.

What Is Camouflage?

At one time or another, most people have dreamed about being invisible. For one thing, if people can't see you, they can't hurt you. You can't make yourself invisible. Neither can animals. Even so, you can make yourself look so much like your surroundings that you are almost invisible.

An animal that does not move, or moves very, very slowly, and looks like its surroundings is camouflaged. **Camouflage** is another important adaptation that helps animals avoid their predators.

There are two basic kinds of camouflage, or blending in with the environment. One has to do with an animal's shape. The other has to do with its color. Let's start off by exploring how shape can camouflage an animal.

What if you were a bird hunting for a butterfly? You would not be tempted to eat a leaf. That is what protects the leaf butterfly from being eaten. The wings of the leaf butterfly are shaped like the leaves of a plant. When this butterfly is perched on the stem of a plant, or resting on a forest floor littered with leaves, it is very hard to see. A bird passes it by as if it were not there.

Leaf butterflies look so much like leaves that a bird looking for a meal will fly right by.

Birds can more easily spot a light-colored peppered moth (right) against a dark background than a dark-colored peppered moth (left) against a dark background.

About 150 years ago, England was home to two kinds of peppered moths. One kind was light colored. The other kind was dark colored. Birds fed on both kinds of moths, many of which clung to the trunks of trees.

However, gradually the light-colored moths seemed to be disappearing. The birds were eating more of these moths than the dark-colored ones. What was causing this?

Nearby factories were pouring dark, sticky smoke into the air. The smoke stuck to the trunks of trees. The light-colored moths stood out against this background. The dark-colored moths blended in with the background.

Since the birds could more easily see the light-colored moths, the birds were eating more light-colored moths than dark-colored moths. This is an example of a kind of camouflage called **protective coloration**. The color of the dark peppered moths protected them from predators.

How does camouflage help an animal survive?

Nest building is an inherited trait. Robins (left) build their nests of twigs. Penguins (above) build their nests of pebbles.

What Is Inherited?

Animals behave in many different ways. They learn some kinds of behavior, like avoiding bad-tasting insects. You may have noticed learned behaviors in your pet. For example, if your cat cries for food every time it hears the electric can opener, your cat has learned that the sound of the can opener can mean mealtime. No wonder your cat acts disappointed when the canned food turns out to be something it doesn't like. However, not all behaviors are learned. Certain other kinds of behavior seem to be automatic.

Young birds will build the same kinds of nests their parents build. They do this even if the young birds have never seen their parents build a nest. In other words, birds do not learn how to build nests. They do it automatically.

Scientists would say that nest building is *inherited*, or passed down from one generation to the next. An inherited behavior is one that is not learned. It is done automatically. This inherited behavior is called *instinct*. The passing of inherited traits from parents to offspring is called **heredity**.

Many physical traits of an animal are also inherited. For example, the shape of a bird's feet and beak is inherited. The color of its feathers is inherited, too. This is easy to see, since young birds have the same-shaped feet and beaks as their parents.

The feet and beaks of birds are inherited physical traits. All woodpeckers have feet adapted for grasping the sides of tree trunks. All hawks have feet armed with claws adapted for grabbing smaller animals. All ducks have webbed feet adapted for swimming.

What physical traits are not inherited? Those that the environment can change. If there is not much food around, an animal's weight and size may be smaller than normal. Weight and size are physical traits, but they may not be inherited. Of course, certain animals—such as elephants—tend to be bigger and heavier than others—such as mice. Such tendencies are inherited.

The average weight and size of an elephant is greater than the average weight and size of a mouse. Even so, some elephants will be larger and heavier than others. Some mice will be larger and heavier than other mice. In other words, some traits are affected by both heredity and the environment.

How are animal behaviors that are inherited different from those that are learned?

Although gerbils are smaller than elephants, the environment can make some gerbils bigger than other gerbils and some elephants bigger than other elephants.

A mule is the hybrid offspring of the mating of a female horse and a male donkey. Many hybrids are sterile and cannot produce offspring of their own. This is true of mules.

What Is a Hybrid?

What looks a little like a horse and a little like a donkey, but isn't either? The answer to this riddle is . . . a mule! It looks the way it does because its male parent was a donkey and its female parent was a horse.

Living things that have parents that are quite different from each other, such as donkeys and horses, are called **hybrids**. People sometimes breed hybrids on purpose, since a hybrid may have more desirable traits than either of its parents.

A mule can do work that a donkey or a horse cannot do. Mules are often used to carry heavy loads through rugged country. That's because mules do not slip as easily as horses. Mules also have more endurance than donkeys. Horses and donkeys do not normally mate. Even so, for thousands of years people have been breeding mules.

Crossbreeds

People often mate closely related living things on purpose. They may mate certain crop plants, flowers, dogs, or cats. They do this to produce hearty crops or plants and animals with desirable traits. This process is sometimes called **crossbreeding**. A crossbreed is a product of the mating of individuals from two distinct breeds or varieties of the same *species* (kind of organism). Crossbreeding has produced new breeds of dogs and cats. Cross-breeding has also given us new kinds of corn that resist disease, produce more food on the same area of land, and are more nutritious.

Crossbreeds also occur naturally. If you have found a shady spot under the branches of a London plane tree, you have run across a hybrid. About 2,000 years ago, the oriental plane tree grew in the southern parts of Europe. It was so pretty that people living in northern Europe wanted to grow it there. Unfortunately, the oriental plane tree could not survive the cold northern winters. Then in about 1670, the oriental plane tree crossbred naturally with another kind of plane tree. The offspring, which came to be called the London plane tree, was a new kind of plant that could survive cold winters. Today these lovely trees are found on many streets in northern Europe and in the northern United States.

Cat Breeds

Cat breeds can be divided into two major groups—cats with short hair and cats with long hair. Different breeds of cats also vary in color, in length and texture of hair, and in temperament. Some are quiet and affectionate. Others tend to be vocal and demanding.

How is a mule an example of a hybrid?

QUICK LAB

Find the New Breed

FOLDABLES™ Make a Three-Tab Book. (See p. R 42.) Label it as shown.

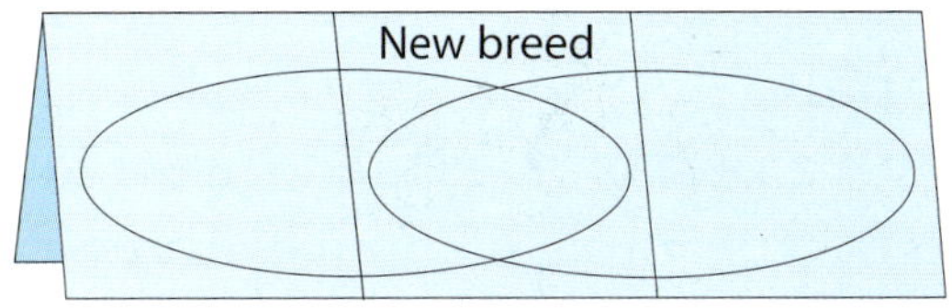

1. **Observe** Make the Three-Tab Book pictured and use it to record your observations. Look at the picture of the Siamese cat. What traits do you think it has been bred for?
2. **Observe** Look at the picture of the Persian cat. What traits do you think it has been bred for?
3. **Observe** Look at the picture of the Himalayan cat. What traits do you think it has been bred for?
4. **Infer** Which cat do you think is the new breed? Explain your answer.

Himalayan cat

Persian cat

Siamese cat

Why Is Diversity Important?

Would you rather have a mutt or a purebred dog? Purebred dogs—or other animals—look very much like their parents. They are bred to have certain traits. Mutts, on the other hand, may not look much like either parent. However, they do have a great mix of traits.

A group of dogs made up of mutts is a good example of animal **diversity**. *Diversity* means "different." Animal diversity refers to a group of the same kind of animal—like dogs—in which there are lots of animals with different traits. A group of mutts is made up of individual dogs with very different traits. Is there an advantage to being a mutt? The answer can be yes! Mutts may be healthier than certain purebred dogs. Some purebred dogs are known to have breathing problems. Some have hip problems. However, other purebred dogs come from very healthy breeds.

Animal diversity is important. When an environment changes, only those animals that can adapt to the change will survive. If the population is made up of animals with the same traits—and those traits do not help the animals survive in a changing environment—the whole population may die out. This fate threatens the cheetahs of Africa. However, if the population holds animals with different traits, it is more likely that some will survive to keep the population going.

Africa's cheetahs are in trouble. The traits of all cheetahs are so much alike, they have little diversity. This could threaten their survival against a new disease or other changes in their environment.

READING Summarize

Why is diversity important in an animal population?

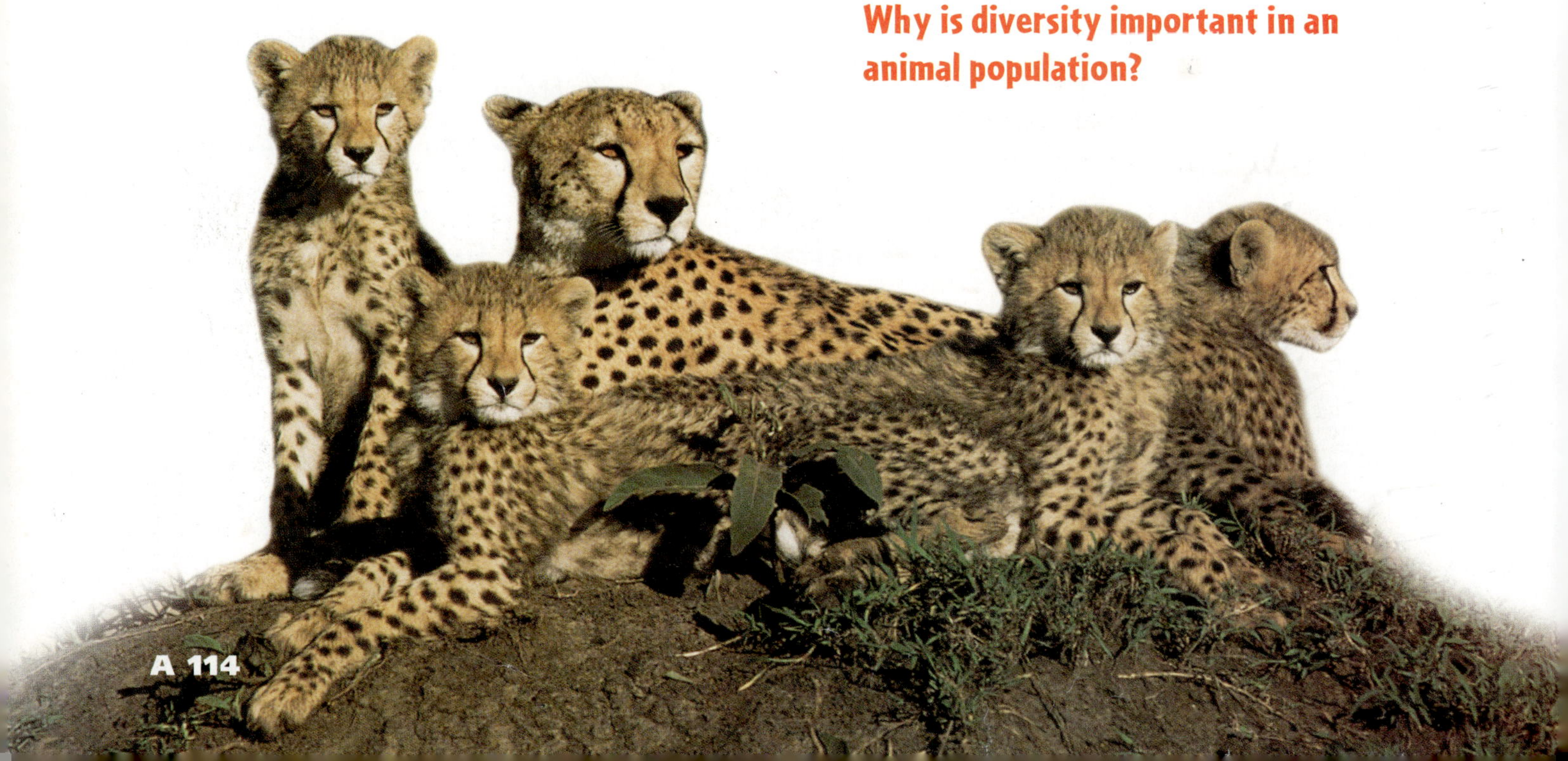

Lesson Review

Why It Matters

Animals need to adapt to changes in their environment to survive. If an animal population is diverse it is likely that at least some of its individuals will be able to adapt to changes in the environment. This ensures species survival.

Sometimes animals carry traits that could be unhealthy for their offspring. Diversity reduces the chances of inheriting such traits. Hybridization, whether natural or artificial, produces animal diversity.

e-Journal Visit our Web site **www.science.mmhschool.com** to do a research project on animal diversity.

Think and Write

1. What is one adaptation that helps an animal escape a predator?
2. What is an example of an inherited behavior?
3. What is an example of an inherited physical trait?
4. Why is diversity important?
5. **Critical Thinking** Dark peppered moths cling to trees covered by black soot from factories. If the factories were not allowed to produce sooty smoke, what might happen to the dark peppered moths? Explain.

L·I·N·K·S

ART LINK

Make a display. Research three hybrid animals other than the ones discussed in this lesson. Make an illustration of these animals and their parents to display.

Tiglon

WRITING LINK

Writing That Compares Think about your favorite animal. Which of its behaviors are automatic? Which are learned? Write an essay that compares the behaviors of your favorite animal with your own behaviors. Which of your responses are automatic? Which are learned? Make a chart of points to compare and contrast before writing.

MATH LINK

Make a bar graph. It is estimated that there were about 100,000 cheetahs in the wild in 1900; about 30,000 in 1950; and there are about 10,000 today. Make a bar graph to show how the population of the cheetah has declined.

TECHNOLOGY LINK

LOG ON Visit **www.science.mmhschool.com** for more links.

Chapter 4 Review

Vocabulary

Fill each blank with the best word or words from the list.

amphibians, A95
camouflage, A108
crossbreeding, A112
diversity, A114
heredity, A110
hybrid, A112
mammals, A95
mimicry, A106
protective coloration, A109
reptiles, A95

1. A group of mutts is a good example of animal ______.
2. An animal uses ______ to blend in with the background.
3. Looking like something a predator would not like to eat is an example of ______.
4. The changing color of an arctic hare's coat is an example of ______.
5. A mule is a(n) ______.
6. Vertebrates that are adapted to live part of their lives in water and part of their lives on land are called ______.
7. Humans are classified as ______.
8. Scientists use ______ to produce heartier crops.
9. The passing down of inherited traits is called ______.
10. Vertebrates that have dry, thick skin are ______.

Test Prep

11. Insects, spiders, lobsters, and crabs are all ______.
    - **A** mammals
    - **B** amphibians
    - **C** arthropods
    - **D** syrphids
12. The skeletons of sharks are made of ______.
    - **F** scales
    - **G** bones
    - **H** fins
    - **J** cartilage
13. A bird's bones ______.
    - **A** are made of cartilage
    - **B** weigh very little for their size
    - **C** weigh a lot for their size
    - **D** are surprisingly thick
14. Animals with fur are ______.
    - **F** amphibians
    - **G** syrphids
    - **H** either arthropods or mollusks
    - **J** mammals
15. As adults, frogs breathe with ______.
    - **A** gills
    - **B** lungs
    - **C** cartilage
    - **D** mollusks

Concepts and Skills

16. Reading in Science Write a paragraph explaining why a predator might avoid eating a syrphid fly.

17. Scientific Methods Describe two ways that adaptation can help animals survive. Write a design for an experiment that would test this.

18. Decision Making A company is planning to build a factory near a river that is home to many different kinds of fish. The only thing the company is planning to dump in the river is clean water. However, the temperature of the water they are dumping is 18°C warmer than the warmest temperature the river usually reaches. You are on the planning committee that will decide whether or not to allow the factory to be built there. What factors do you need to consider when making your decision? Write a paragraph discussing these factors and explaining what your decision would be.

19. INQUIRY SKILL **Classify** Many members of different animal groups are found in water. Create a classification key to identify a whale among a hagfish, a shark, and a sea turtle. Write a paragraph explaining how your key works.

20. Critical Thinking You are a marine biologist, a scientist who studies living things in the ocean. You are exploring under the water and come upon a strange fish. You catch it in a net and take it back to your laboratory. What must you find out about the fish in order to classify it? Write your ideas.

Did You Ever Wonder?

INQUIRY SKILL **Experiment** Suppose you were a naturalist. How would you set up an experiment to determine if the snowshoe hare's color change helps it to survive?

LOG ON Visit **www.science.mmhschool.com** to boost your test scores.

Meet a Scientist

Students of Professor Paul Sereno follow him around the world for one of his classes. Sereno is a paleontologist — a scientist who studies the remains of plants and animals that lived millions of years ago. He and his students travel the world in search of dinosaur fossils.

Fossils are the remains of ancient life forms. They can be bones, shells, impressions of feathers—even footprints! They are usually found in rocks. Fossils give scientists information about Earth's past. They can unlock mysteries about what life was like in the past.

Sereno and a team of students working in the field.

Sereno's hand showing jaws of "super croc."

One of Sereno's most interesting finds was the bones of a 40-foot-long crocodile. He found the bones in Niger, a nation in Africa. The "super croc" lived about 110 million years ago. It weighed as much as a small whale. Its jaws were about five feet long!

Sereno knows it's important to back up his discoveries with science that's available today. By measuring live crocodiles in the wild, Sereno and his team were able to figure out how long the super croc may have been and how much it probably weighed. Members of his team literally got on the backs of living crocodiles to measure them!

LOG ON Visit **www.science.mmhschool.com** to learn more about the work of paleontologists.

TOP 5 Most Extreme Dinosaurs

Here are five dinosaurs that paleontologists think were tops in their fields:

1. Largest dinosaur: *Seismosaurus* Grew to about 120 feet long
2. Smallest dinosaur: *Compsognathus* Weighed about $6\frac{1}{3}$ pounds
3. Longest neck: *Mamenchisaurus* Possessed a neck 46 feet long
4. Fastest: *Ornithomimu* Could run about 40 to 50 miles per hour
5. Smartest: *Troodon* Had the largest brain-to-body ratio of all dinosaurs

Write About It

1. What are fossils?
2. What can paleontologists learn by studying fossils?

Performance Assessment

Classifying Your World

Your goal is to design a key to classify living things.

What to Do

Make a list of all the living things you encounter on a daily basis. How would you classify them? Design a key that you can use to classify them.

Analyze Your Results

1. Use your key to classify all the living things you listed.
2. Make a diagram to show how you grouped your list of living things.

Plant Parts Do Their Part

Your goal is to identify plant parts and diagram water movement in a plant.

What to Do

1. Using a hand lens, identify veins and petioles in a leaf; root hairs, cortex, and xylem in a root; and xylem and phloem in a stem. Draw and label diagrams of each part.

Root	Stem	Leaf	Fruit
Seed	Flower	Bark	Sap

2. Draw and label a tree. Show water movement from soil to leaf.

Analyze Your Results

Using the words ***light***, ***chlorophyll***, and ***energy*** describe how leaf cells use water.

Cactus Creature

Your goal is to make a model animal adapted to life in the desert.

What to Do

BE CAREFUL! Handle sharp objects carefully! Examine a cactus with a hand lens. Think of how an animal that lives among cactus would look. Make a model of it.

Analyze Your Results

Describe the adaptations you gave your model animal. How would each of these adaptations help the animal survive in the desert? Compare it to a cactus.

For Your Reference

Science Handbook

Health Handbook

Units of Measurement

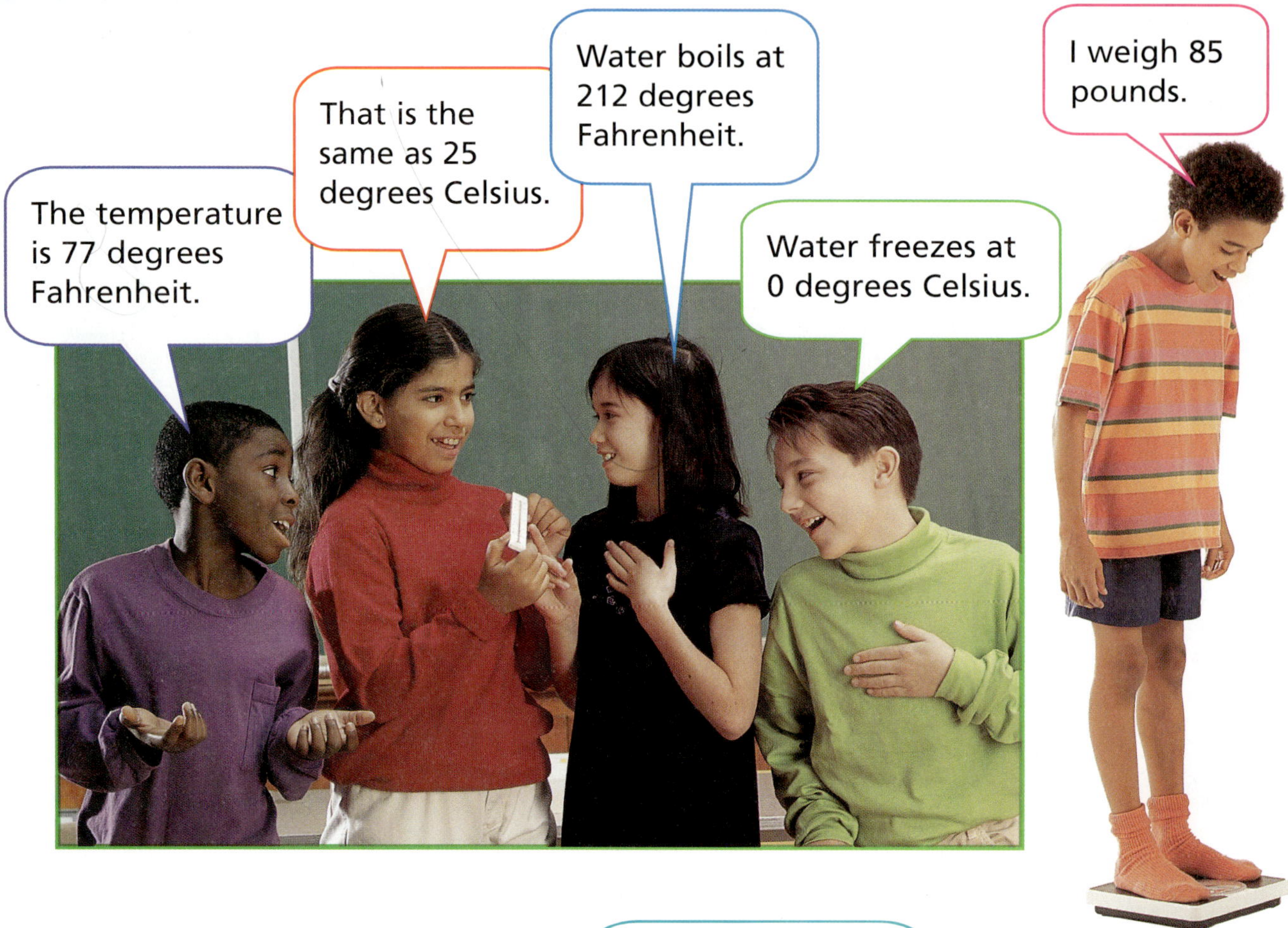

Units of Measurement

Table of Measurements

International System of Units (SI)

Temperature

Water freezes at 0°C and boils at 100°C.

Length and Distance

1,000 meters (m) = 1 kilometer (km)

100 centimeters (cm) = 1 meter

10 millimeters (mm) = 1 centimeter

Volume

1,000 milliliters (mL) = 1 liter (L)

1 cubic centimeter (cm^3) = 1 milliliter

Mass

1,000 grams (g) = 1 kilogram (kg)

English System of Units

Temperature

Water freezes at 32°F and boils at 212°F.

Length and Distance

5,280 feet = 1 mile

3 feet = 1 yard

12 inches = 1 foot

Volume of Fluids

4 quarts = 1 gallon

2 pints = 1 quart

2 cups = 1 pint

8 fluid ounces = 1 cup

Weight

2,000 pounds = 1 ton

16 ounces = 1 pound

Use a Hand Lens

You use a hand lens to magnify an object, or make the object look larger. With a hand lens, you can see details that would be hard to see without the hand lens.

Magnify a Piece of Cereal

1. Place a piece of your favorite cereal on a flat surface. Look at the cereal carefully. Draw a picture of it.
2. Look at the cereal through the large lens of a hand lens. Move the lens toward or away from the cereal until it looks larger and in focus. Draw a picture of the cereal as you see it through the hand lens. Fill in details that you did not see before.
3. Look at the cereal through the smaller lens, which will magnify the cereal even more. If you notice more details, add them to your drawing.
4. Repeat this activity using objects you are studying in science. It might be a rock, some soil, or a seed.

Observe Seeds in a Petri Dish

Can you observe a seed as it sprouts? You can if it's in a petri dish. A petri dish is a shallow, clear, round dish with a cover.

1. Line the sides and bottom of a petri dish with a double layer of filter paper or paper towel. You may have to cut the paper to make it fit.
2. Sprinkle water on the paper to wet it.
3. Place three or four radish seeds on the wet paper in different areas of the dish. Put the lid on the dish, and keep it in a warm place.
4. Observe the seeds every day for a week. Use a hand lens to look for a tiny root pushing through the seed. Record how long it takes each seed to sprout.

Use a Microscope

Hand lenses make objects look several times larger. A microscope, however, can magnify an object to look hundreds of times larger.

Examine Salt Grains

1. Look at the photograph to learn the different parts of your microscope.
2. Place the microscope on a flat surface. Always carry a microscope with both hands. Hold the arm with one hand, and put your other hand beneath the base.
3. Move the mirror so that it reflects light up toward the stage. Never point the mirror directly at the Sun or a bright light. Bright light can cause permanent eye damage.
4. Place a few grains of salt on the slide. Put the slide under the stage clips. Be sure that the salt grains you are going to examine are over the hole in the stage.
5. Look through the eyepiece. Turn the focusing knob slowly until the salt grains come into focus.
6. Draw what the grains look like through the microscope.
7. Look at other objects through the microscope. Try a piece of leaf, a human hair, or a pencil mark.

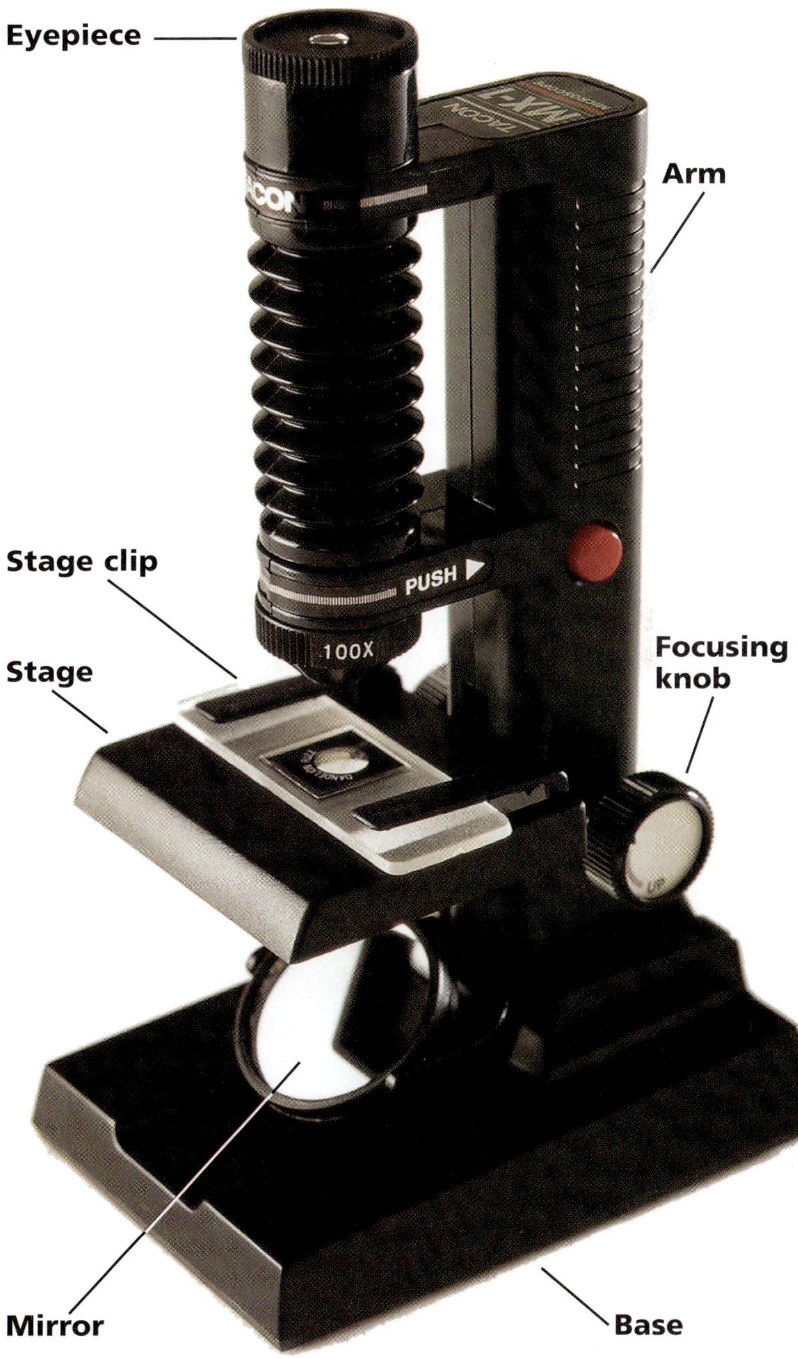

Measure Time

You use timing devices to measure how long something takes to happen. Some timing devices you use in science are a clock with a second hand and a stopwatch. Which one is more accurate?

Comparing a Clock and Stopwatch

1. Look at a clock with a second hand. The second hand is the hand that you can see moving. It measures seconds.
2. Get an egg timer with falling sand or some device like a wind-up toy that runs down after a certain length of time. When the second hand of the clock points to 12, tell your partner to start the egg timer. Watch the clock while the sand in the egg timer is falling.
3. When the sand stops falling, count how many seconds it took. Record this measurement. Repeat the activity, and compare the two measurements.
4. Switch roles with your partner.
5. Look at a stopwatch. Click the button on the top right. This starts the time. Click the button again. This stops the time. Click the button on the top left. This sets the stopwatch back to zero. Notice that the stopwatch tells time in minutes, seconds, and hundredths of a second.
6. Repeat the activity in steps 1–3, using the stopwatch instead of a clock. Make sure the stopwatch is set to zero. Click the top right button to start timing the reading. Click it again when the sand stops falling. Make sure you and your partner time each other twice.

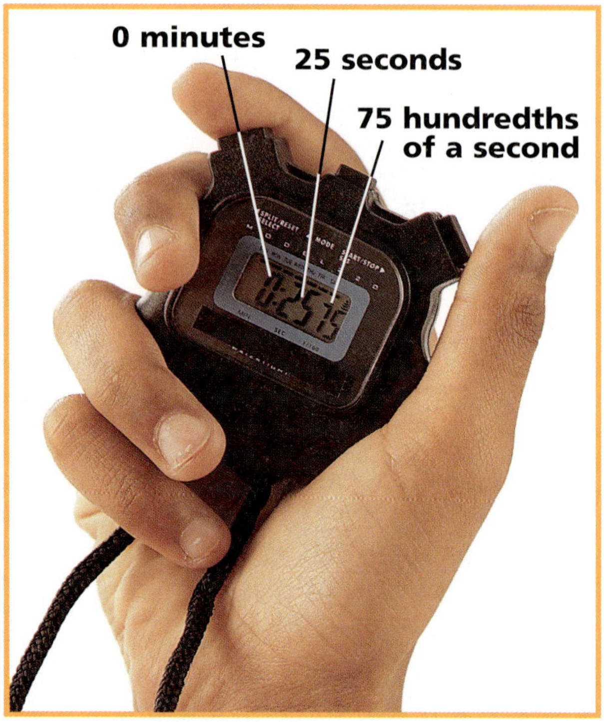

More About Time

1. Use the stopwatch to time how long it takes an ice cube to melt under cold running water. How long does an ice cube take to melt under warm running water?
2. Match each of these times with the action you think took that amount of time.

   a. 00:14:55
   b. 44:39:45
   c. 10:23:00

   1. Taking a shower
   2. Saying the Pledge of Allegiance
   3. Recess

Measure Length

Find Length with a Ruler

1. Look at this section of a ruler. Each centimeter is divided into 10 millimeters. How long is the paper clip?
2. The length of the paper clip is 3 centimeters plus 2 millimeters. You can write this length as 3.2 centimeters.
3. Place the ruler on your desk. Lay a pencil against the ruler so that one end of the pencil lines up with the left edge of the ruler. Record the length of the pencil.
4. Trade your pencil with a classmate. Measure and record the length of each other's pencil. Compare your answers.

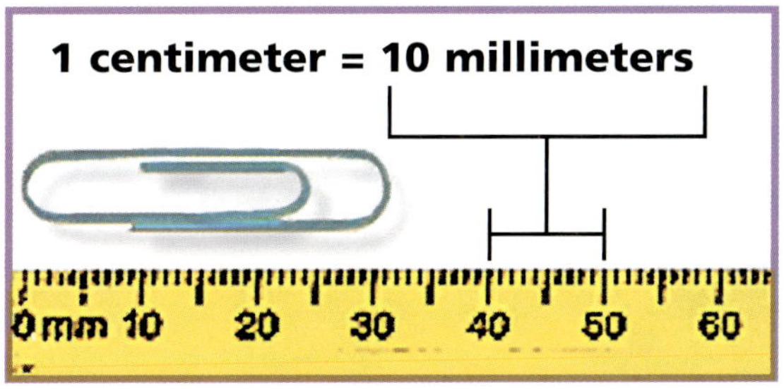

Measuring Area

Area is the amount of surface something covers. To find the area of a rectangle, multiply the rectangle's length by its width. For example, the rectangle here is 3 centimeters long and 2 centimeters wide. Its area is 3 cm x 2 cm = 6 square centimeters. You write the area as 6 cm^2.

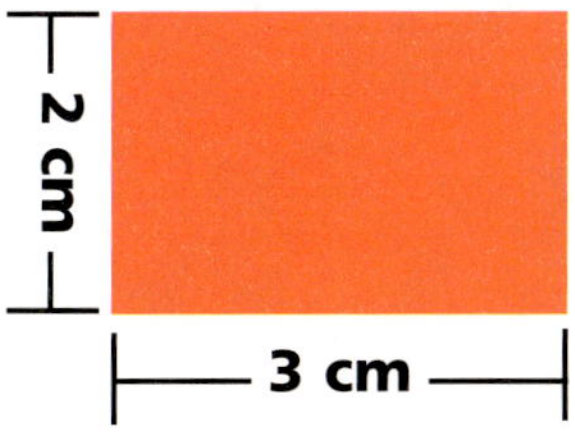

Opposite sides of a rectangle are parallel. The adjacent sides are perpendicular to each other (at right angles). Rectangles have symmetry. When folded in half, both halves are identical in size and shape. This is known as congruence.The two halves fit over each other exactly.

Find Length with a Meterstick

1. Line up the meterstick with the left edge of the chalkboard. Make a chalk mark on the board at the right end of the meterstick.
2. Move the meterstick so that the left edge lines up with the chalk mark. Keep the stick level. Make another mark on the board at the right end of the meterstick.
3. Continue to move the meterstick and make chalk marks until the meterstick meets or overlaps the right edge of the board.
4. Record the length of the chalkboard in centimeters by adding all the measurements you've made. Remember, a meterstick has 100 centimeters.

Estimating Length

Try estimating the length of objects in the room. Then measure the length, and compare the estimation with the measurement.

Measure Mass

Mass is the amount of matter an object has. You use a balance to measure mass. To find the mass of an object, you balance it with objects whose masses you know. Let's find the mass of a box of crayons.

Measure the Mass of a Box of Crayons

1. Place the balance on a flat, level surface. Check that the two pans are empty and clean.
2. Make sure the empty pans are balanced with each other. The pointer should point to the middle mark. If it does not, move the slider a little to the right or left to balance the pans.
3. Gently place a box of crayons on the left pan. This pan will drop lower.
4. Add masses to the right pan until the pans are balanced.
5. Add the numbers on the masses that are in the right pan. The total is the mass of the box of crayons, in grams. Record this number. After the number write a *g* for "grams."

Estimating Mass

Once you become familiar with the mass of objects, you can try estimating the masses of objects. Then you can compare the estimation with the actual mass.

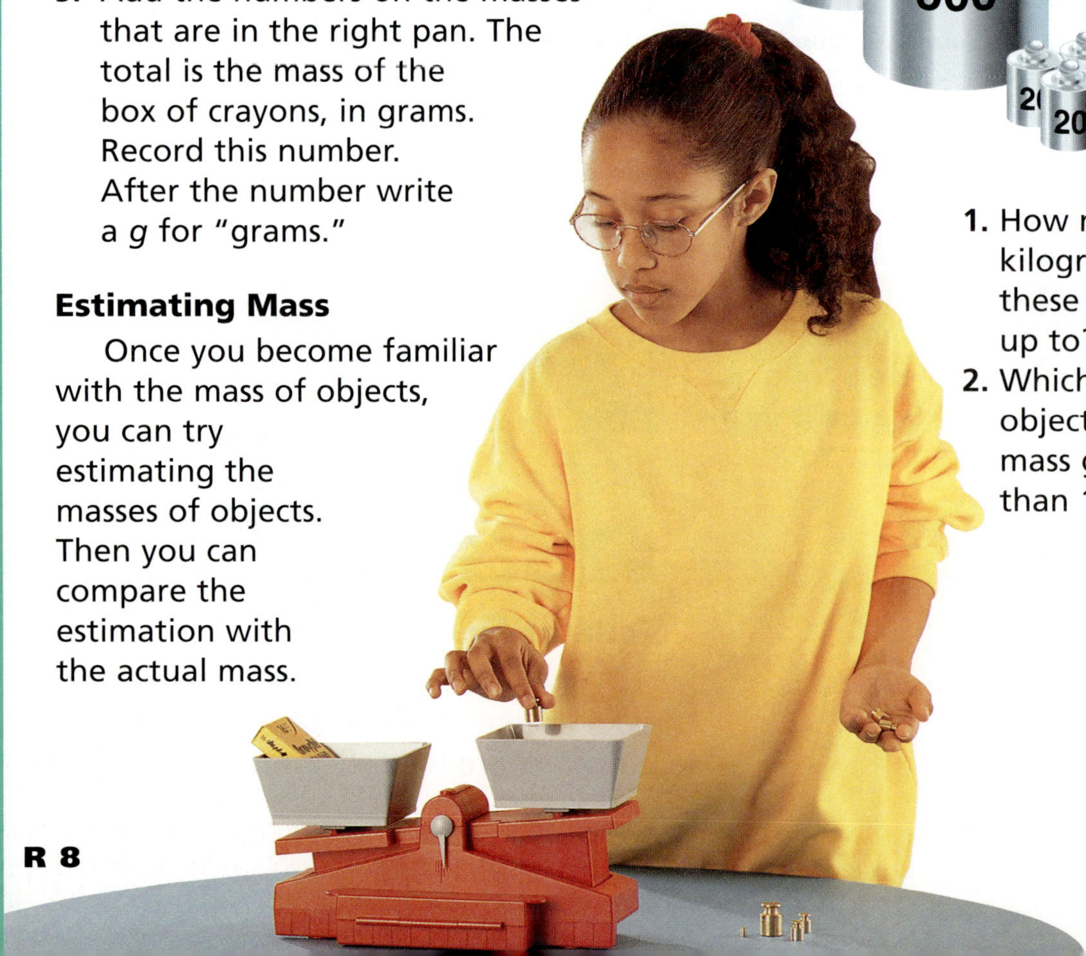

More About Mass

The mass of your crayons was probably less than 100 grams. You may not have enough masses to balance a pineapple. It has a mass of about 1,000 grams. That's the same as 1 kilogram, because *kilo* means "1,000."

1. How many kilograms do all these masses add up to?
2. Which of these objects have a mass greater than 1 kilogram?

Measure Volume

Volume is the amount of space something takes up. In science you usually measure the volume of liquids by using beakers and graduated cylinders. These containers are marked in milliliters (mL).

Measure the Volume of a Liquid

1. Look at the beaker and at the graduated cylinder. The beaker has marks for each 25 mL up to 200 mL. The graduated cylinder has marks for each 1 mL up to 100 mL.
2. The surface of the water in the graduated cylinder curves up at the sides. You measure the volume by reading the height of the water at the flat part. What is the volume of water in the graduated cylinder? How much water is in the beaker? They both contain 75 mL of water.
3. Pour 50 mL of water from a pitcher into a beaker.
4. Now pour the 50 mL of water into a graduated cylinder.

Find the Volume of a Solid

Here's a way to find the volume of a solid, such as a rock.

1. Start with 50 mL of water in a graduated cylinder.
2. Place a small rock in the water. The water level rises.
3. Measure the new water level. Subtract 50 mL from the new reading. The difference is the volume of the rock. Record the volume in cm^3.

Estimating Volume

Once you become familiar with the volumes of liquids and solids, you can estimate volumes. Estimate the amount of liquid in a glass or can. Estimate the volume of an eraser.

Measure Weight/Force

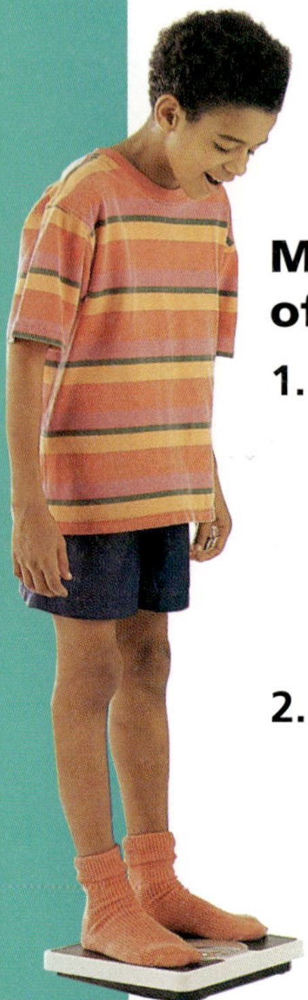

You use a spring scale to measure weight. An object has weight because the force of gravity pulls down on the object. Therefore, weight is a force. Weight is measured in newtons (N) like all forces.

Measure the Weight of an Object

1. Look at your spring scale to see how many newtons it measures. See how the measurements are divided. The spring scale shown here measures up to 5 N. It has a mark for every 0.1 N.
2. Hold the spring scale by the top loop. Put the object to be measured on the bottom hook. If the object will not stay on the hook, place it in a net bag. Then hang the bag from the hook.
3. Let go of the object slowly. It will pull down on a spring inside the scale. The spring is connected to a pointer. The pointer on the spring scale shown here is a small bar.
4. Wait for the pointer to stop moving. Read the number of newtons next to the pointer. This is the object's weight. The mug in the picture weighs 4 N.

More About Spring Scales

You probably weigh yourself by standing on a bathroom scale. This is a spring scale. The force of your body stretches a spring inside the scale. The dial on the scale is probably marked in pounds—the English unit of weight. One pound is equal to about 4.5 newtons.

A bathroom scale, a grocery scale, and a kitchen scale are some other spring scales you may have seen.

Measure Temperature

You use a thermometer to measure temperature—how hot or cold something is. A thermometer is made of a thin tube with colored liquid inside. When the liquid gets warmer, it expands and moves up the tube. When the liquid gets cooler, it contracts and moves down the tube. You may have seen most temperatures measured in degrees Fahrenheit (°F). Scientists measure temperature in degrees Celsius (°C).

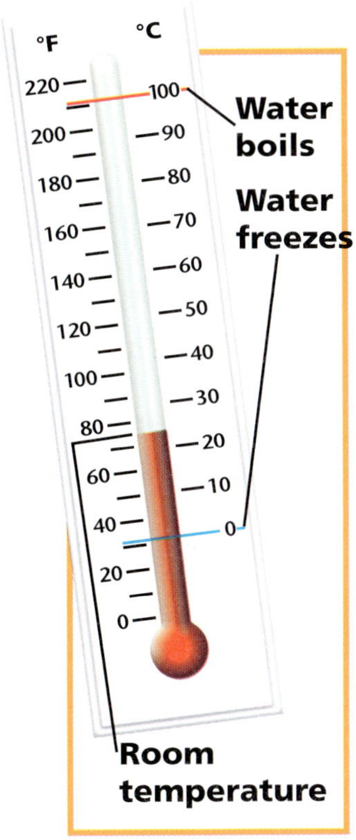

Read a Thermometer

1. Look at the thermometer shown here. It has two scales—a Fahrenheit scale and a Celsius scale.
2. What is the temperature shown on the thermometer? At what temperature does water freeze?

What Is Convection?

1. Fill a large beaker about two-thirds full of cool water. Find the temperature of the water by holding a thermometer in the water. Do not let the bulb at the bottom of the thermometer touch the sides or bottom of the beaker.
2. Keep the thermometer in the water until the liquid in the tube stops moving—about 1 minute. Read and record the temperature in °C.
3. Sprinkle a little fish food on the surface of the water in the beaker. Do not knock the beaker, and most of the food will stay on top.
4. Carefully place the beaker on a hot plate. A hot plate is a small electric stove. Plug in the hot plate, and turn the control knob to a middle setting.
5. After 1 minute measure the temperature of water near the bottom of the beaker. At the same time, a classmate should measure the temperature of water near the top of the beaker. Record these temperatures. Is water near the bottom of the beaker heating up faster than near the top?
6. As the water heats up, notice what happens to the fish food. How do you know that warmer water at the bottom of the beaker rises and cooler water at the top sinks?

Use Calculators

Sometimes after you make measurements, you have to analyze your data to see what it means. This might involve doing calculations with your data. A calculator helps you do time-consuming calculations.

Find an Average

After you collect a set of measurements, you may want to get an idea of a typical measurement in that set. What if, for example, you are doing a weather project? As part of the project, you are studying rainfall data of a nearby town. The table shows how much rain fell in that town each week during the summer.

Week	Rain (cm)
1	2.0
2	1.4
3	0.0
4	0.5
5	1.2
6	2.5
7	1.8
8	1.4
9	2.4
10	8.6
11	7.5

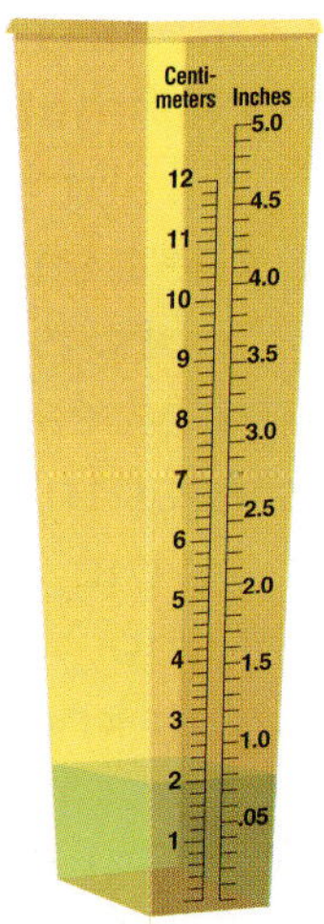

What if you want to get an idea of how much rain fell during a typical week in the summer? In other words, you want to find the average for the set of data. There are three kinds of averages—mean, median, and mode. Does it matter which one you use?

Find the Mean

The mean is what most people think of when they hear the word *average*. You can use a calculator to find the mean.

1. Make sure the calculator is on.
2. Add the numbers. To add a series of numbers, enter the first number and press [+]. Repeat until you enter the last number. See the hints below. After your last number, press [=]. Your total should be 29.3.
3. While entering so many numbers, it's easy to make a mistake and hit the wrong key. If you make a mistake, correct it by pressing the clear entry key, [CE]. Then continue entering the rest of the numbers.
4. Find the mean by dividing your total by the number of weeks. If 29.3 is displayed, press [÷] [1] [1] [=]. Rounded up to one decimal point, your mean should be 2.7.

Hints:

- If the only number to the right of the decimal point is 0, you don't have to enter it into the calculator. To enter 2.0, just press [2].
- If the only number to the left of the decimal point is 0, you don't have to enter it into the calculator. To enter 0.5, just press [.] [5].

Find the Median

The median is the middle number when the numbers are arranged in order of size. When the rainfall measurements are arranged in order of size, they look like this.

0.0
0.5
1.2
1.4
1.4
1.8 — The median is 1.8. This number is in the middle; there are five numbers above it and five numbers below it.
2.0
2.4
2.5
7.5
8.6

Find the Mode

The mode is the number that occurs most frequently. From the ranked set of data above, you can see that the most frequent number is 1.4. It occurs twice. Here are your three different averages from the same set of data.

Average Weekly Rainfall (cm)

Mean	2.7
Median	1.8
Mode	1.4

Why is the mean so much higher than the median or mode? The mean is affected greatly by the last two weeks when it rained a lot. A typical week for that summer was much drier than either of those last two weeks. The median or mode gives a better idea of rainfall for a typical week.

Find the Percent

Sometimes numbers are given as percents (%). *Percent* literally means "per hundred." For example, 28% means 28 out of 100. What if there are about 14,000 trees in the forest and 28% are over 50 years old? How many of them are over 50 years old? Use your calculator. You want to find 28% of 14,000. Press [1][4][0][0][0] [×] [2][8][%]. The answer should be 3,920.

Mathematical Operations

Addition and subtraction are reverse operations, or inverses of each other. For example:

$2 + 3 = 5;$
$5 - 3 = 2;$
$5 - 2 = 3.$

Similarly, multiplication and division are also inverses of each other. For example:

$6 \times 3 = 18;$
$18 \div 6 = 3;$
$18 \div 3 = 6.$

Mathematical Statements

Mathematical statements using symbols may be true only when the symbols are replaced by certain numbers. For example:

$A < B$

If $A = 2$ and $B = 3$, the statement is true.
If $A = 3$ and $B = 2$, the statement is false.

Use Computers

A computer has many uses. The Internet connects your computer to many other computers around the world, so you can collect all kinds of information. You can use a computer to show this information and write reports. Best of all you can use a computer to explore, discover, and learn.

You can also get information from CD-ROMs. They are computer disks that can hold large amounts of information. You can fit a whole encyclopedia on one CD-ROM.

Use Computers for a Project

Here is how one group of students uses computers as they work on a weather project.

1. The students use instruments to measure temperature, wind speed, wind direction, and other parts of the weather. They input this information, or data, into the computer. The students keep the data in a table. This helps them compare the data from one day to the next.

Use Technology

2. The teacher finds out that another group of students in a town 200 kilometers to the west is also doing a weather project. The two groups use the Internet to talk to each other and share data. When a storm happens in the town to the west, that group tells the other group that it's coming their way.
3. The students want to find out more. They decide to stay on the Internet and send questions to a local TV weather forecaster. She has a Web site and answers questions from students every day.

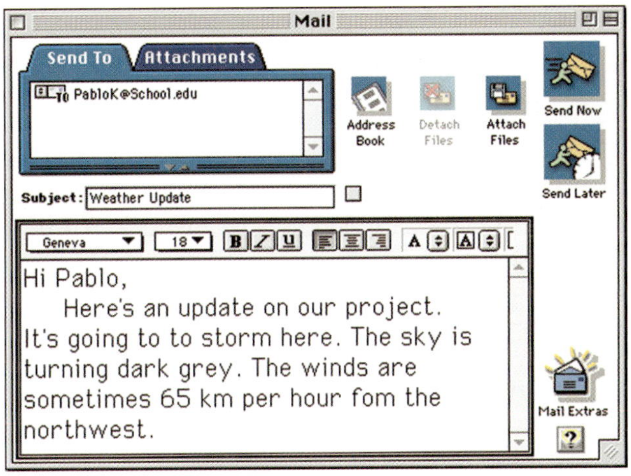

4. Meanwhile some students go to the library to gather more information from a CD-ROM. The CD-ROM has an encyclopedia that includes movie clips. The clips give examples of different kinds of storms.
5. The students have kept all their information in a folder called Weather Project. Now they use that information to write a report about the weather. On the computer they can move around paragraphs, add words, take out words, put in diagrams, and draw weather maps. Then they print the report in color.

Make Graphs to Organize Data

When you do an experiment in science, you collect information. To find out what your information means, you can organize it into graphs. There are many kinds of graphs.

Bar Graphs

A bar graph uses bars to show information. For example, what if you do an experiment by wrapping wire around a nail and connecting the ends of the wire to a battery? The nail then becomes a magnet that can pick up paper clips. The graph shows that the more you wrap the wire around the nail, the more paper clips it picks up. How many paper clips did the nail with 20 coils pick up? With 50 coils?

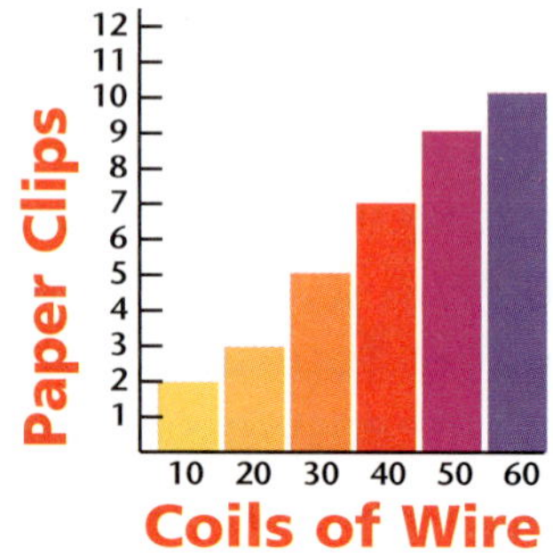

Pictographs

A pictograph uses symbols, or pictures, to show information. What if you collect information about how much water your family uses each day? The table shows what you find.

You can organize this information into the pictograph shown here. The pictograph has to explain what the symbol on the graph means. In this case each bottle means 20 liters of water. A half bottle means half of 20, or 10 liters of water.

1. Which activity uses the most water?
2. Which activity uses the least water?

Activity	Water Used Each Day (L)
Drinking	10
Showering	180
Bathing	240
Brushing teeth	80
Washing dishes	140
Washing hands	30
Washing clothes	280
Flushing toilet	90

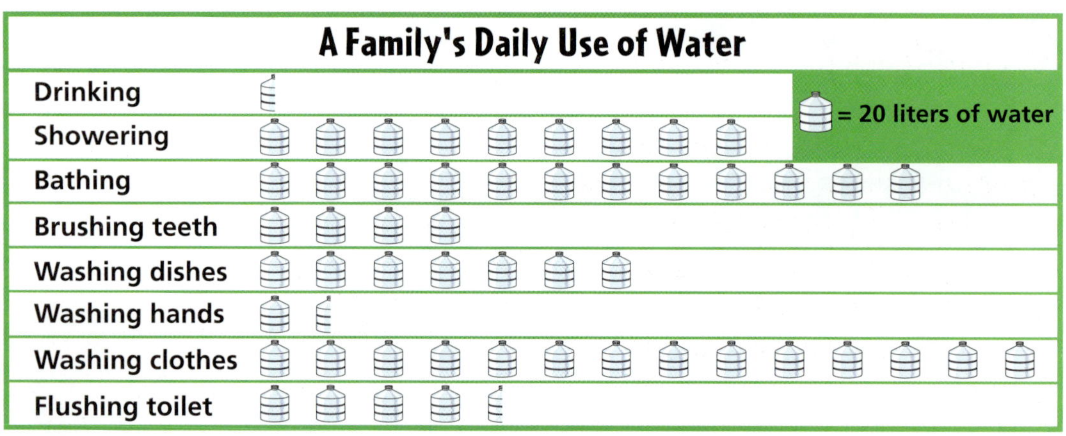

Represent Data

Circle Graphs

A circle graph is helpful to show how a complete set of data is divided into parts. The circle graph here shows how water is used in the United States. What is the single largest use of water?

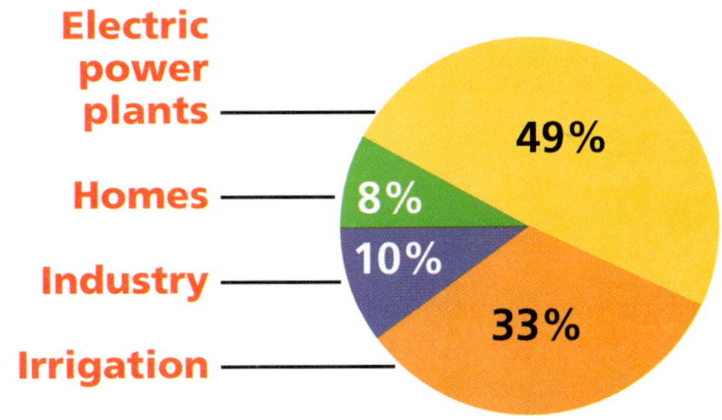

Line Graphs

A line graph shows information by connecting dots plotted on the graph. It shows change over time. For example, what if you measure the temperature out of doors every hour starting at 6 A.M.? The table shows what you find.

Time	Temperature (°C)
6 A.M.	10
7 A.M.	12
8 A.M.	14
9 A.M.	16
10 A.M.	18
11 A.M.	20

You can organize this information into a line graph. Follow these steps.

1. Make a scale along the bottom and side of the graph. The scales should include all the numbers in the chart. Label the scales.
2. Plot points on the graph. For example, place your finger at the "6 A.M." on the bottom line. Place a finger from your other hand on the "10" on the left line. Move your "6 A.M." finger up and your "10" finger to the right until they meet, and make a pencil point. Plot the other points in this way.
3. Connect the points with a line.

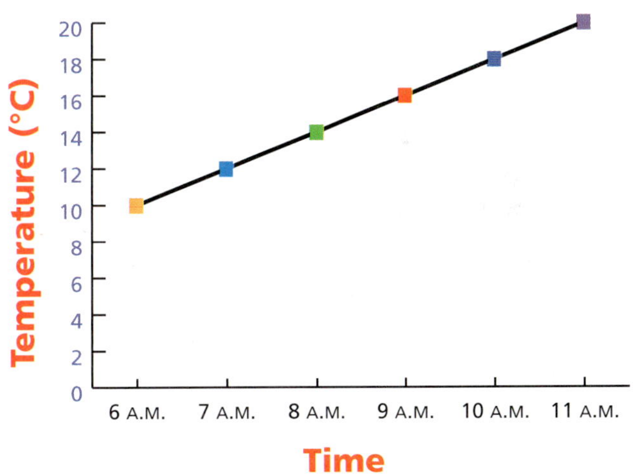

The line graph to the right organizes measurements you collected so that you can easily compare them.

1. Between which two weeks did the plant grow most?
2. When did plant growth begin to level off?

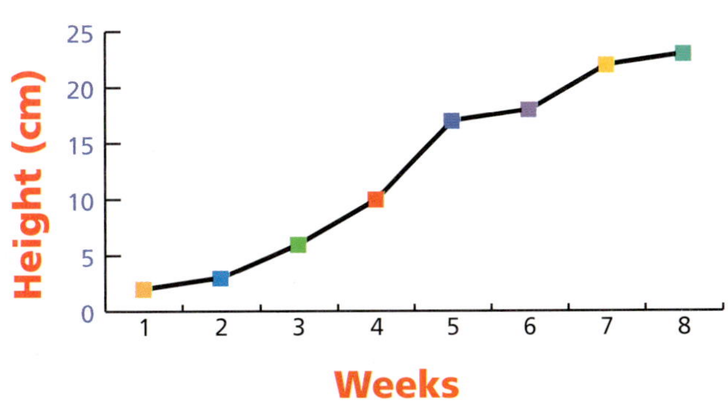

Represent Data

Make Maps to Show Information

Locate Places

A map is a drawing that shows an area from above. Most maps have coordinates—numbers and letters along the top and side. Coordinates help you find places easily. For example, what if you wanted to find the library on the map? It is located at B4. Place a finger on the letter B along the side of the map, and another finger on the number 4 at the top. Then move your fingers straight across and down the map until they meet. The library is located where the coordinates B and 4 meet, or very nearby.

1. What color building is located at F6?
2. The hospital is located three blocks north and two blocks east of the library. What are its coordinates?
3. Make a map of an area in your community. It might be a park or the area between your home and school. Include coordinates. Use a compass to find north, and mark north on your map. Exchange maps with classmates, and answer each other's questions.

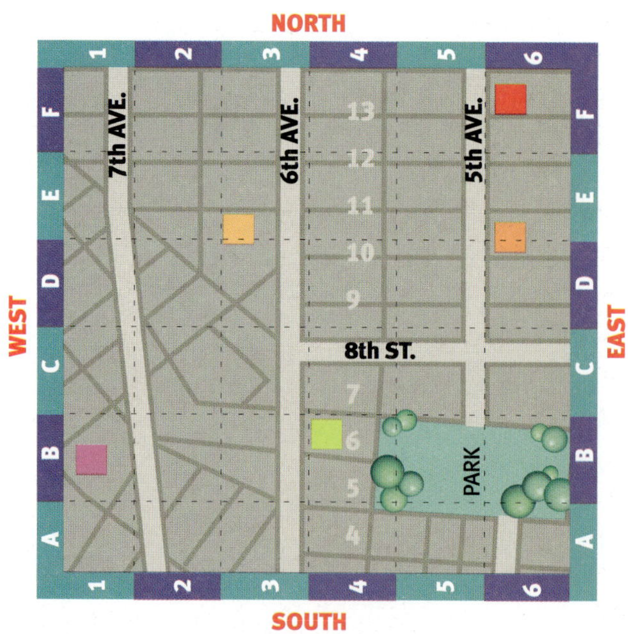

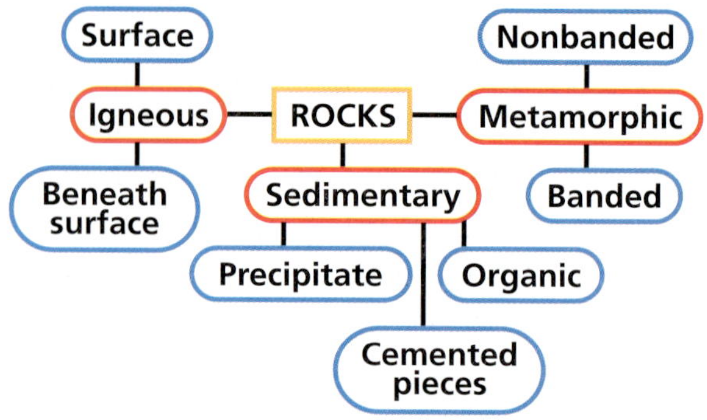

Idea Maps

The map below shows how places are connected to each other. Idea maps, on the other hand, show how ideas are connected to each other. Idea maps help you organize information about a topic.

The idea map above connects ideas about rocks. This map shows that there are three major types of rock—igneous, sedimentary, and metamorphic. Connections to each rock type provide further information. For example, this map reminds you that igneous rocks are classified into those that form at Earth's surface and far beneath it.

Make an idea map about a topic you are learning in science. Your map can include words, phrases, or even sentences. Arrange your map in a way that makes sense to you and helps you understand the ideas.

Represent Data

Make Tables and Charts to Organize Information

Tables help you organize data during experiments. Most tables have columns that run up and down, and rows that run across. The columns and rows have headings that tell you what kind of data goes in each part of the table.

A Sample Table

What if you are going to do an experiment to find out how long different kinds of seeds take to sprout? Before you begin the experiment, you should set up your table. Follow these steps.

1. In this experiment you will plant 20 radish seeds, 20 bean seeds, and 20 corn seeds. Your table must show how many radish seeds, bean seeds, and corn seeds sprouted on days 1, 2, 3, 4, and 5.

2. Make your table with columns, rows, and headings. You might use a computer to make a table. Some computer programs let you build a table with just the click of a mouse. You can delete or add columns and rows if you need to.
3. Give your table a title. Your table could look like the one here.

Make a Table

Now what if you are going to do an experiment to find out how temperature affects the sprouting of seeds? You will plant 20 bean seeds in each of two trays. You will keep each tray at a different temperature, as shown below, and observe the trays for seven days. Make a table you can use for this experiment.

Make a Chart

A chart is simply a table with pictures as well as words to label the rows or columns.

HEALTH Handbook

The Human Body

Like all organisms, humans are made up of cells. In fact, the human body is made of trillions of cells. These cells are organized into tissues, a group of similar cells that perform a specific function. Tissues, in turn, form organs. Your heart and lungs are examples of organs. Finally, organs work together as part of organ systems. Your heart, for example, is part of the circulatory system.

Levels of Organization

- Cells
- Tissues
- Organs
- Organ Systems
- Organism

Including the skin, or integumentary system, the human body has 11 major organ systems. These body systems each have specific functions, and they also work together as parts of the human body as a whole.

Human Body Systems

System	Function
Nervous System	control
Skeletal System	support
Integumentary System	protection
Muscular System	movement
Circulatory System	transport
Respiratory System	oxygen/ carbon dioxide exchange
Digestive System	food absorption
Excretory System	waste removal
Endocrine System	regulation and control
Reproductive System	reproduction
Immune System	protection

The Nervous System

The nervous system has two parts. The brain and the spinal cord are the central nervous system. All other nerves are the outer, or peripheral, nervous system.

The largest part of the brain is the cerebrum. A deep groove separates the right half, or hemisphere, of the cerebrum from the left half. Both the right and left hemispheres of the cerebrum contain control centers for the senses.

The cerebellum lies below the cerebrum. It coordinates the skeletal muscles so they work smoothly together. It also helps in keeping balance.

The brain stem connects to the spinal cord. The lowest part of the brain stem is the medulla. It controls heartbeat, breathing, blood pressure, and the muscles in the digestive system.

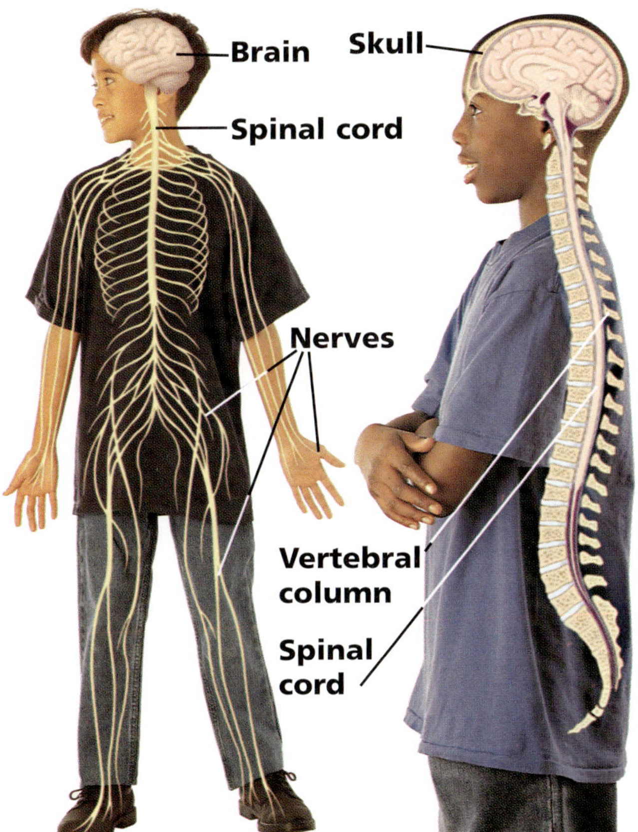

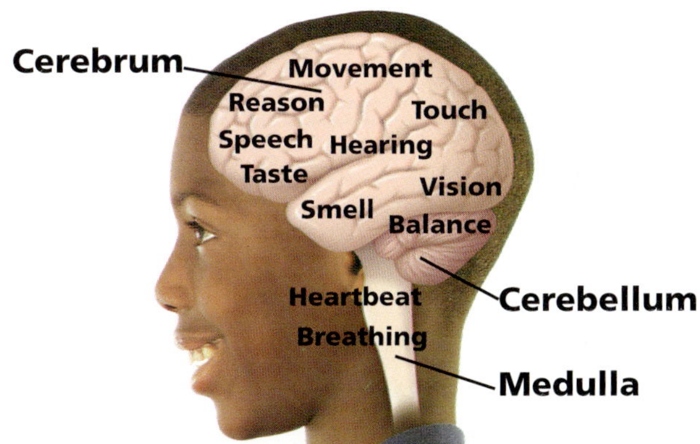

CARE!

- Wear protective headgear when you play sports or exercise.
- Stay away from drugs, such as stimulants, which can speed up the nervous system.
- Stay away from alcohol, which is a depressant and slows down the nervous system.

Parts of a Neuron

The nerves in the nervous system are made up of nerve cells called *neurons.* Each neuron has three main parts—a cell body, dendrites, and an axon. Dendrites are branching nerve fibers that carry impulses, or electrical signals, toward the cell body. An axon is a nerve fiber that carries impulses away from the cell body.

When an impulse reaches the tip of an axon, it must cross a tiny gap to reach the next neuron. This gap between neurons is called a *synapse.*

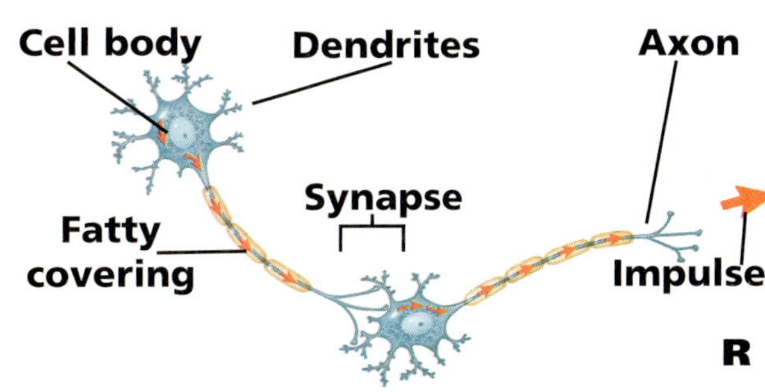

The Senses

Seeing

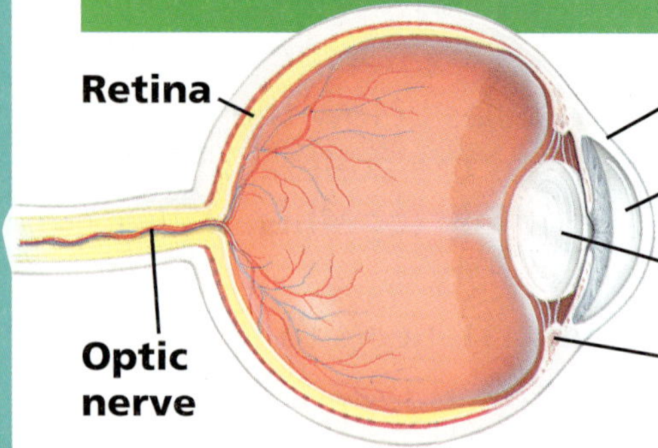

Light reflected from an object enters the eye and falls on the retina. Receptor cells change the light into electrical signals, or impulses. These impulses travel along the optic nerve to the vision center of the brain.

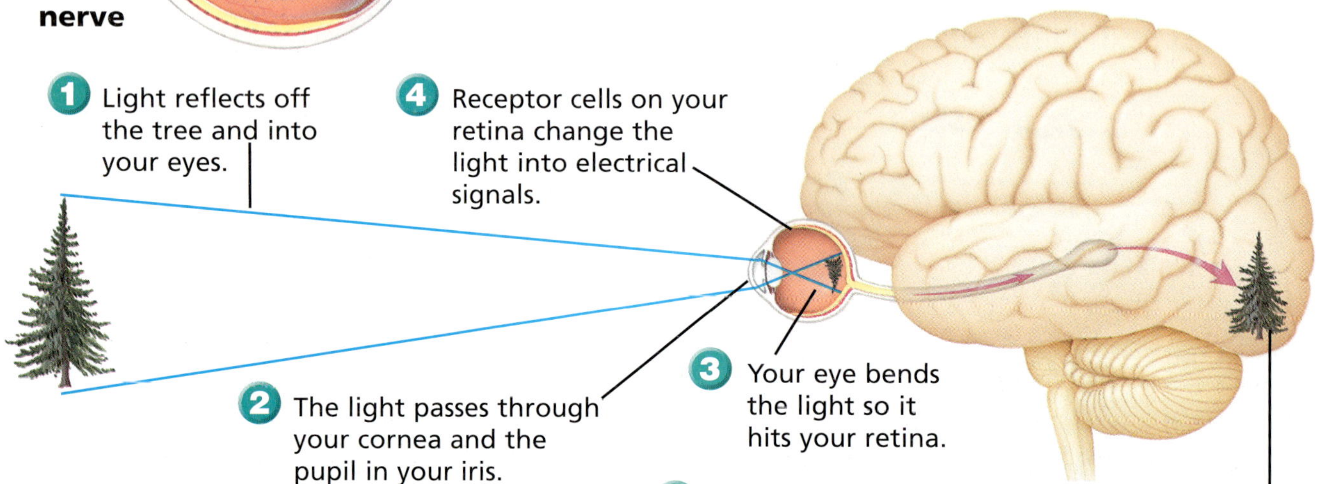

Hearing

Sound waves enter the ear and cause the eardrum to vibrate. Receptor cells in the ear change the sound waves into impulses that travel along the auditory nerve to the hearing center of the brain.

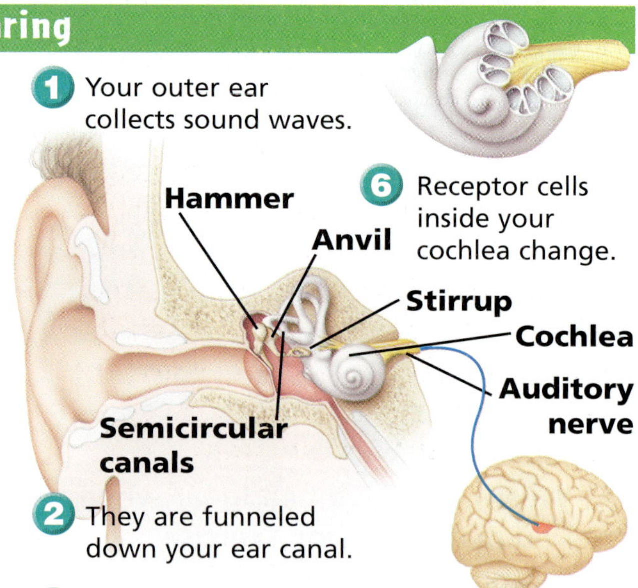

CARE!

- To avoid straining your eye muscles, don't sit too close to the TV screen or computer monitor.
- Avoid loud music. Turn down the volume when wearing headphones.

The Senses

Smelling

The sense of smell is really the ability to detect chemicals in the air. When a person breathes, chemicals dissolve in mucus in the upper part of the nose. When the chemicals come in contact with receptor cells, the cells send impulses along the olfactory nerve to the smelling center of the brain.

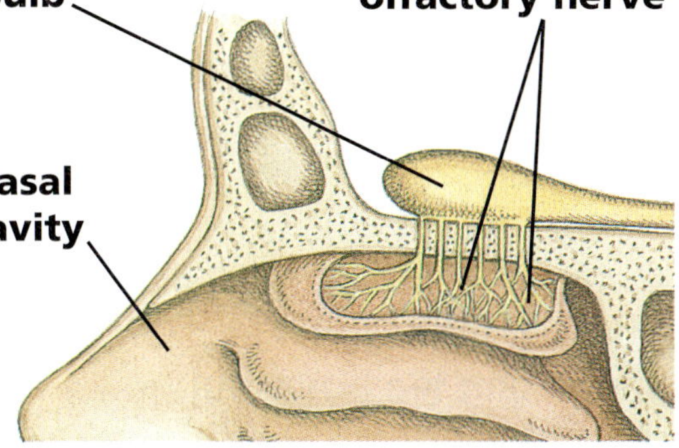

Tasting

When a person eats, chemicals in food dissolve in saliva. Saliva carries the chemicals to taste buds on the tongue. Inside each taste bud are receptors that can sense the four main tastes—sweet, sour, salty, and bitter. The receptors send impulses along a nerve to the taste center of the brain. The brain identifies the taste of the food, which is usually a combination of the four main tastes.

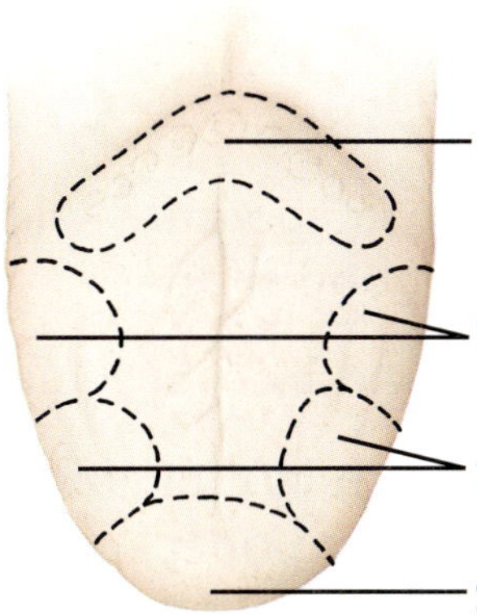

Touching

Receptor cells in the skin help a person tell hot from cold, wet from dry, and the light touch of a feather from the pressure of stepping on a stone. Each receptor cell sends impulses along sensory nerves to the spinal cord. The spinal cord then sends the impulses to the touch center of the brain.

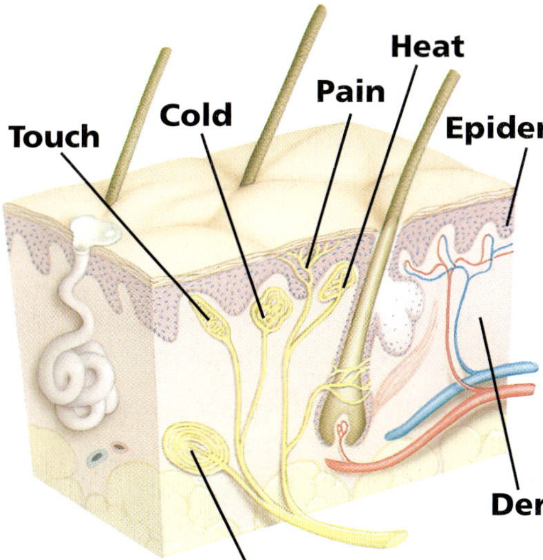

CARE!

- **To prevent the spread of germs, always cover your mouth and nose when you cough or sneeze.**

The Skeletal System

The body has a supporting frame, called a skeleton, which is made up of bones. The skeleton has several jobs.

- It gives the body its shape.
- It protects organs in the body.
- It works with muscles to move the body.

Each of the 206 bones of the skeleton is the size and shape best fitted to do its job. For example, long and strong leg bones support the body's weight.

The Skeleton

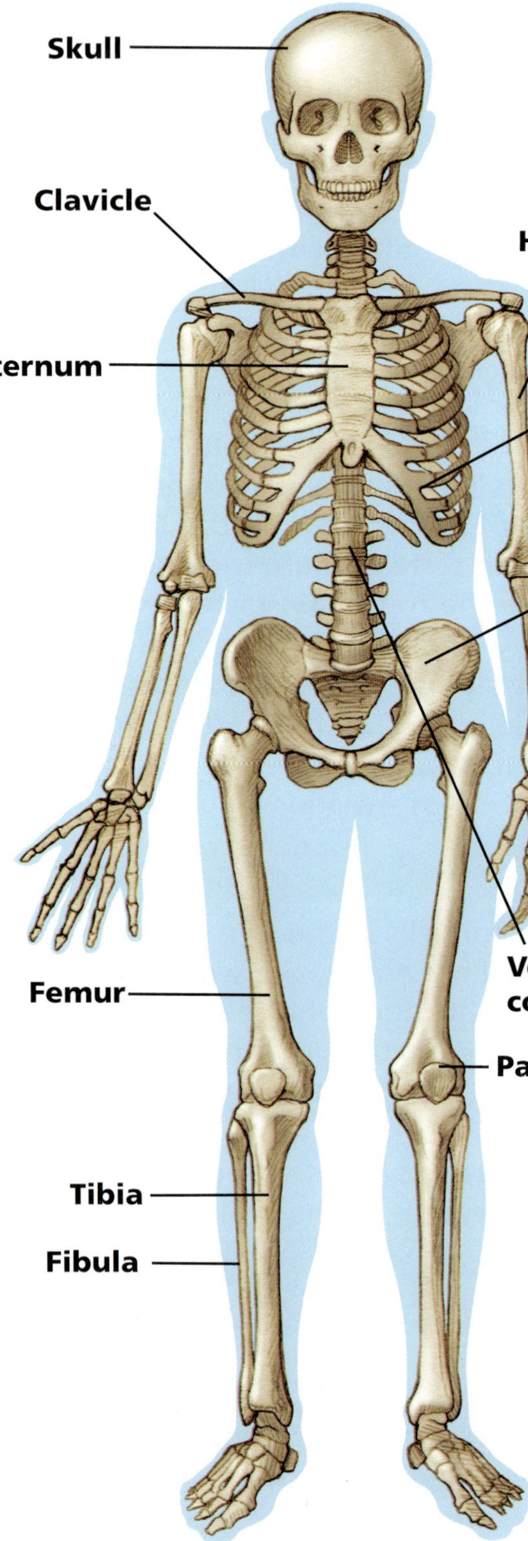

CARE!

- **Exercise to keep your skeletal system in good shape.**
- **Don't overextend your joints.**
- **Eat foods rich in vitamins and minerals. Your bones need the minerals, calcium, and phosphorus to grow strong.**

The Integumentary System

The skeleton and the organ systems are covered by an outer layer of skin. The skin is the largest organ of the human body. It is part of the integumentary system. Other parts of the integumentary system are your hair, nails, and glands in the skin. The skin has several functions.

- It protects your internal organs.
- It protects your body from injury and infection.
- It helps regulate body temperature.
- It helps remove wastes.

Joints

The skeleton has different types of joints. A joint is a place where two or more bones meet. Joints can be classified into three major groups—immovable joints, partly movable joints, and movable joints.

Types of Joints

Immovable Joints

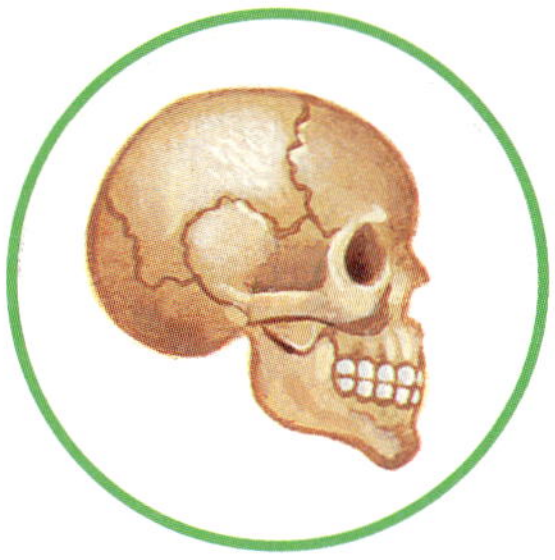

Head

Immovable joints are places where bones fit together too tightly to move. Nearly all the 29 bones in the skull meet at immovable joints. Only the lower jaw can move.

Partly Movable Joints

Partly movable joints are places where bones can move only a little. Ribs are connected to the sternum, or breastbone, with these joints.

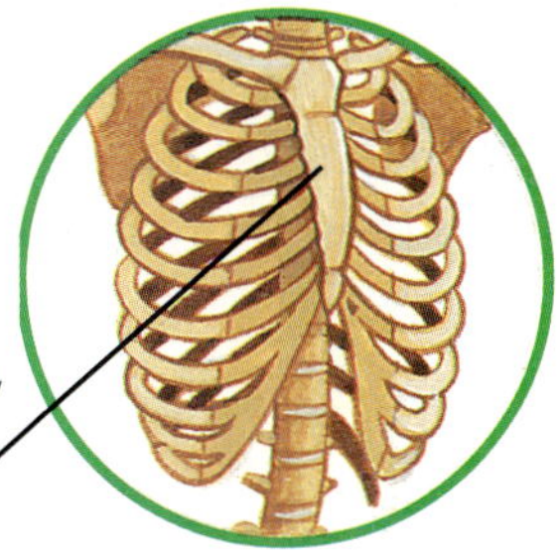

Sternum

Ribs

Movable Joints

Movable joints are places where bones can move easily.

Gliding joint

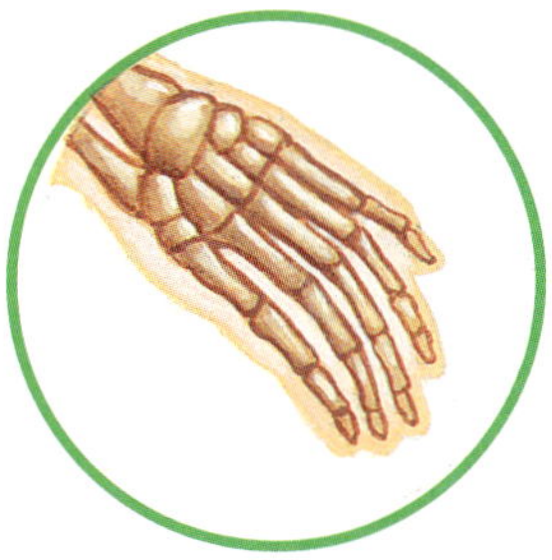

Hand and wrist

Small bones in the wrists and ankles meet at gliding joints. The bones can slide against one another. These joints allow some movement in all directions.

Ball-and-socket joint

The hips are examples of ball-and-socket joints. The ball of one bone fits into the socket, or cup, of another bone. These joints allow bones to move back and forth, in a circle, and side to side.

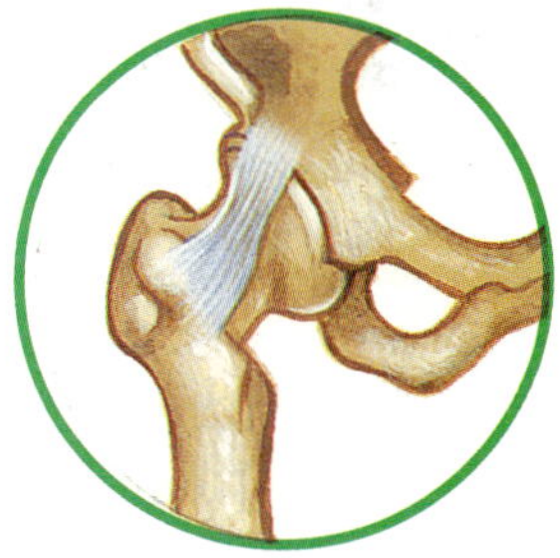

Hip

Hinge joint

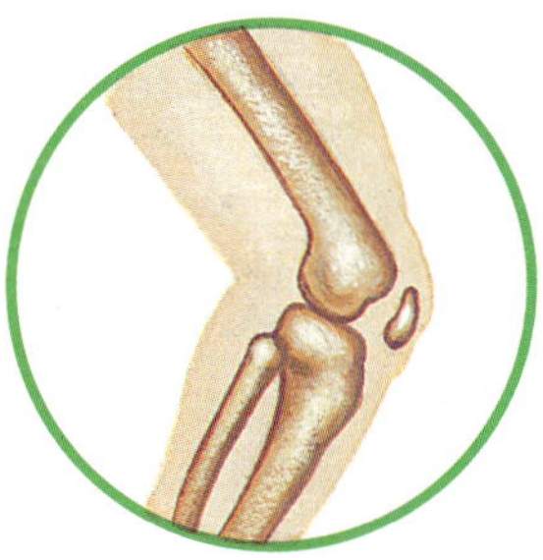

Knee

The knees are hinge joints. A hinge joint is similar to a door hinge. It allows bones to move back and forth in one direction.

Pivot joint

The joint between the skull and neck is a pivot joint. It allows the head to move up and down, and side to side.

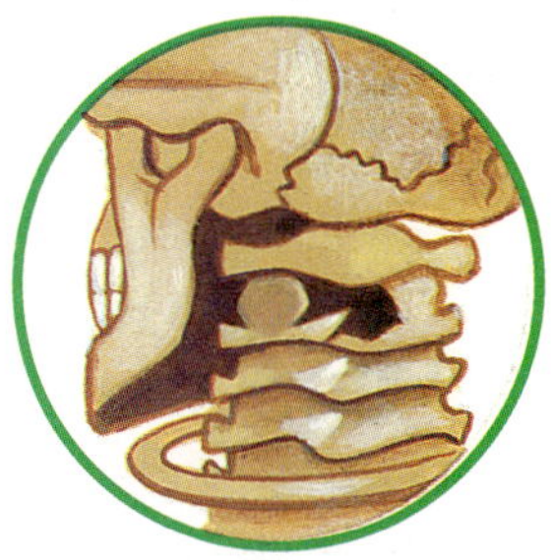

Neck

The Muscular System

Three types of muscles make up the body—skeletal muscle, cardiac muscle, and smooth muscle.

The muscles that are attached to and move bones are called *skeletal muscles.* These muscles are attached to bones by a tough cord called a *tendon.* Skeletal muscles pull bones to move them. Muscles do not push bones.

Cardiac muscles are found in only one place in the body—the heart. The walls of the heart are made of strong cardiac muscles. When cardiac muscles contract, they squeeze blood out of the heart. When cardiac muscles relax, the heart fills with more blood.

Smooth muscles make up internal organs and blood vessels. Smooth muscles in the lungs help a person breathe. Those in the blood vessels help control blood flow around the body.

CARE!

- **Exercise to strengthen your muscles.**
- **Eat the right foods.**
- **Get plenty of rest.**
- **Never take steroids unless your doctor tells you to.**

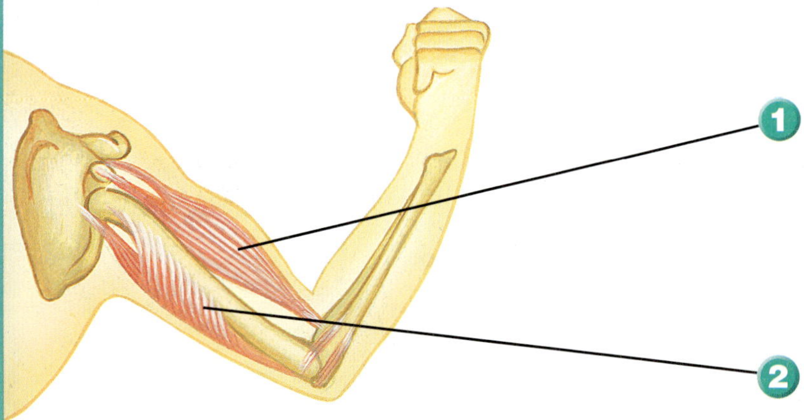

1. A message from your brain causes this muscle, called the biceps (BIGH·seps), to contract. When a muscle contracts, it becomes shorter and thicker. As the biceps contracts, it pulls on the arm bone it is attached to.

2. Most muscles work in pairs to move bones. This muscle, called the triceps (TRIGH·seps), relaxes when the biceps contracts. When a muscle relaxes, it becomes longer and thinner.

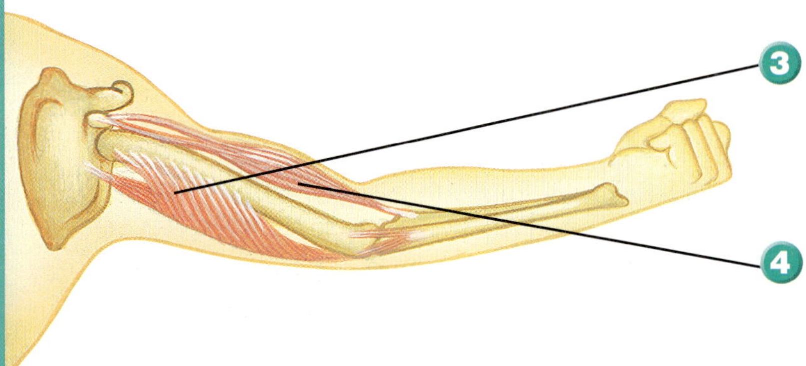

3. To straighten your arm, a message from your brain causes the triceps to contract. When the triceps contracts, it pulls on the bone it is attached to.

4. As the triceps contracts, the biceps relaxes. Your arm straightens.

Stimulus and Response

The nervous system, the skeletal system, and the muscular system work together to help you adjust to your surroundings. Anything in the environment that requires your body to adjust is called a *stimulus* (plural: stimuli). A reaction to a stimulus is called a *response*.

As you learned, nerve cells are called *neurons.* There are three kinds of neurons: sensory, associative, and motor. Each kind does a different job to help your body respond to stimuli.

- The job of your sensory neurons is to collect information from stimuli and send it to your brain and spinal cord. When you touch a sharp tack, sensory neurons alert your brain. The sensory neurons carry the message that your finger has touched a tack (stimulus) to the associative neurons in the brain and spinal cord.
- Associative neurons pass impulses from sensory to motor neurons. The message is interpreted and sent to the motor neurons.
- Motor neurons carry impulses from your brain and spinal cord to your muscles. The motor neurons cause your finger to move away from the tack (response).

In addition to responding to external stimuli, your body also responds to internal changes. Your body regulates its internal environment to maintain a stable condition for survival. This is called a *steady-state* condition.

Nerve Response

Nerves respond to a sharp object.

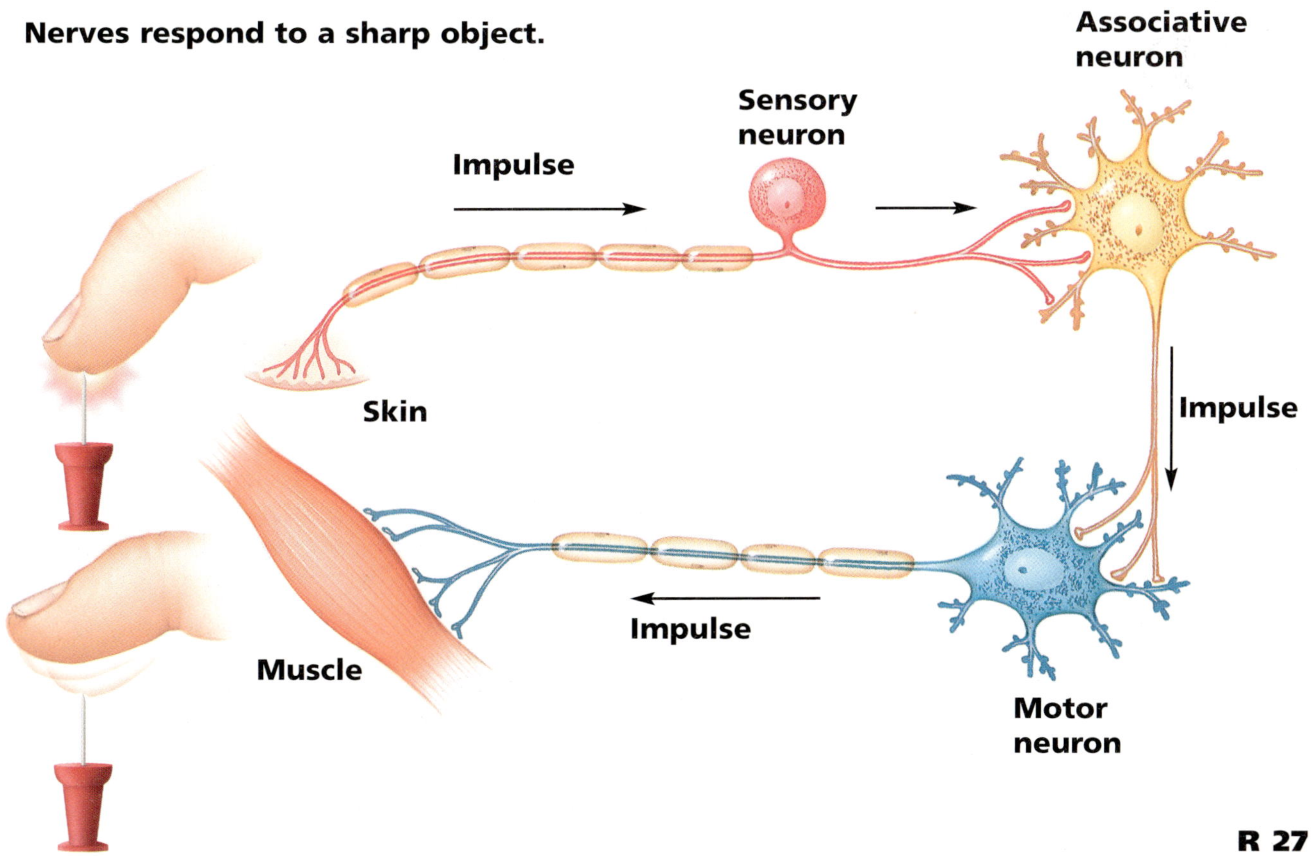

The Circulatory System

The circulatory system consists of the heart, blood vessels, and blood. Circulation is the flow of blood through the body. Blood is a liquid that contains red blood cells, white blood cells, and platelets. Red blood cells carry oxygen and nutrients to cells. White blood cells work to fight germs that enter the body. Platelets are cell fragments that make the blood clot.

The heart is a muscular organ about the size of a fist. It beats about 70 to 90 times a minute, pumping blood through the blood vessels. Arteries carry blood away from the heart. Some arteries carry blood to the lungs, where the cells pick up oxygen. Other arteries carry oxygen-rich blood from the lungs to all other parts of the body. Veins carry blood from other parts of the body back to the heart. Blood in most veins carries the wastes released by cells and has little oxygen. Blood flows from arteries to veins through narrow vessels called capillaries.

Pulse Rate and Pulse Points

You can tell how fast your heart is beating by checking your *pulse rate*. Take your pulse by putting the first and second fingers of one hand on the inside of the wrist of the other hand, just below the thumb. What you feel is the blood being pumped by your heart through arteries that lie close to the surface of the skin. Count the number of times you feel your heart pump in one minute. This is your pulse rate.

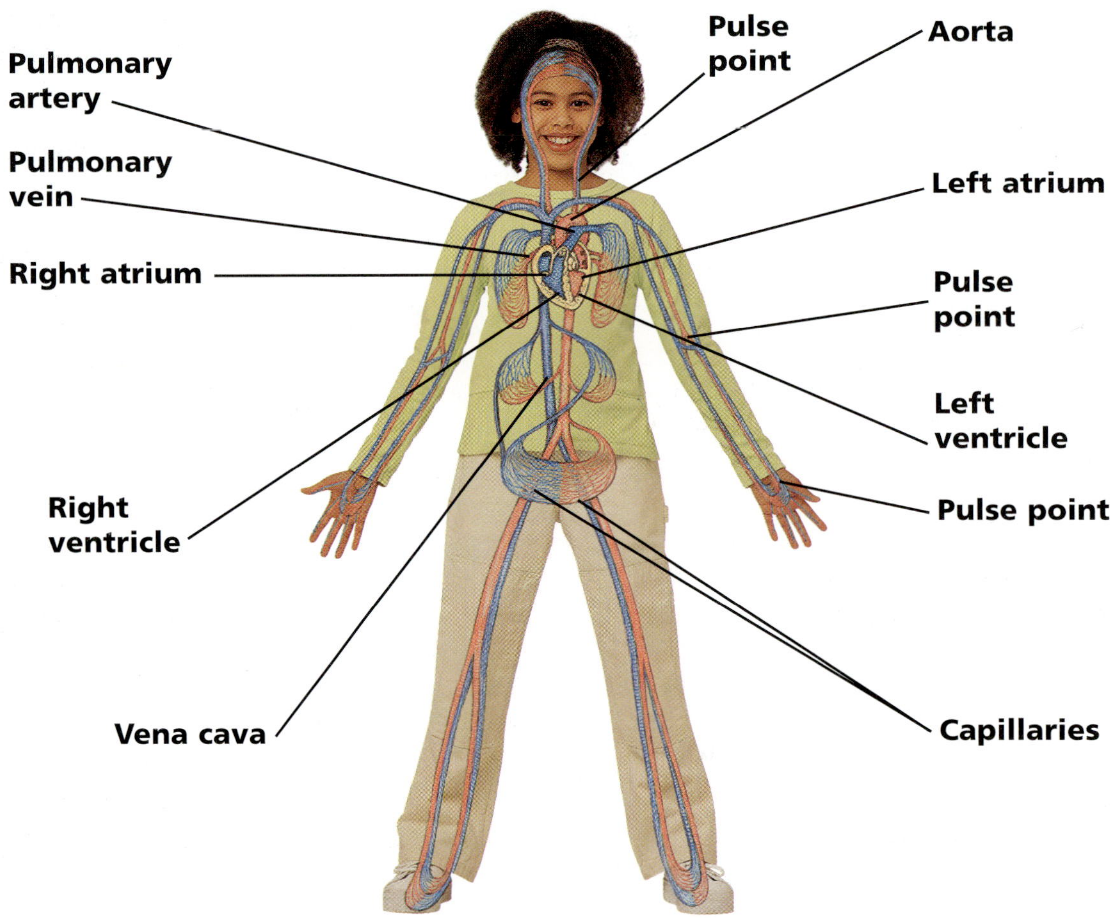

The Heart

The heart has two sides, right and left, separated by a thick muscular wall. Each side has two chambers for blood. The upper chamber is the atrium. The lower chamber is the ventricle. Blood enters the heart through the vena cava. It leaves the heart through the aorta.

The pulmonary artery carries blood from the body into the lungs. Here carbon dioxide leaves the blood to be exhaled by the lungs. Fresh oxygen enters the blood to be carried to every cell in the body. Blood returns from the lungs to the heart through the pulmonary veins.

CARE!

- **Don't smoke. The nicotine in tobacco makes the heart beat faster and work harder to pump blood.**
- **Never take illegal drugs, such as cocaine or heroin. They can damage the heart and cause heart failure.**

How the Heart Works

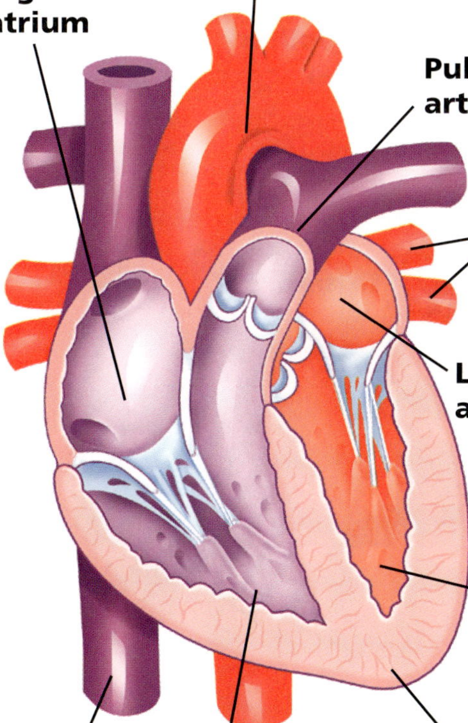

To the Lungs

1. The right atrium fills.
2. Right atrium squeezes blood into right ventricle.
3. Right ventricle squeezes blood into pulmonary artery.

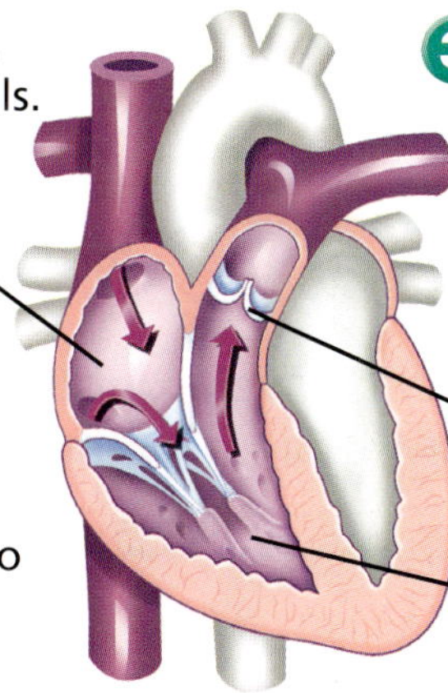

From the Lungs

1. The left atrium fills.
2. Left atrium squeezes blood into left ventricle.
3. Left ventricle squeezes blood into aorta.

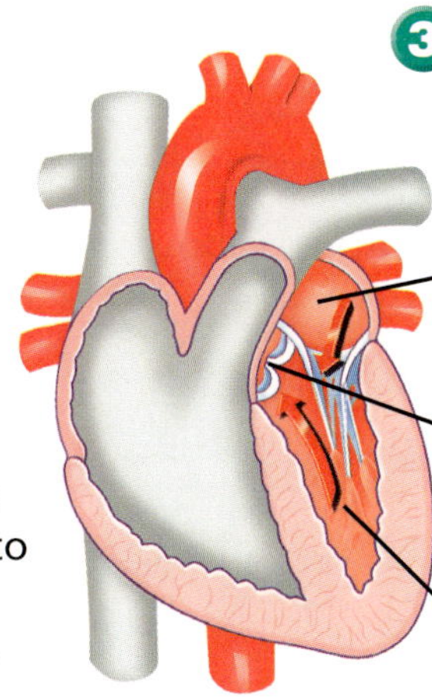

The Respiratory System

The process of getting and using oxygen in the body is called respiration. When a person inhales, air is pulled into the nose or mouth. The air travels down into the trachea. In the chest the trachea divides into two bronchial tubes. One bronchial tube enters each lung. Each bronchial tube branches into smaller tubes called bronchioles.

At the end of each bronchiole are tiny air sacs called alveoli. The alveoli exchange carbon dioxide for oxygen.

Oxygen comes from the air a person breathes. Two main muscles control breathing. One is located between the ribs. The other is a dome-shaped sheet of muscle called the diaphragm.

To inhale, the diaphragm contracts and pulls down. Other muscles pull the ribs up and out. This makes more room in the chest. Air rushes into the lungs and fills the space.

To exhale, the diaphragm relaxes and returns to its dome shape. The lungs get smaller and force the air out.

CARE!

- **Don't smoke. Smoking damages your respiratory system.**
- **Exercise to strengthen your breathing muscles.**
- **If you ever have trouble breathing, tell an adult at once.**

1. Carbon dioxide diffuses into the alveoli. From there it is exhaled.
2. Fresh oxygen diffuses from the alveoli to the blood.

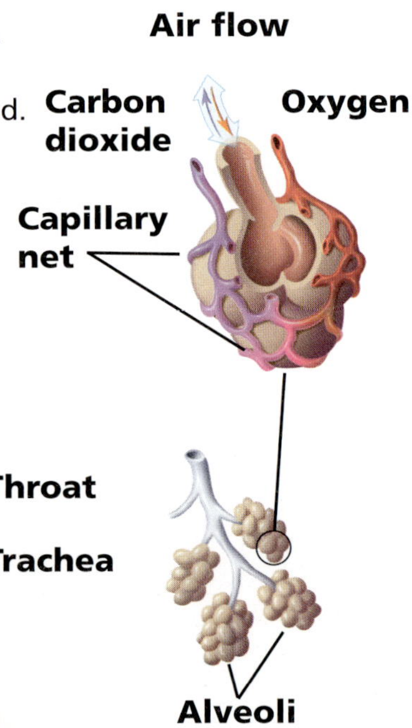

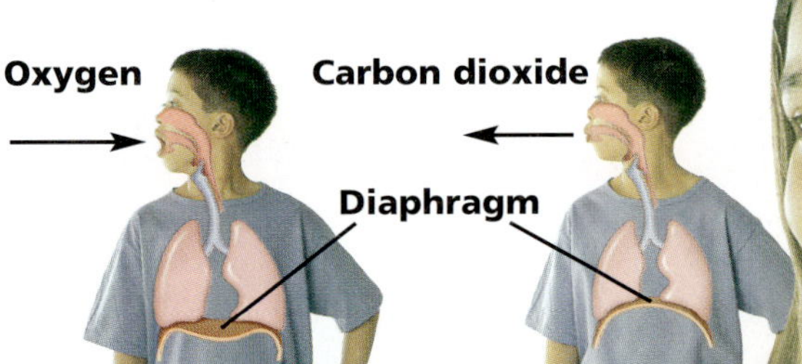

The air you breathe is about 21 percent oxygen.

The blood in the capillaries of your lungs has very little oxygen.

The blood has a higher concentration of carbon dioxide than air.

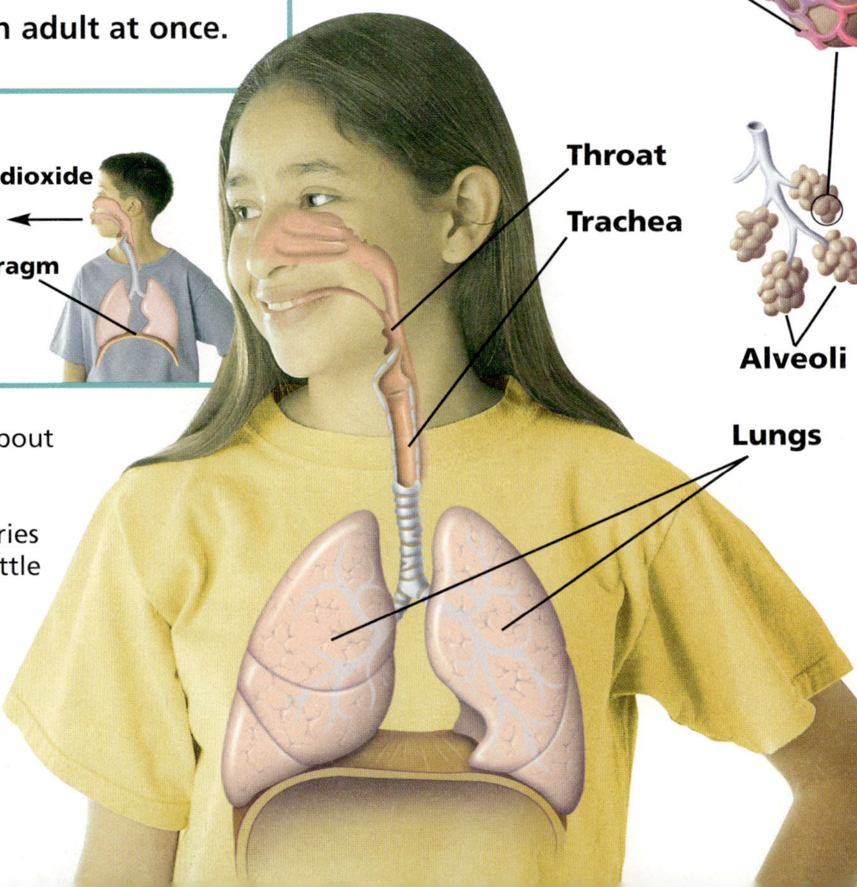

Effects of Exercise

Any type of exercise uses your muscles. When you exercise, your muscles need three things:

- They need oxygen.
- They need to remove wastes.
- They need to get rid of heat.

When you exercise, several things happen to your body. Your heart beats faster, you breathe heavier and faster, and you sweat.

If you are going to be exercising for more than a couple of minutes, your body needs to get oxygen to the muscles or the muscles will stop working. Your body increases the flow of oxygen-rich blood to working muscle as follows:

- Your rate and depth of breathing increase to take in more oxygen.
- Your heart beats faster so that it can pump more oxygen-rich blood to the muscles.

Sweating helps remove both wastes and heat that result from exercise.

The Digestive System

Digestion is the process of breaking down food into simple substances the body can use. Digestion begins when a person chews food. Chewing breaks the food down into smaller pieces and moistens it with saliva. Saliva is produced by the salivary glands.

Digested food is absorbed in the small intestine. The walls of the small intestine are lined with villi. Villi are tiny fingerlike projections that absorb digested food. From the villi the blood transports nutrients to every part of the body.

CARE!

- Chew your food well.
- Drink plenty of water to help move food through your digestive system.

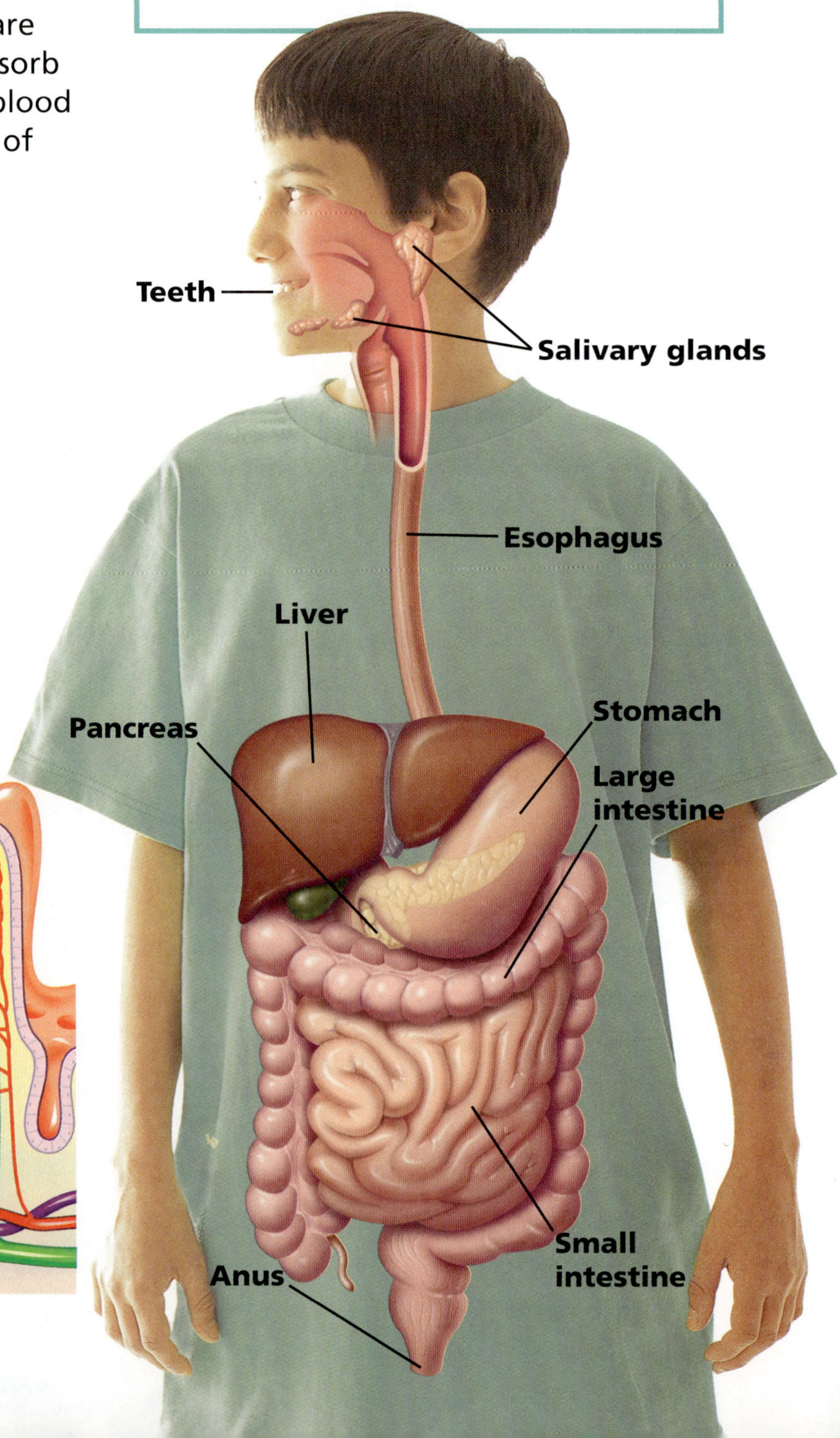

The shape of the small intestine's villi increases the amount of nutrients that can be absorbed from the food.

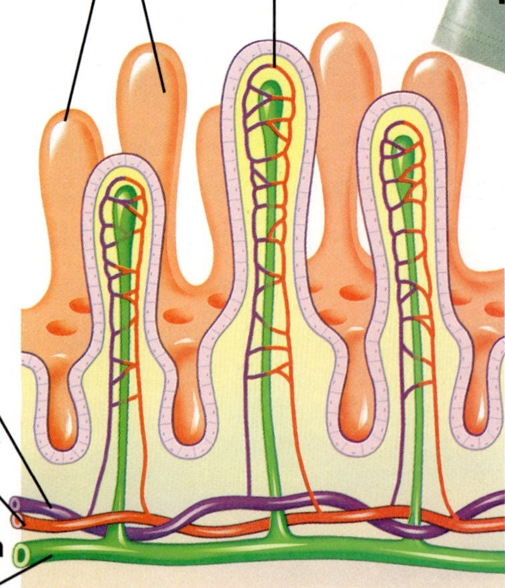

The Digestive System

Mechanical and Chemical Digestion

Digestion is both mechanical and chemical. Chewing is the first step in digestion. Chewing is *mechanical digestion*, the physical process of breaking food down into smaller pieces. As you chew, saliva begins to break the food into simpler molecules. This is *chemical digestion*.

After you swallow your food, both mechanical and chemical digestion continue in the stomach. Stomach muscles churn food particles into smaller pieces. Glands lining the stomach produce strong digestive juices.

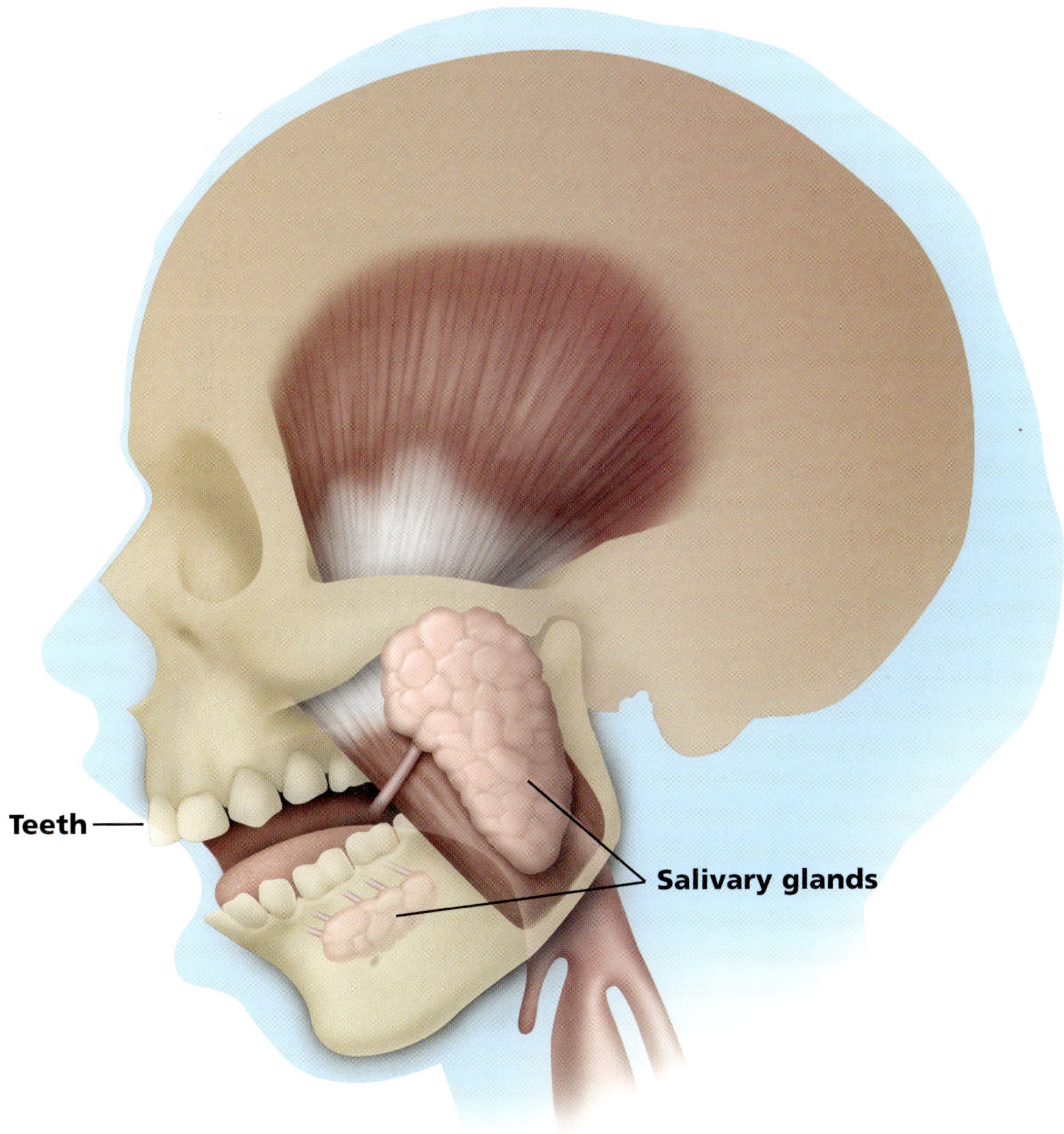

The Excretory System

Excretion is the process of removing waste products from the body. The liver filters wastes from the blood and converts them into urea. Urea is then carried to the kidneys for excretion. Each kidney contains more than a million nephrons. Nephrons are structures in the kidneys that filter blood.

The skin takes part in excretion when a person sweats. Glands in the inner layer of the skin produce sweat. Sweat is mostly water. Sweat tastes salty because it contains mineral salts the body doesn't need. There is also a tiny amount of urea in sweat.

Sweat is excreted by the sweat glands onto the outer layer of the skin. There it evaporates into the air. Evaporation takes place in part because of body heat. When sweat evaporates, a person feels cooler. On hot days or when exercising, a person sweats more to keep the body from overheating.

How You Sweat

Glands under your skin push sweat up to the surface, where it collects.

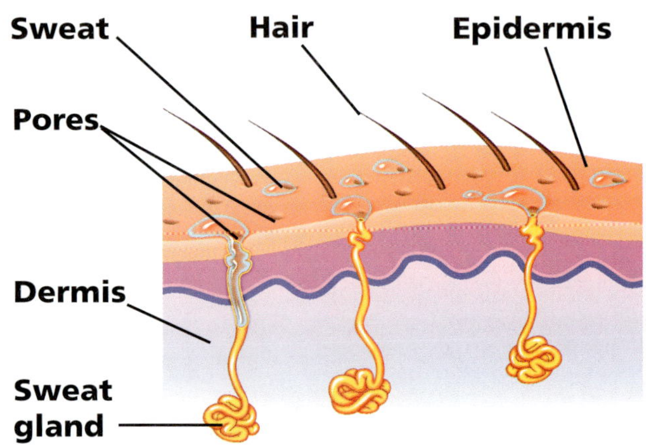

How Your Kidneys Work

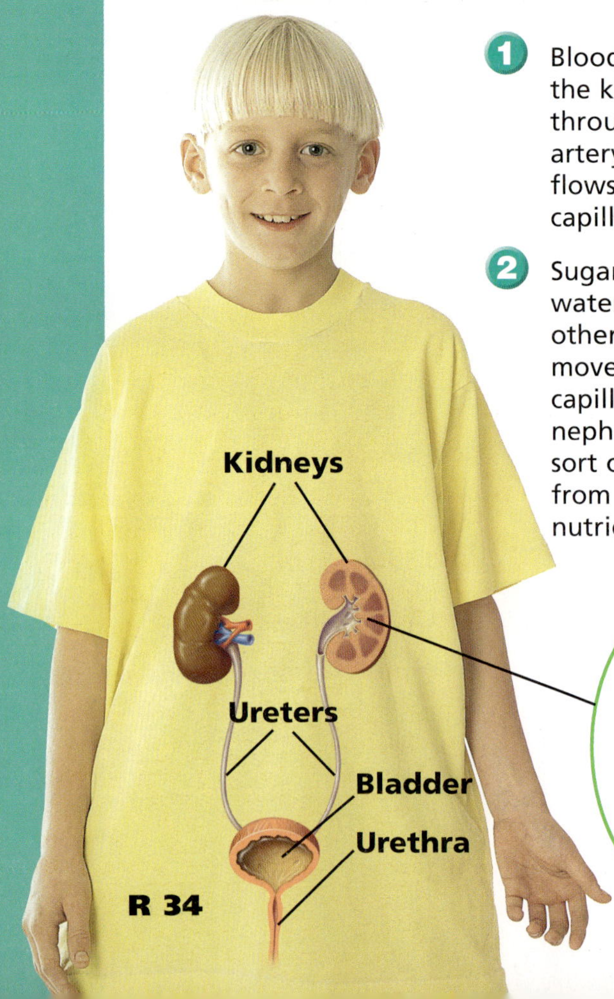

1. Blood enters the kidney through an artery and flows into capillaries.
2. Sugars, salts, water, urea, and other wastes move from the capillaries to tiny nephrons, which sort out wastes from the useful nutrients.
3. The nutrients return to the blood and flow back out through veins.
4. Urea and other wastes become urine, which flows down the ureters.
5. Urine is stored in the bladder and excreted through the urethra.

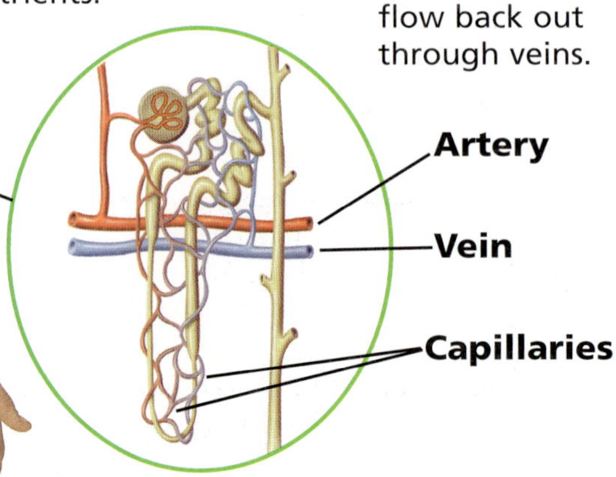

CARE!

- **Drink plenty of water to help the kidneys do their job and to replace water loss from sweating.**
- **Wash regularly to avoid body odor, clogged pores, and skin irritation.**

The Excretory System

Removing Excess Heat

In addition to waste removal, one of the skin's most important jobs is to maintain internal body temperature. The skin does this by removing excess heat. Two things happen when you exercise: your face gets red and you sweat. Both are ways of getting rid of excess heat.

The nervous system, the circulatory system, and the skin all work together to regulate body temperature. The diagram below shows what happens when your body heats up as a result of exercise.

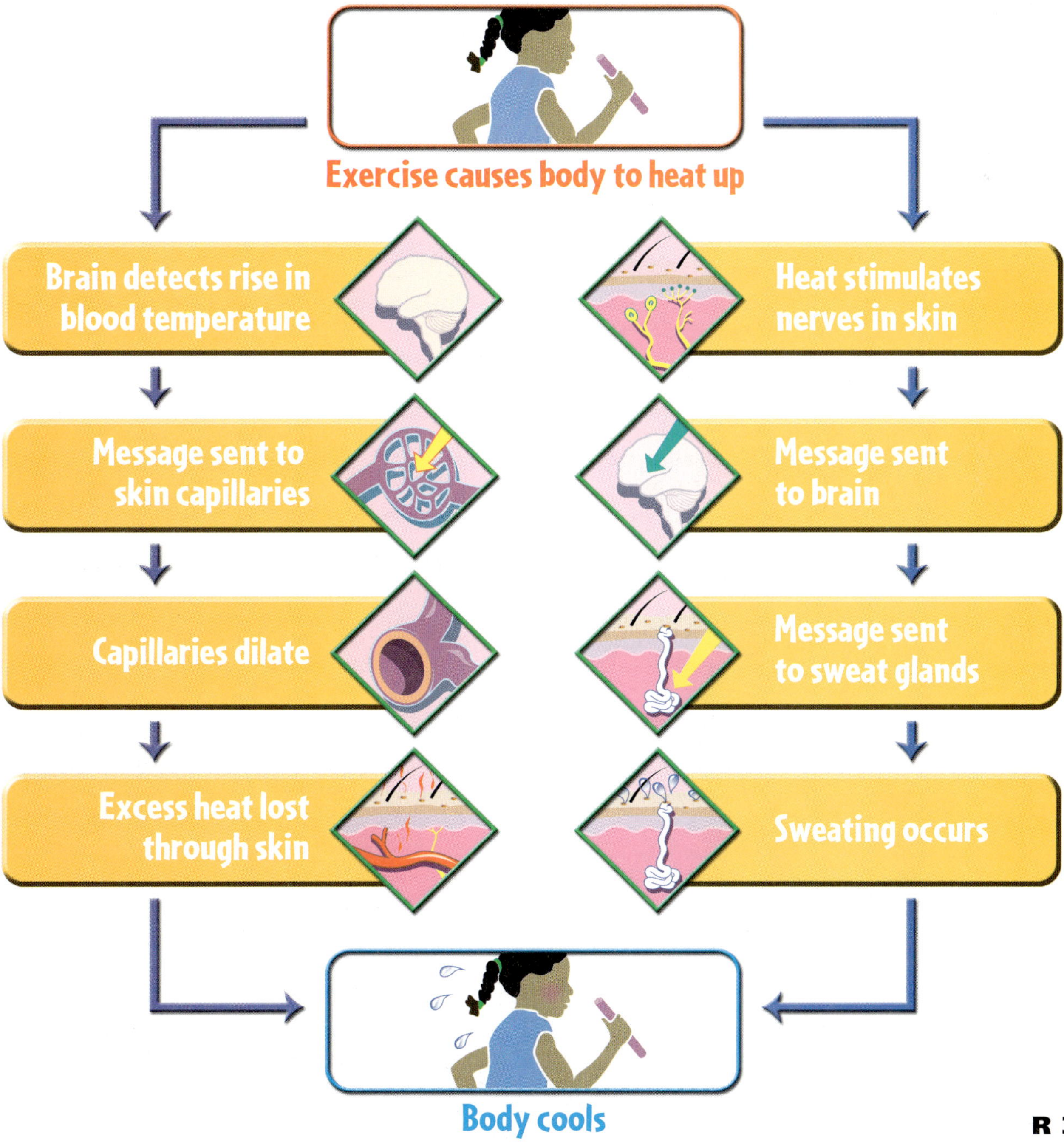

The Endocrine System

Hormones are chemicals that control body functions. A gland that produces hormones is called an endocrine gland. Sweat from sweat glands flows out of tubes called ducts. Endocrine glands have no ducts.

The endocrine glands are scattered around the body. Each gland makes one or more hormones. Every hormone seeks out a target organ, the place in the body where the hormone acts.

The endocrine glands help to maintain a *steady-state* condition in your body. They can turn the production of hormones on or off when they sense that too little or too much is being produced.

CARE!

- **Doctors can treat many diseases, such as diabetes, caused by endocrine glands that produce too little or too much of a hormone.**

Some Glands in the Endocrine System

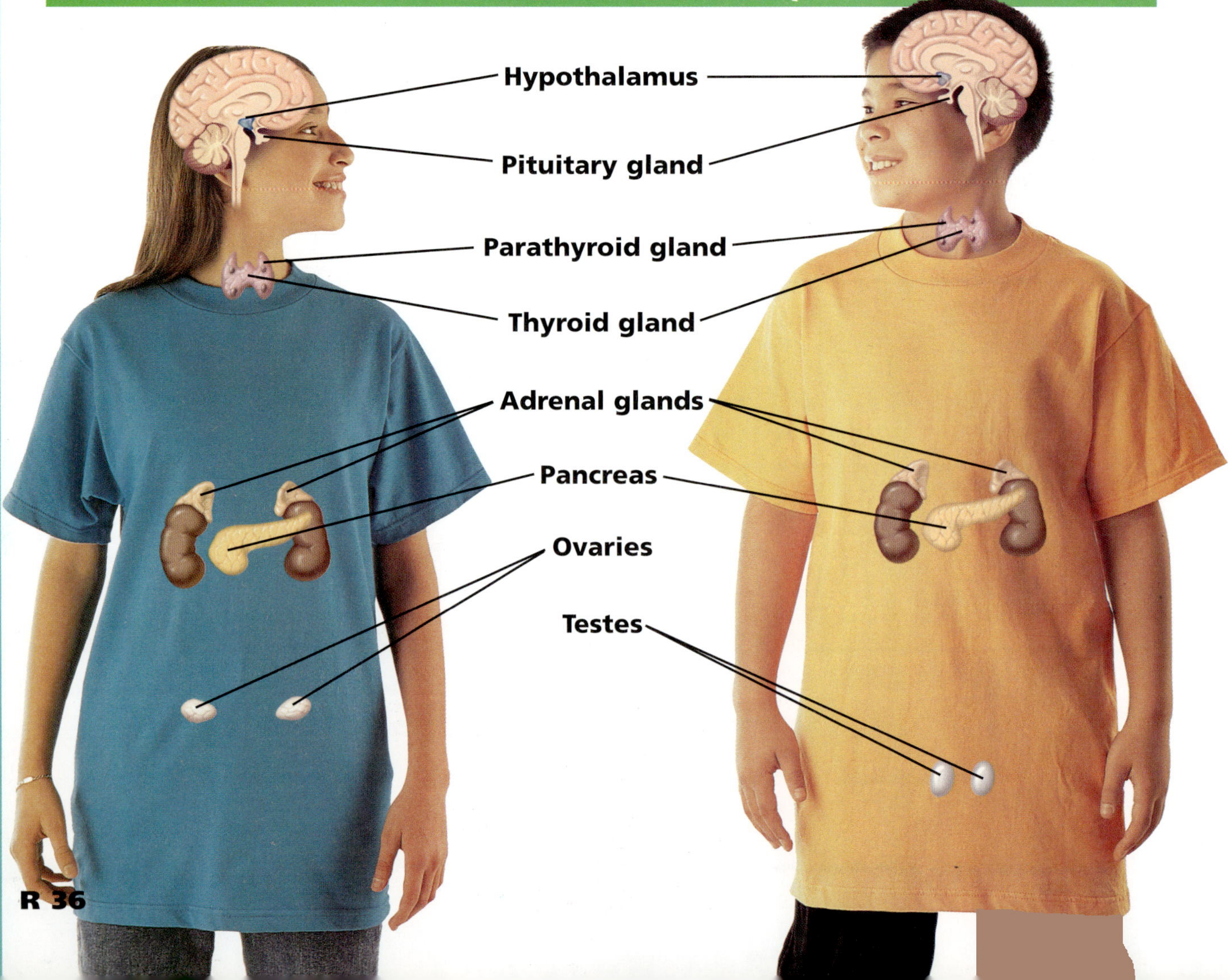

The Reproductive System

The testes are the male reproductive organs. At puberty the testes begin to produce sperm. Sperm move through sperm ducts, where they mix with fluid from endocrine glands.

The ovaries are the female reproductive organs, which contain eggs. After puberty one mature egg is released about once every 28 days. The egg moves to the oviduct, a narrow tube leading from the ovary.

CARE!

- **Abstinence is the only sure way to avoid sexually transmitted diseases.**

The Male Reproductive System

Sperm move from the testes through sperm ducts, where they mix with fluid from the glands. The sperm and fluid move through the urethra.

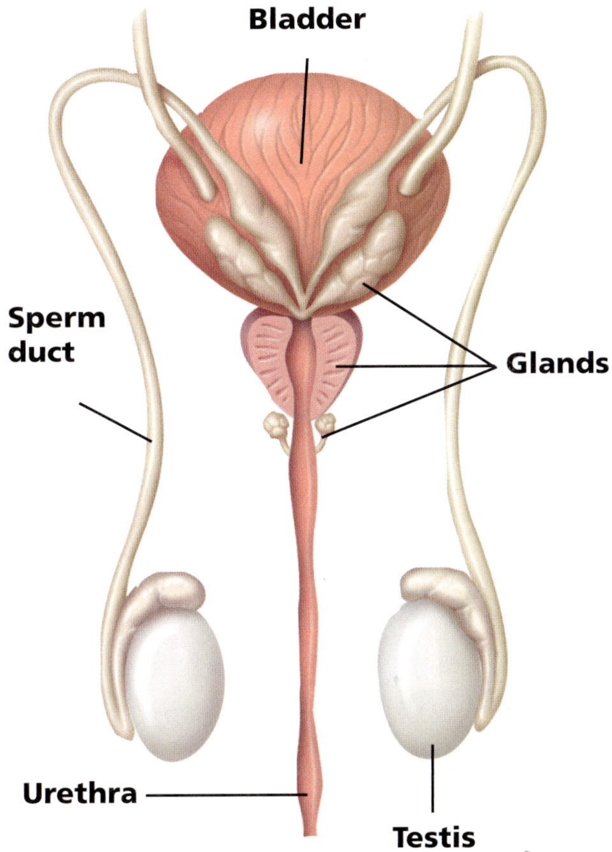

The Female Reproductive System

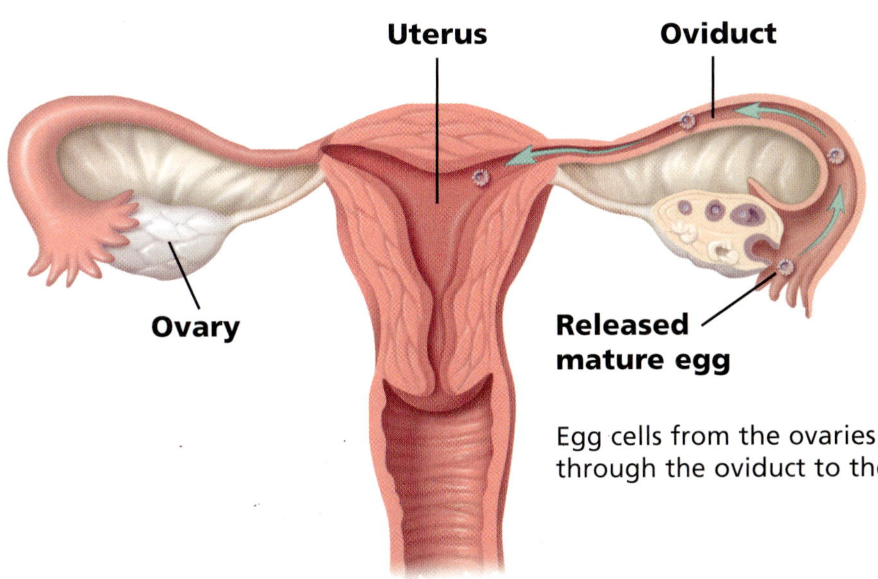

Egg cells from the ovaries move through the oviduct to the uterus.

The Immune System

The immune system helps the body fight disease. Inside some bones is a soft tissue known as red marrow that fills the spaces in spongy bone. Red marrow makes new red blood cells, platelets that stop a cut from bleeding, and germ-fighting white blood cells.

There are white blood cells in the blood vessels and in the lymph vessels. Lymph vessels are similar to blood vessels. Instead of blood, they carry lymph. Lymph is a straw-colored fluid surrounding body cells.

Lymph nodes filter out harmful materials in lymph. Like red marrow, they also produce white blood cells to fight infections. Swollen lymph nodes in the neck are a clue that the body is fighting germs.

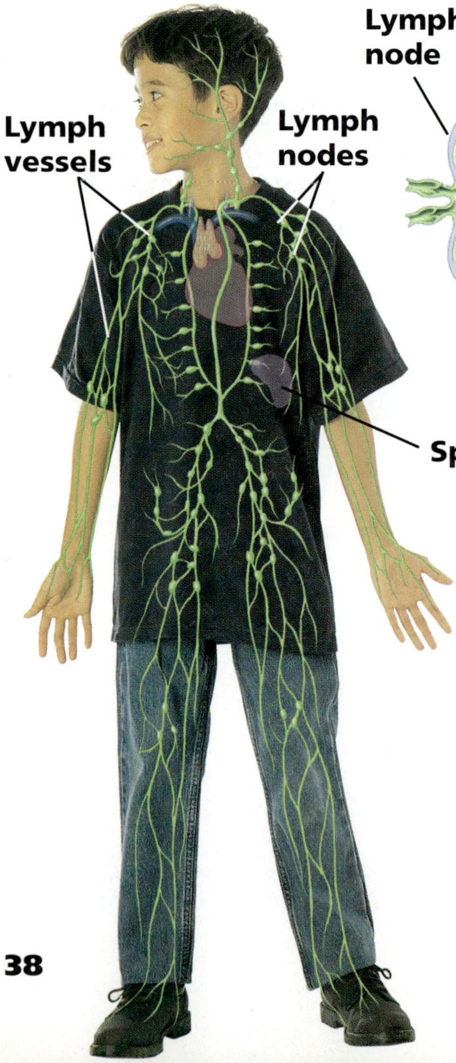

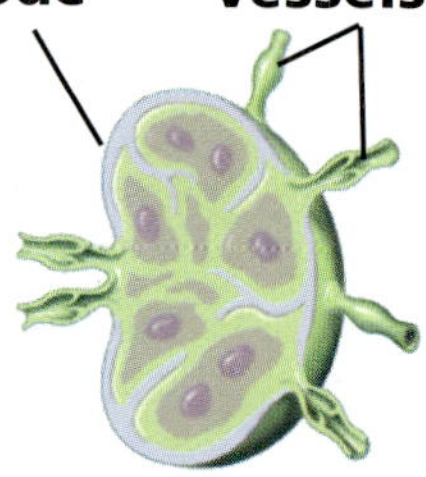

CARE!

- **Be sure to get immunized against common diseases.**
- **Keep cuts clean to prevent infection.**

1. A bone is covered with a tough but thin membrane that has many small blood vessels. The blood vessels bring nutrients and oxygen to the living parts of the bone and remove wastes.

2. Inside some bones is a soft tissue known as marrow. Yellow marrow is made mostly of fat cells and is one of the body's energy reserves. It is usually found in the long, hollow spaces of long bones.

3. Part of the bone is compact, or solid. It is made up of living bone cells and nonliving materials. The nonliving part is made up of layers of hardened minerals such as calcium and phosphorus. In between the mineral layers are living bone cells.

4. Red marrow fills the spaces in spongy bone. Red marrow makes new red blood cells, germ-fighting white blood cells, and platelets that stop a cut from bleeding.

5. Part of the bone is made of bone tissue that looks like a dry sponge. It is made of strong, hard tubes. It is also found in the middle of short, flat bones.

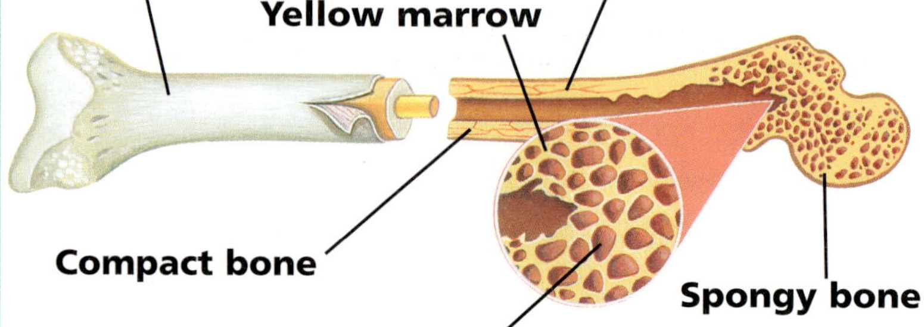

Infectious Diseases

A disease is anything that breaks down the normal functions of the body. Some diseases are inherited. Others are caused by harmful materials in the environment. Many diseases, however, are caused by organisms. Disease-causing organisms include bacteria and viruses. Diseases caused by these organisms are called *infectious diseases* because the organisms enter, or infect, the body.

Human Infectious Diseases		
Disease	**Caused by**	**Organ System Affected**
Chicken pox	Virus	Skin
Smallpox	Virus	Skin
Polio	Virus	Nervous system
Rabies	Virus	Nervous system
Influenza	Virus	Respiratory system
Measles	Virus	Skin
Mumps	Virus	Salivary glands
Tuberculosis	Bacteria	Respiratory system
Tetanus	Bacteria	Nervous system
Food poisoning	Bacteria	Digestive system

White blood cells are your body's main protection against infectious disease. The white blood cells leave the blood vessels or lymph vessels to fight disease organisms in your tissues.

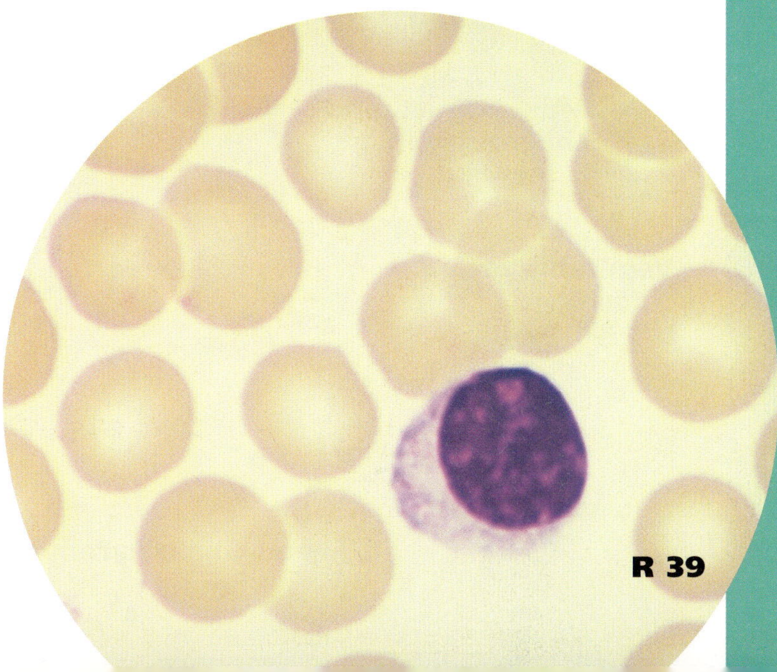

Staying Healthy

Physical fitness is the condition in which the body is healthy and works the best it can. It involves working the skeletal muscles, bones, joints, heart, and respiratory system.

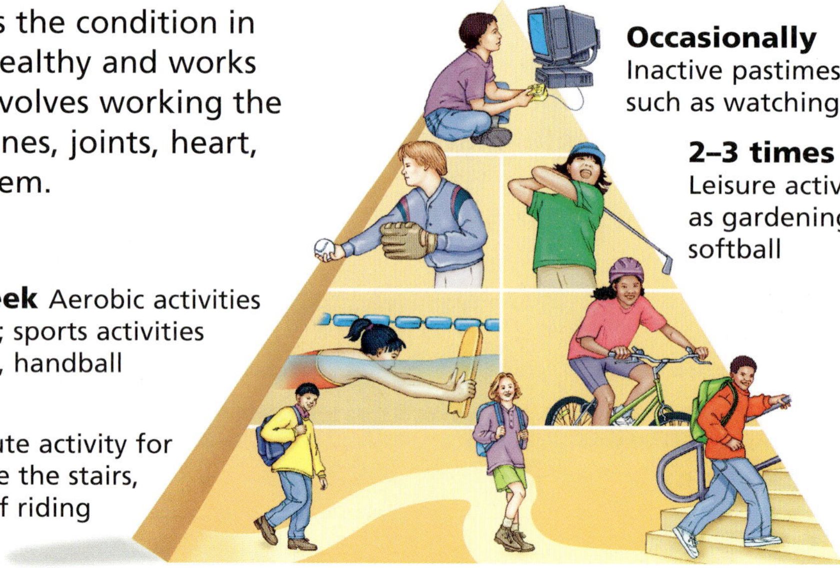

Occasionally Inactive pastimes such as watching TV

2–3 times a week Leisure activities such as gardening, golf, softball

3–5 times a week Aerobic activities such as swimming; sports activities such as basketball, handball

Daily Substitute activity for inactivity—take the stairs, walk instead of riding

Activity Pyramid

CARE!

- **Stay active every day.**
- **Eat a balanced diet.**
- **Drink plenty of water—6 to 8 large glasses a day.**

There is more to fitness than exercise. To make sure your body gets all the nutrients you need, you should eat a balanced diet. *A balanced diet* includes all the major food groups.

A balanced diet provides the calories, or energy from food, that you need to stay healthy. The number of calories needed varies from person to person, depending on their metabolism. *Metabolism* is the rate at which you burn energy. It is determined by weight, age, sex, and level of activity.

Fats, oils, and sweets Use sparingly

Milk, yogurt, and cheese group 2–3 servings

Meat, poultry, fish, dry beans, eggs, and nuts group 2–3 servings

Vegetable group 3–5 servings

Fruit group 2–4 servings

Bread, cereal, rice, and pasta group 6–11 servings

Food Guide Pyramid

FOLDABLES™

by Dinah Zike

Folding Instructions

So how do you make a Foldables data organizer? The following pages offer step-by-step instructions—where and when to fold, where to cut—for making 11 basic Foldables data organizers. The instructions begin with the basic shapes, such as the hot dog fold, that were introduced on page xv.

Half-Book

Fold a sheet of paper ($8\frac{1}{2}$" x 11") in half.

1. This book can be folded vertically like a hot dog or …
2. … it can be folded horizontally like a hamburger.

Folded Book

1. Make a Half-Book.
2. Fold in half again like a hamburger.

This makes a ready-made cover and two small pages inside for recording information.

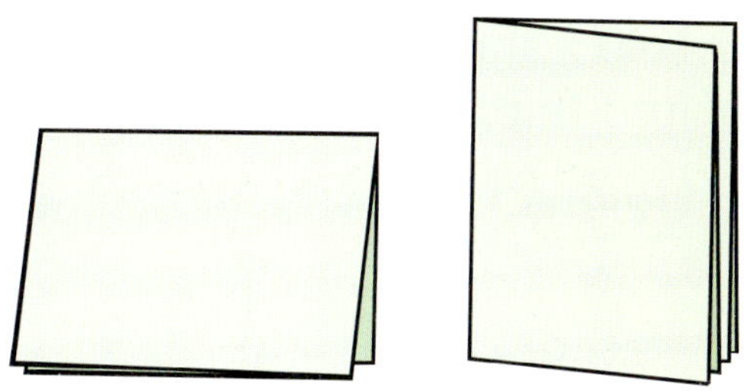

Two-Tab Book

Take a Folded Book and cut up the valley of the inside fold toward the mountain top.

This cut forms two large tabs that can be used front and back for writing and illustrations.

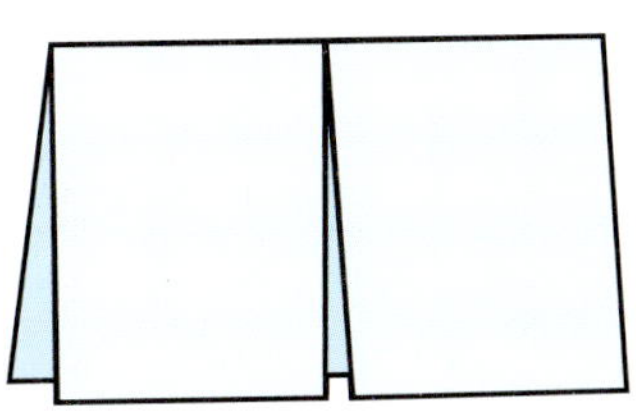

Pocket Book

1. Fold a sheet of paper ($8\frac{1}{2}$" x 11") in half like a hamburger.
2. Open the folded paper and fold one of the long sides up two inches to form a pocket. Refold along the hamburger fold so that the newly formed pockets are on the inside.
3. Glue the outer edges of the two-inch fold with a small amount of glue.

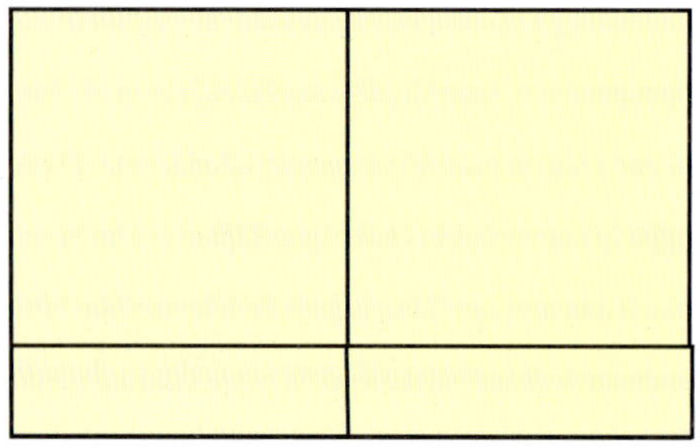

Shutter Fold

1. Begin as if you were going to make a hamburger, but instead of creasing the paper, pinch it to show the midpoint.
2. Fold the outer edges of the paper to meet at the pinch, or midpoint, forming a Shutter Fold.

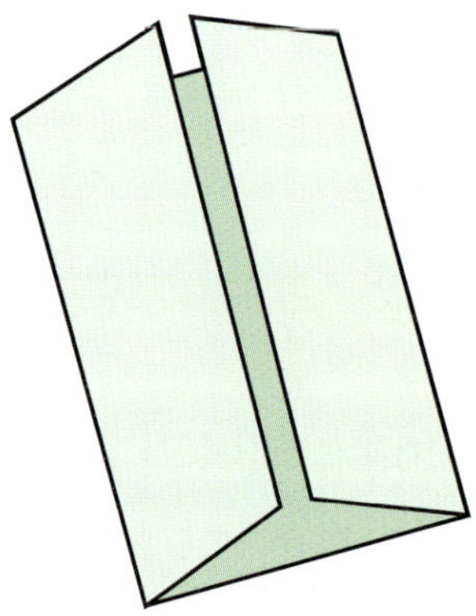

Trifold Book

1. Fold a sheet of paper ($8\frac{1}{2}$" x 11") into thirds.
2. Use this book as is, or cut into shapes.

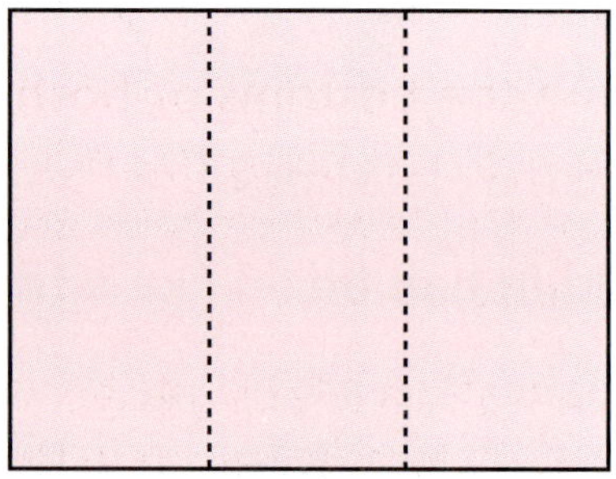

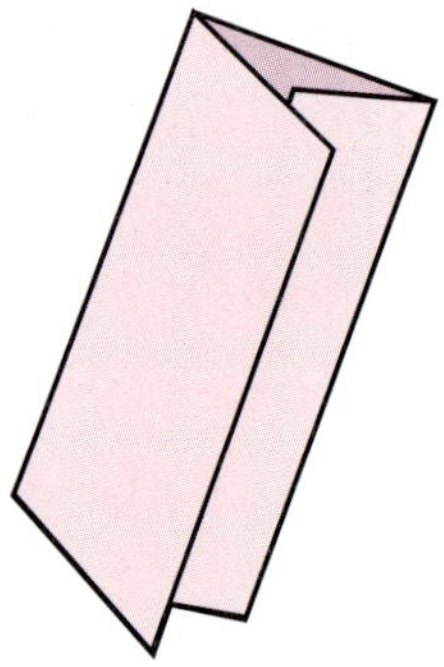

Three-Tab Book

1. Fold a sheet of paper like a hot dog.
2. With the paper horizontal and the fold of the hot dog up, fold the right side toward the center, trying to cover one half of the paper.
3. Fold the left side over the right side to make a book with three folds.
4. Open the folded book. Place one hand between the two thicknesses of paper and cut up the two valleys on one side only. This will create three tabs.

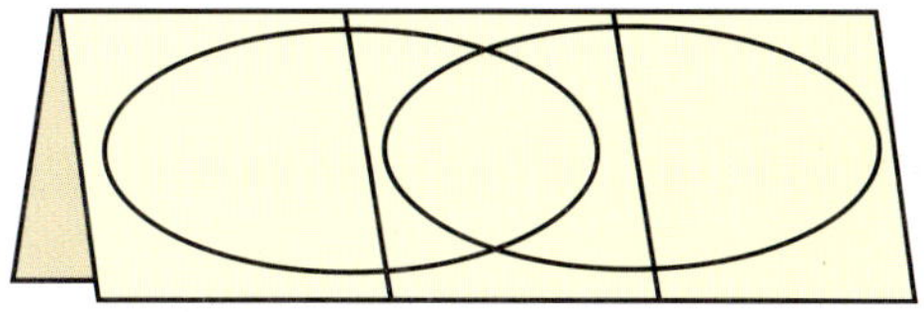

Layered-Look Book

1. Stack two sheets of paper ($8\frac{1}{2}$" x 11") so that the back sheet is one inch higher than the front sheet.
2. Bring the bottoms of both sheets upward and align the edges so that all of the layers or tabs are the same distance apart.
3. When all the tabs are an equal distance apart, fold the papers and crease well.
4. Open the papers and glue them together along the valley, or inner center fold, or staple them along the mountain.

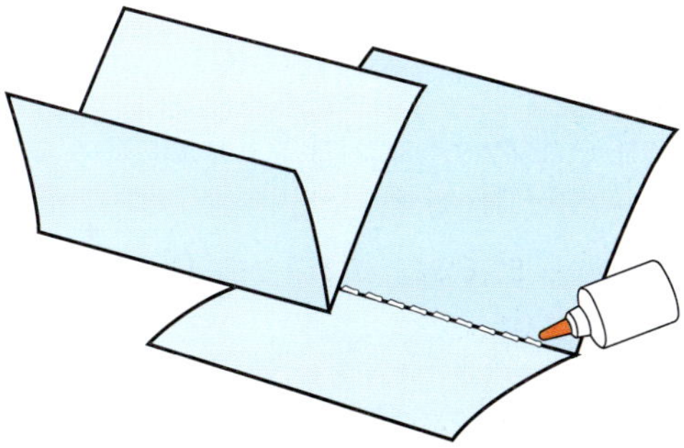

Four-Tab Book

1. Fold a sheet of paper ($8\frac{1}{2}$" x 11") in half like a hot dog.
2. Fold this long rectangle in half like a hamburger.
3. Fold both ends back to touch the mountain top or fold it like an accordion.
4. On the side with two valleys and one mountain top, make vertical cuts through one thickness of paper, forming four tabs.

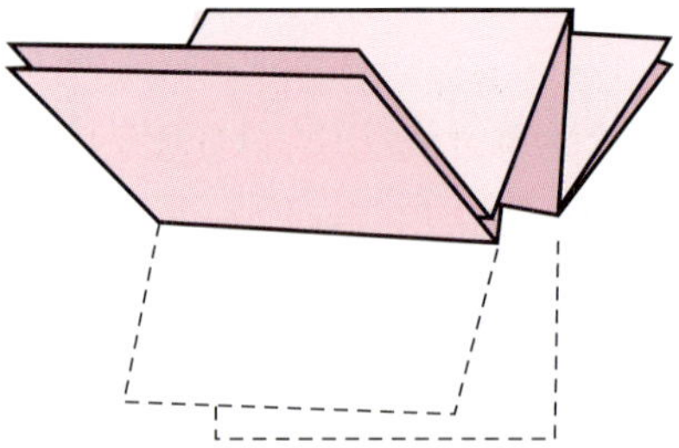

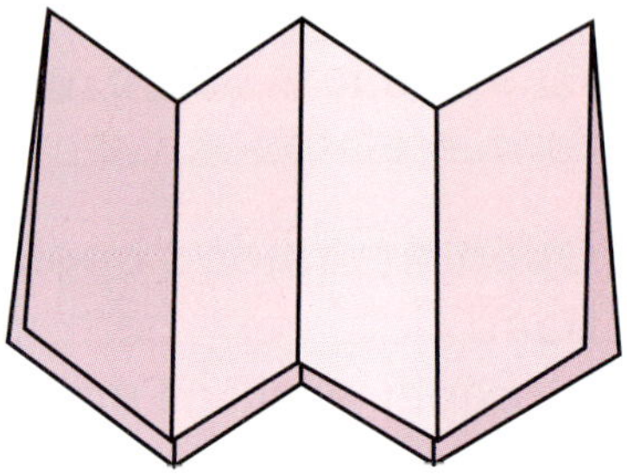

Four-Door Book

1. Make a Shutter Fold using 11" x 17" or 12" x 18" paper.
2. Fold the Shutter Fold in half like a hamburger. Crease well.
3. Open the project and cut along the two inside valley folds.

These cuts will form four doors on the inside of the project.

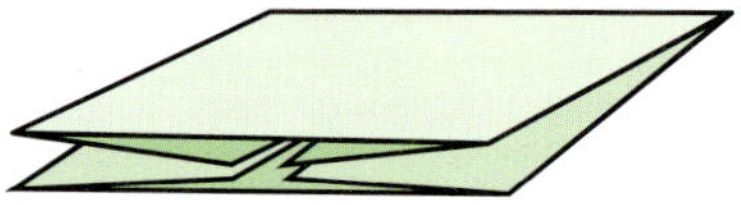

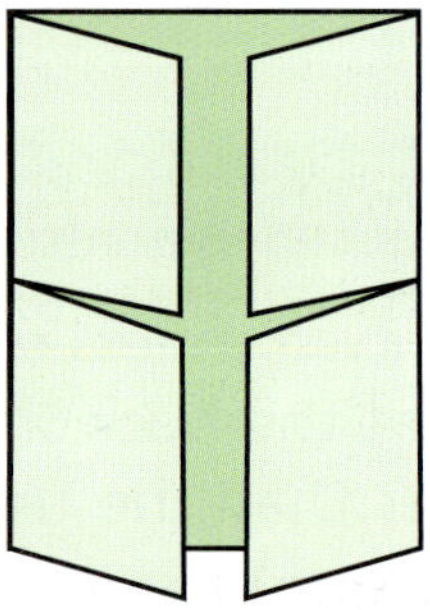

Folded Table or Chart

1. Fold the number of vertical columns needed to make the table or chart.
2. Fold the horizontal rows needed to make the table or chart.
3. Label the rows and columns.

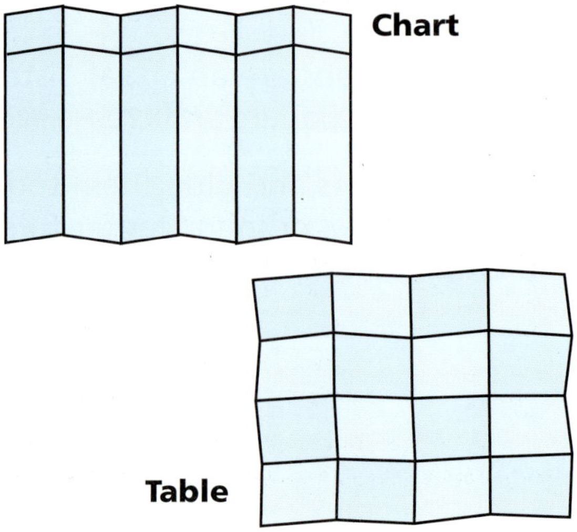

Glossary

This Glossary will help you to pronounce and understand the meanings of the Science Words introduced in this book. The page number at the end of the definition tells where the word appears.

A

abiotic factor (ā′bī ot′ik fak′tər) A nonliving part of an ecosystem. (p. B6)

absorption (əb sôrp′shən) The disappearance of a sound wave into a surface. (p. F66)

abyssal plain (ə bis′əl plān) The vast flat lands beyond the continental shelf that cover almost half of the deep ocean floor. (p. C90)

acceleration (ak sel′ə rā′shən) Change in velocity with respect to time. (pp. F13, F22)

acid (as′id) A substance that tastes sour and turns blue litmus paper red. (p. E82)

acid rain (as′id rān) Moisture that falls to Earth after being mixed with wastes from burned fossil fuels. (p. C65)

acidity (ə sid′ə tē) The strength of an acid. (p. E86)

action (ak′shən) The force one object applies to a second, as in Newton's third law of motion, which states, "For every action, there is an equal but opposite reaction." *See* **reaction**. (p. F24)

adaptation (ad′əp tā′shən) A characteristic that enables a living thing to survive in its environment. (pp. A46, A106)

aerial root (âr′ē əl rüt) A root that never touches the ground but can take in moisture from the air. (p. A31)

aerosol (ār′ə sōl′) A type of colloid in which liquid drops or solid particles are spread throughout a gas. (p. E60)

air mass (âr mas) A large region of the atmosphere where the air has similar properties throughout. (p. D70)

air pressure (âr presh′ər) The force put on a given area by the weight of the air above it. (p. D33)

alkalinity (al′kə lin′i tē) The strength of a base. (p. E86)

alternative energy source (ōl tûr′nə tiv en′ər jē sôrs) A source of energy other than the burning of a fossil fuel. (p. C104)

amphibian (am fib′ē ən) A vertebrate that lives part of its life in water and part of its life on land. (p. A95)

anemometer (an′ə mom′i tər) A device that measures wind speed. (p. D64)

PRONUNCIATION KEY

The following symbols are used throughout the McGraw-Hill Science Glossaries.

a	**a**t	e	**e**nd	o	h**o**t	u	**u**p	hw	**wh**ite	ə	**a**bout
ā	**a**pe	ē	m**e**	ō	**o**ld	ū	**u**se	ng	so**ng**		tak**e**n
ä	f**a**r	i	**i**t	ôr	f**or**k	ü	r**u**le	th	**th**in		penc**i**l
âr	c**ar**e	ī	**i**ce	oi	**oi**l	u̇	p**u**ll	th	**th**is		lem**o**n
ô	l**aw**	îr	p**ier**ce	ou	**ou**t	ûr	t**ur**n	zh	mea**s**ure		circ**u**s

′ = primary accent; shows which syllable takes the main stress, such as **kil** in **kilogram** (kil′ə gram′).

′ = secondary accent; shows which syllables take lighter stresses, such as **gram** in **kilogram.**

aneroid barometer (an′ə roid bə rom′i tər) A spring enclosed in a pleated metal can that expands or contracts to indicate changes in air pressure. (p. D34)

angiosperm (an′jē ə spûrm′) A seed plant that produces flowers. *See* **gymnosperm.** (p. A68)

aquifer (ak′wə fər) An underground layer of rock or soil filled with water. (p. C75)

asexual reproduction (a sek′shü əl rē′prō duk′shən) The production of a new organism from only one cell. (p. A62)

asteroid (as′tə roid′) "Minor planet." One of many small, rocky objects that orbit the Sun between the orbits of Mars and Jupiter. (p. D19)

asteroid belt (as′tə roid′ belt) Region between Mars and Jupiter where most asteroids are found. (p. D19)

atmosphere (at′məs fîr′) The blanket of gases that surrounds Earth. (pp. C26, D32)

atom (at′əm) The smallest unit of an element that retains the properties of that element. *See* **molecule**. (p. E26)

aurora (ə rôr′ə) The northern or southern lights that appear in the night sky, especially in polar regions. (p. D32)

B

bacterium (bak tîr′ē əm) *sing., n. pl.* **bacteria** (-ē ə) A member of either of two kingdoms of one-celled living things that have no nucleus, or center, in their cell body. (p. A19)

balanced forces (bal′ənst fôrs′əz) Forces that cancel each other out when acting together on a single object. (p. F21)

barometer (bə rom′i tər) A device for measuring air pressure. (p. D34)

base (bās) A substance that tastes bitter and turns red litmus paper blue. (p. E82)

basin (bās′in) The floor of an ocean, containing mountains, valleys, and plains. (p. C84)

bench mark (bench′ märk′) A plaque left by surveyors to tell the exact location and elevation of a place. (p. C6)

benthos (ben′thos) Organisms that live on the bottom in aquatic ecosystems. (p. B72)

bird (bûrd) A vertebrate that has both feathers and wings. (p. C95)

biomass (bī′ō mas′) Energy from plant matter or animal waste. (p. C106)

biome (bī′ōm) One of Earth's large ecosystems, with its own kind of climate, soil, plants, and animals. (p. B64)

biotic factor (bī ot′ik fak′tər) A living part of an ecosystem. (p. B7)

boiling point (boil′ing point) The particular temperature for each substance at which it changes state from a liquid to a gas. (p. E37)

buoyancy (boi′ən sē) The upward push of a liquid on an object placed in it. (p. E12)

C

cambium (kam′be əm) The layer in plants that separates the xylem from the phloem. (p. A31, A32)

camouflage (kam′ə fläzh′) An adaptation in which an animal protects itself against predators by blending in with the environment. (p. A108)

carbon cycle (kär′bən sī′kəl) The continuous exchange of carbon dioxide and oxygen among living things. (p. B53)

carnivore (kär′nə vôr′) An animal that eats another animal. (p. B20)

carrying capacity (kar′ē ing kə pas′i tē) The maximum population size that an area can support. (p. B35)

cell (sel) The smallest unit of living matter. (p. A6)

chemical change (kem′i kəl chānj) A change of matter that occurs when atoms link together in a new way, creating a new substance different from the original substances. (p. E71)

chemical formula (kəm′i kəl fôr′myə lə) A way to write a compound's name using symbols. The letters tell what elements are in the compound, and the subscripts tell the number of particles in the compound. (p. E25)

chemical reaction (kem′i kəl rē ak′shən) Another name for chemical change. (p. E71)

chemosynthesis (kē′mō sin′thə sis) In tube worms the process by which bacteria create nutrients from hydrogen sulfide and oxygen, using chemical reactions rather than light. (p. C93)

chlorophyll (klôr′ə fil′) A green chemical in plant cells that allows plants to use the Sun's energy for making food. (p. A6)

cirrus cloud (sir′əs kloud) A high-altitude cloud with a featherlike shape, made of ice crystals. (p. D44)

classification (klas′ə fi kā′shən) The science of finding patterns among living things. (p. A10)

cleavage (klē′vij) The tendency of a mineral to break along flat surfaces. (p. C34)

climate (klī′mit) The average weather pattern of a region. (p. D84)

climate zone (klī mat′ zōn) A region that has similar weather patterns based on temperature, precipitation, wind, distance from a coast, mountain ranges, ocean currents, and vegetation. (p. D84)

climax community (klī′maks kə mū′ni tē) The final stage of succession in an area, unless a major change happens. (p. B84)

cold front (kōld frunt) A front where cold air moves in under a warm air mass. (p. D72)

colloid (kol′oid) A special type of mixture in which the particles of one material are scattered through another and block the passage of light without settling out. (pp. E54, E60)

comet (kom′ it) A "dirty snowball" orbiting the Sun — a mixture of ices, frozen gases, rock, and dust left over from the formation of the solar system. (p. D19)

commensalism (kə men′sə liz′əm) A relationship between two kinds of organisms that benefits one without harming the other. (p. B27)

community (kə mū′ni tē) All the living things in an ecosystem. (p. B11)

complete flower (kəm plēt′ flou′ər) A flower that has sepals, petals, stamens, and pistils. (p. A78)

compound (kom′pound) Any substance that is formed by the chemical combination of two or more elements and acts like a single substance. (p. E24)

compression (kəm presh′ən) **1.** The part of a sound wave where molecules are crowded together. (p. F51) **2.** A movement of plates that presses together or squeezes Earth's crust. (p. C8)

concave lens (kon kāv′ lenz) A lens that is thicker at the edges than at the middle. As it curves inward, it spreads light rays apart, making images appear smaller. (p. F100)

concave mirror (kon kāv′ mir′ər) A mirror that curves in on the shiny side. (p. F88)

condensation (kon′den sā′shən) *n.* The changing of a gas into a liquid. (pp. B50, D39) —**condense** (kən dens′) *v.* (p. E37)

PRONUNCIATION KEY

a **at**; ā **ape**; ä **far**; âr **care**; ô **law**; e **end**; ē **me**; i **it**; ī **ice**; îr **pierce**; o **hot**; ō **old**; ôr **fork**; oi **oil**; ou **out**; u **up**; ū **use**; ü **rule**; ú **pull**; ûr **turn**; hw **white**; ng **song**; th **thin**; th **this**; zh **measure**; ə about, taken, pencil, lemon, circus

conduction (kən duk′shən) *n.* The passing of heat through a material while the material itself stays in place. (p. E97) **—conduct** (kən dukt′) *v.* (p. E14)

conifer (kon′ə fər) Any of a group of gymnosperms that produce seeds in cones and have needlelike leaves. (p. A69)

conserve (kən′sûrv′) To save, protect, or use resources wisely. (p. C39)

constellation (kon′stə lā′shən) Patterns formed by groups of stars in the night sky. (p. D12)

consumer (kən sü′mər) Any animal that eats plants or eats other plant-eating animals. (pp. B7, B20)

continental rise (kon′tə nen′təl rīz) A buildup of sediment on the sea floor at the bottom of the continental slope. It is a zone of sand and mud that stretches from the slope down to the deep-sea floor. (p. C90)

continental shelf (kon′tə nen′təl shelf) The underwater edge of a continent. (p. C90)

continental slope (kon′tə nen′təl slōp) The steep slope leading down from the continental shelf toward the sea floor. (p. C90)

contour plowing (kon′tür plou′ing) Preventing erosion by plowing across rather than up and down a slope. (p. C51)

contract (kən trakt′) To shrink, as when a material gets colder. (p. E41)

convection (kən vek′shən) The flow of heat through a liquid or a gas, causing hot parts to rise and cooler parts to sink. (p. E97)

convection cell (kən vek′shən sel) A circular pattern of air rising, air sinking, and wind. (p. D55)

convex lens (kon veks′ lenz) A lens that is thicker at the middle than at the edges. As it curves outward, it brings light together, making images appear larger. (p. F100)

convex mirror (kon veks′ mir′ər) A mirror that curves out on the shiny side. (p. F88)

coquina (kō kē′nə) A sedimentary rock formed from seashell fragments. (p. C44)

Coriolis effect (kôr′ē ō′lis i fekt′) The curving of the path of a moving object caused by Earth's rotation. (p. D57)

cortex (kôr′teks) The layer of tissue just inside the epidermis of a plant's roots and stems. (p. A30)

cotyledon (ko′tə lē′dən) A tiny leaflike structure, also called a seedleaf, inside the seed of an angiosperm. (p. A72)

crop rotation (krop rō tā′shən) Growing different crops each year so that the soil does not use up the same kinds of minerals year after year. (p. C51)

crossbreeding (krôs′brēd′ing) Producing offspring by mating individuals from two distinct breeds or varieties of the same species. (p. A112)

cross-pollination (krôs′pol′ə nā′shən) The transfer of pollen from one flower to another. (p. A80)

crust (krust) The rocky surface that makes up the top of the lithosphere and includes the continents and the ocean floor. (p. C7)

crystal (kris′təl) The geometric shape a mineral forms when its atoms and molecules get into fixed patterns. (p. C32)

cumulus cloud (kū′myə ləs kloud) A puffy cloud that appears to rise up from a flat bottom. (p. D44)

current (kûr′ənt) An ocean movement; a large stream of water that flows in the ocean. (p. C86)

cycad (sī′kad) One of the evergreen gymnosperms that resemble palms and have seed-bearing cones. (p. A69)

D

decibel (dB) (des′ə bel′) A unit that measures loudness. (p. F58)

deciduous (di sij′ü əs) Said of a plant that loses its leaves each fall. *See* **evergreen.** (pp. A69, B70)

deciduous forest (di si′jə wəs fôr′ist) A forest biome with many kinds of trees that lose their leaves each autumn. (p. B70)

decomposer (dē′kəm pōz′ər) Any of the fungi or bacteria that break down dead plants and animals into useful things like minerals and rich soil. (pp. B7, B21, B56)

delta (del′tə) Fan-shaped region formed by deposits of sediments found at the mouth of a river. (p. C21)

density (den′si tē) A measure of how tightly packed the matter in an object is. (pp. C35, E8)

deposition (dep′ə zish′ən) The dropping off of bits of eroded rock. (p. C13)

desalination (dē sal′ə nā′shən) Getting fresh water from seawater. (p. C73)

desert (dez′ərt) A sandy or rocky biome, with little precipitation and little plant life. (p. B69)

dicot (dī′kot′) An angiosperm with two cotyledons in each seed. *See* **monocot.** (p. A72)

dinoflagellate (din′ə flaj′ə lāt′) A protist containing chlorophyll that has two flagella for motion. When they overreproduce, they can cause "red tides." (p. A14)

distillation (dis′tə lā′shən) The process of separating the parts of a mixture by evaporation and condensation. (p. E64)

diversity (di vûr′si tē) A wide variety of traits in individuals from the same population. (p. A114)

Doppler effect (dop′lər i fekt′) The change in frequency (and pitch) as a source of sound moves toward or away from you. (p. F71)

downdraft (doun′draft′) A downward rush of air caused by the falling of rain during a thunderstorm. (pp. D55, D76)

E

echo (e′kō) A reflected sound wave. (p. F68)

echolocation (ek′ō lō kā′shən) Finding an object by using reflected sound. (p. F70)

ecological succession (ek′ə loj′i kəl sək sesh′ən) The gradual replacement of one community by another. (p. B82)

ecology (ē kol′ə jē) The study of how living and nonliving things interact. (p. B11)

ecosystem (ek′ō sis′təm) All the living and non-living things in an environment, including their interactions with each other. (p. B6)

effort arm (ef′ərt arm) The part of a lever that applies force to the resistance arm. (p. F26)

electromagnetic spectrum (i lek′trō mag net′ik spek′trəm) All the wavelengths of visible and invisible light in order, from short (gamma rays) to long (radio). (p. F119)

electromagnetism (i lek′trō mag′ni tiz′əm) The production of magnetism by electricity (and the production of electricity by magnets). (p. F118)

electron (i lek′tron) A particle in the space outside the nucleus of an atom that carries one unit of negative electric charge. (p. E27)

element (el′ə mənt) A pure substance that cannot be broken down into any simpler substances. (p. E22)

PRONUNCIATION KEY

a **at**; ā **ape**; ä **far**; âr **care**; ô **law**; e **end**; ē **me**; i **it**; ī **ice**; îr **pierce**; o **hot**; ō **old**; ôr **fork**; oi **oil**; ou **out**; u **up**; ū **use**; ü **rule**; ù **pull**; ûr **turn**; hw **white**; ng **song**; th **thin**; th **this**; zh **measure**; ə **about**, **taken**, **pencil**, **lemon**, **circus**

elevation (el′ə vā′shən) The height of a place above sea level. (p. C6)

embryo (em′brē ō′) The immature plant inside a seed. (p. A82)

emulsion (i mul′shən) A type of colloid in which one liquid is spread throughout another. (p. E60)

endangered species (en dān′jərd spē′shēz) A species that is in danger of becoming extinct. (p. B36)

epidermis (ep′i dûr′mis) An outermost layer of such plant parts as roots and leaves. (pp. A30, A34)

erosion (i rō′zhən) The picking up and carrying away of pieces of rocks. (p. C10)

evaporation (i vap′ə rā′shən) The slow changing of a liquid into a gas. (pp. B50, D38, E38)

evergreen (ev′ər grēn′) Said of a gymnosperm that keeps its leaves for at least a few years. *See* **deciduous.** (p. A69)

expand (ek spand′) To spread out, as when a material gets hotter. (p. E41)

extinct (ek stingkt′) A species that has died out completely. (p. B36)

F

fault (fôlt) A crack in Earth's crust whose sides show evidence of motion. (p. C6)

fault-block mountain (fôlt blok moun′tən) A mountain formed by blocks of Earth's crust moving along a fault. (p. C9)

fertilization (fûr′tə lə zā′shən) The joining of a sperm cell with an egg cell to make one new cell, a fertilized egg. (pp. A62, A81)

fertilizer (fûr′tə lī′zər) A substance used to add minerals to the soil. (p. B56)

fibrous root (fī′brəs rüt) One of the many hairy branching roots that some plants have. (p. A31)

filament (fil′ə mənt) The wire in a light bulb that gives off light and heat. (p. E92)

fish (fish) A vertebrate that lives its whole life in water. (p. A95)

flood plain (flud′ plān′) Land that is likely to be underwater during a flood. (p. C21)

foam (fōm) A type of colloid in which a gas is spread throughout a liquid. (p. E60)

fog (fôg) A cloud at ground level. (p. D44)

fold mountain (fōld moun′tən) A mountain made up mostly of rock layers folded by being squeezed together. (p. C8)

food chain (füd chān) The path of the energy in food from one organism to another. (p. B18)

food web (füd web) The overlapping food chains in an ecosystem. (p. B20)

force (fôrs) A push or pull exerted by one object on another, causing a change in motion. (p. F6)

fossil (fos′əl) Any remains or imprint of living things of the past. (p. C45)

fossil fuel (fos′əl fū′əl) A fuel formed from the decay of ancient forms of life. (p. C64)

fracture (frak′chər) The characteristic way some minerals break in uneven patterns. (p. C35)

freezing point (frēz′ing point) The temperature at which a substance changes state from a liquid to a solid. (p. E37)

frequency (frē′kwən sē) The number of times an object vibrates per second. (p. F57)

friction (frik′ shen′) A force that opposes the motion of one object moving past another. (p. F8)

frond (frond) The leaf of a fern. (p. A61)

front (frunt) A boundary between air masses with different temperatures. (p. D71)

fruit (früt) The ripened ovary of a flowering seed plant. (p. A70)

fulcrum (fu̇l′krəm) The pivot point of a lever. (p. F26)

fundamental frequency (fun′də men′təl frē′kwən sē) The lowest frequency at which an object vibrates. (p. F72)

fungus (fung′gəs) *n.,* **fungi** (fun′jī) *pl.* Members of a kingdom that contains one-celled and many-celled living things that absorb food from their environment. (p. A17)

G

galaxy (gal′ək sē) A collection of billions of stars. Our Sun belongs to the Milky Way galaxy. (p. D20)

gas (gas) A form of matter that does not take up a definite amount of space and has no definite shape. (p. E36)

gel (jel) A type of colloid in which a solid is spread throughout a liquid. (p. E60)

gem (jem) A mineral valued for being rare and beautiful. (p. C38)

geologist (jē ol′ə jist) A scientist who studies rocks to tell how they formed and to predict when an earthquake may occur. (p. C16)

geothermal energy (jē′ō thûr′məl en′ər jē) Earth's internal energy. (p. C104)

germination (jûr′mə nā′shən) The sprouting of a seed into a new plant. (p. A83)

ginkgo (ging′kō) *n., pl.* **ginkgoes** A large gymnosperm with fan-shaped leaves. (p. A69)

gnetophyte (ne′tō fīt′) One of the gymnosperms that are closely related to flowering plants and live in both deserts and the tropics. (p. A69)

grassland (gras′land′) A biome where grasses, not trees, are the main plant life. Prairies are one kind of grassland region. (p. B66)

gravitropism (grav′ī trō′pi′zəm) The response of a plant to gravity. (p. A44)

gravity (grav′i tē) The force of attraction between any two objects due to their mass. (pp. D8, F35)

groundwater (ground wô′tər) Precipitation that seeps into the ground and is stored in tiny holes, or pores, in soil and rocks. (pp. B51, C74)

gymnosperm (jim′nə spûrm′) A seed plant that does not produce flowers. *See* **angiosperm**. (p. A68)

H

habitat (hab′i tat) The place where a plant or animal naturally lives and grows. (p. B12)

hail (hāl) Pellets made of ice and snow. (p. D47)

hardness (härd′nis) How well a mineral resists scratching. (p. C34)

herbivore (hûr′bə vôr′) An animal that eats plants, algae, and other producers. (p. B20)

heredity (hə red′i tē) The passing down of inherited traits from parents to offspring. (p. A110)

hertz (Hz) (hûrts) A unit for measuring frequency. One hertz equals a frequency of one vibration per second. (p. F57)

heterogeneous (het′ər ə jē′nē əs) Differing in kind or nature; dissimilar; not homogeneous. (p. E54)

high-pressure system (hī′presh′ər sis′təm) A pattern surrounding a high pressure center, from which winds blow outward. In the Northern Hemisphere these winds curve to the right in a clockwise pattern. (p. D59)

PRONUNCIATION KEY

a **at**; ā **ape**; ä **far**; âr **care**; ô **law**; e **end**; ē **me**; i **it**; ī **ice**; îr **pierce**; o **hot**; ō **old**; ôr **fork**; oi **oil**; ou **out**; u **up**; ū **use**; ü **rule**; ů **pull**; ûr **turn**; hw **white**; ng **song**; th **thin**; th **this**; zh **measure**; ə **about, taken, pencil, lemon, circus**

host (hōst) The organism a parasite lives in or on and is harmed by. (p. B26)

humidity (hū mid′i tē) The amount of water vapor in the air. (p. D38)

humus (hü′məs) Decayed plant or animal material in soil. (pp. B9, C49)

hurricane (hûr′i kān′) A very large, swirling storm with very low pressure at the center. (p. D78)

hybrid (hī′brid) An organism produced by the crossing of parents that have different forms of the same trait. (p. A112)

hydrocarbon (hī′drə kär′bən) Compound made only of hydrogen and carbon atoms. (p. E32)

hydroelectric plant (hī′drō i lek′trik plant) A factory where running or falling water spins a generator to make electricity. (p. C104)

hydrosphere (hī′drə sfîr′) Earth's water, found in continents and oceans, including the fresh water in ice, lakes, rivers, and underground water. (p. C26)

hydrotropism (hī drot′rə piz′əm) The response of a plant to a nearby source of water. (p. A45)

hyperthermia (hī′pər thûr′mē ə) The overheating of the body that can be caused by overexposure in a hot, dry climate. (p. D90)

I

igneous rock (ig′nē əs rok) A rock formed when melted rock material cools and hardens (p. C43)

image (im′ij) A "picture" of the light source that light rays make in bouncing off a polished, shiny surface. (p. F89)

imperfect flower (im pûr′fikt flou′ər) A flower with either a stamen or a pistil, but not both. (p. A78)

incomplete flower (in′kəm plēt′ flou′ər) A flower that lacks sepals, petals, stamens or pistils. (p. A78)

indicator (in′di kā′tər) A substance such as litmus paper whose color changes when it is mixed with an acid or a base. (p. E84)

inertia (i nûr′shə) The tendency of a moving object to keep moving in a straight line or of any object to resist a change in motion. (pp. D8, F7)

inexhaustible resource (in′eg zôs′tə bəl rē′sôrs′) A resource that cannot be depleted or used up easily. (p. B58)

inherited trait (in her′i təd trāt) A characteristic that is passed from parents to offspring. (p. A110)

inner planet (in′ər plan′it) A planet between the Sun and the asteroid belt (Mercury, Venus, Earth, Mars). (p. D16)

insolation (in′sə lā′shən) The amount of the Sun's energy that reaches Earth at a given time and place. *Insolation* is short for *in*coming *sol*ar radi*ation*. (p. D30)

instinct (in′stingkt′) An inherited behavior, one that is not learned but is done automatically. (p. A110)

insulate (in′sə lāt′) To prevent heat from passing through. (p. E14)

intertidal zone (in′tər tī′dəl zōn) The shallowest section of the marine, or ocean, ecosystem, where the ocean floor is covered and uncovered as the tide goes in and out. (p. B73)

invertebrate (in vûr′tə brit) An animal that does not have a backbone. (p. A16)

ionized (ī′ə nīzd′) Electrically charged by radiation, as gas particles of auroras in the night sky. (p. D32)

isobar (ī′sə bär′) A line on a weather map connecting places with equal air pressure. (p. D59)

K

kinetic energy (ki net′ik en′ər jē) The energy of any moving object. (p. E95)

L

land breeze (land brēz) Wind that blows from land to sea. (p. D56)

laser (lā′zər) A device that produces a thin stream of light of just a few close wavelengths. (p. F122)

lava (lä′və) Magma that reaches Earth's surface. (pp. C9, C43)

law of reflection (lô uv ri flek′shən) The angle between an incoming light ray and a surface equals the angle between the reflected light ray and the surface. (p. F87)

lever (lev′ər) A simple machine made of a rigid bar and a fixed pivot point, called the fulcrum. (p. F26)

light ray (līt rā) A straight-line beam of light as it travels outward from its source. (p. F85)

lightning (līt′ning) One of the huge electric sparks that leap from clouds to the ground in thunderstorms. (p. D76)

limiting factor (lim′ə ting fak′tər) Anything that controls the growth or survival of a population. (p. B34)

liquid (lik′wid) A form of matter that takes up a definite amount of space and has no definite shape. (p. E36)

lithosphere (lith′ə sfîr′) The hard outer layer of Earth, about 100 km thick. (p. C26)

long-day plant (lông′dā plant) A plant that blooms when there is much more daylight than darkness. (p. A46)

low-pressure system (lō′presh′ər sis′təm) A pattern surrounding a low-pressure center, in which winds blow in toward the center. In the Northern Hemisphere, these winds blow to the right in a counterclockwise pattern. (p. D59)

luster (lus′tər) The way light bounces off a mineral's surface. (p. C33)

M

magma (mag′mə) Hot, molten rock deep below Earth's surface. (p. C9)

magnetic (mag net′ik) The property of a material like iron in which the particles line up pole to pole, causing it to be attracted or repelled by a magnet. (p. E15)

mammal (mam′əl) A vertebrate that feeds its young milk. (p. A95)

mare (mär′ā) *n., pl.* **maria** (mär′ē ə) Dark-colored land on the Moon that is dry and flat and is surrounded by mountains and ridges. (p. D10)

mass (mas) A measure of the amount of matter in an object. (p. E6)

matter (ma′tər) Anything that has mass and takes up space. (pp. E6, F51)

meander (mē an′dər) Bends or s-shaped curves in a river. (p. C21)

melting point (melt′ing point) The particular temperature for each substance at which it changes state from a solid to a liquid. (p. E37)

membrane (mem′brān) A thin envelope surrounding the nucleus of a cell. (p. A18)

metal (met′əl) Any of a group of elements found in the ground that conducts heat and electricity. (p. C38)

PRONUNCIATION KEY

a **a**t; ā **a**pe; ä f**a**r; âr c**are**; ô l**aw**; e **e**nd; ē m**e**; i **i**t; ī **i**ce; îr p**ier**ce; o h**o**t; ō **o**ld; ôr f**or**k; oi **oi**l; ou **ou**t; u **u**p; ū **u**se; ü r**u**le; u̇ p**u**ll; ûr t**ur**n; hw **wh**ite; ng so**ng**; th **th**in; t͟h **th**is; zh mea**s**ure; ə **a**bout, tak**e**n, penc**i**l, lem**o**n, circ**u**s

metamorphic rock (met′ə môr′fik rok) A rock formed under heat and pressure from another kind of rock. (p. C46)

meteor (mē′ tē or) A chunk of rock from space that burns up as it travels through Earth's atmosphere. A "shooting star." (p. D19)

meteorite (mē′tē ə rīt′) A chunk of rock from space that strikes the surface of Earth or the Moon. (pp. C14, D19)

mid-ocean ridge (mid ō′shun rij) Chain of mountains that wind along all the world's major oceans. (p. C91)

mimicry (mim′i krē) An adaptation in which an animal is protected against predators by its resemblance to another, unpleasant animal. (p. A106)

mineral (min′ə rəl) A solid material of Earth's crust with a definite composition. (p. C32)

mixture (miks′chər) A physical combination of two or more substances that are blended together without forming new substances. (p. E52)

molecule (mol′ə kūl′) A particle that contains more than one atom joined together. (p. E30) *See* **atom**. (p. E26)

monocot (mon′ə kot′) An angiosperm with one cotyledon in each seed. *See* **dicot.** (p. A72)

mountain breeze (moun′tən brēz) A cool night wind that blows down a mountain slope to replace the warmer air in the valley. (p. D56)

mutualism (mū′chü ə liz′əm) A relationship between two kinds of organisms that benefits both. (p. B24)

N

neap tide (nēp tīd) The slightest changes from high to low tide that occur when the Sun, the Moon, and Earth form a right angle or are perpendicular to each other. (p. C89)

nekton (nek′tən) Organisms that swim through the water in aquatic ecosystems. (p. B72)

neutral (nü′trəl) Neither acid nor base. (p. E82)

neutron (nü′tron) A particle in the nucleus of an atom that has no net electric charge. (p. E27)

newton (nü′tən) A basic unit measuring the amount of pull or push a force produces. (pp. E7, F20)

NEXRAD (neks′rad′) A new form of Doppler radar that is used to track storms. The word stands for *NEXt generation of weather RADar.* (p. D81)

niche (nich) The role of an organism in a community. (p. B12)

nitrogen cycle (nī′trə jən sī′kəl) The continuous trapping of nitrogen gas into compounds in the soil and its return to the air. (p. B54)

nonrenewable resource (non′ri nü′ə bəl rē′sôrs′) A resource that cannot be replaced within a short period of time or at all. (pp. B58, C64)

nonvascular (non vas′kyə lər) Containing no plant tissue through which water and food move. (p. A15)

nucleus (nü′klē əs) **1.** A dense structure inside the cell. (p. A18) **2.** One of the airborne dust particles around which water condenses as droplets or ice crystals before falling as precipitation. (p. D46) **3.** An atom's dense center, where most of its mass is. (p. E27)

O

omnivore (om′nə vôr′) An animal that eats both plants and animals. (p. B21)

opaque (ō pāk′) Completely blocking light from passing through it. (p. F96)

orbit (ôr′bit) The path of a planet traveling around a star. (p. D6)

ore (ôr) A mineral containing a useful substance. (p. C38)

organ (ôr′gən) A group of tissues that work together to do a certain job. (p. A9)

organism (ôr′gə niz′əm) Any living thing that can carry out its life on its own. (p. A6)

organ system (ôr′gən sis′təm) A group of organs that work together to do a certain job. (p. A9)

outer planet (out′er plan′it) One of the five planets beyond the asteroid belt (Jupiter, Saturn, Uranus, Neptune, Pluto). (p. D16)

ovary (ō′və rē) A structure containing egg cells; the base of a pistil in a flower. (p. A78)

overtone (ō′vər tōn′) One of a series of pitches that blend to give a sound its quality. (p. F72)

ozone layer (ō′zōn lā′ər) A layer of ozone gas in the atmosphere that screens out much of the Sun's UV (ultraviolet) rays. (p. C63)

P

parasitism (par′ə sī tiz′əm) A relationship in which one organism lives in or on another organism and benefits from that relationship while the other organism may be harmed by it. (p. B26) —**parasite** (par′ə sīt′) (pp. A71, B26)

perfect flower (pûr′fikt flou′ər) A flower with both male and female parts, that is, both a stamen and a pistil. (p. A78)

permafrost (pûr′mə frôst′) A layer of permanently frozen soil found in arctic and antarctic regions. (p. B68)

pH (pē′aitch′) The scale that tells how acidic or basic a solution is. (p. E86)

phloem (flō′em) The tissue through which food from the leaves moves down through the rest of a plant. (pp. A31, A32)

photon (fō′ton) The tiny bundles of energy by means of which light travels. (p. F119)

photoperiodism (fō′tō pîr′ē ə diz′əm) The flowering response of a plant to changing periods of daylight and darkness. (p. A46)

photosynthesis (fō′tə sin′thə sis) The food-making process in green plants that uses sunlight. (p. A36)

phototropism (fō tot′rə piz′əm) The response of a plant to changes in light. (p. A44)

phylum (fī′ləm) *n., pl.* **phyla** (-lə) One of the large groups in the animal kingdom. (p. A16)

physical change (fiz′i kəl chānj) A change of matter in size, shape, or state without any change in identity. (p. E70)

pioneer community (pī′ə nîr′ kə mū′ni tē) The first community thriving in a once lifeless area. (p. B83)

pioneer species (pī′ə nîr′ spē′shēz) The first species living in an otherwise lifeless area. (p. B83)

pitch (pich) How high or low a sound is. (p. F56)

planet (plan′it) Any of the nine major objects that travel around the Sun and shine by reflecting its light. (p. D6)

plankton (plangk′tən) Organisms that float on the water in aquatic ecosystems. (p. B72)

plate (plāt) One of the moving pieces of Earth's crust that has been broken by upward pressure from the mantle. (p. C7)

plate tectonics (plāt tek ton′iks) A scientific theory that Earth's crust is made of moving plates. (pp. B90, C7)

polarization (pō′lər ə zā′shən) Allowing light vibrations to pass through in only one direction. (p. F97)

pollen (pol′ən) Dustlike grains in the flower of a plant that contain its male sex cells. (pp. A70, A74, A84)

PRONUNCIATION KEY

a **at**; ā **ape**; ä **far**; âr **care**; ô **law**; e **end**; ē **me**; i **it**; ī **ice**; îr **pierce**; o **hot**; ō **old**; ôr **fork**; oi **oil**; ou **out**; u **up**; ū **use**; ü **rule**; ů **pull**; ûr **turn**; hw **white**; ng **song**; th **thin**; <u>th</u> **this**; zh **measure**; ə **about, taken, pencil, lemon, circus**

pollination (pol′ə nā′shən) The transfer of a pollen grain to the egg-producing part of a plant. (p. A74)

pollute (pə lüt′) *v.* To add harmful substances to Earth's land, water, or air. (p. C50) —**pollutant** (pə lü′tənt) *n.* Something that pollutes. (p. C50) —**pollution** (pə lü′shən) *n.* A polluted condition. (p. C50)

population (pop′yə lā′shən) All the members of one species in an area. (p. B11)

potential energy (pə ten′shəl en′ər jē) Stored energy. (p. E95)

precipitation (pri sip′i tā′shən) Any form of water particles that falls from the atmosphere and reaches the ground. (pp. B51, D46)

predator (pred′ə tər) An animal that hunts other animals for food. (pp. A106, B21)

prey (prā) A living thing that is hunted for food. (p. B21)

primary color (prī′mer′ē kul′ər) Red, green, or blue. Mixing these colors can produce all the colors of the spectrum. (p. F110)

primary pigment (prī′mer′ē pig′mənt) Magenta, cyan, or yellow. Materials with any of these colors absorb one primary color of light and reflect the other two. (p. F112)

primary succession (prī′mer′ē sək sesh′ən) The beginning of a community where few, if any, living things exist, or where earlier communities were wiped out. (p. B82)

prism (priz′əm) A cut piece of clear glass (or plastic) with two opposite sides in the shape of a triangle or other geometric shape. (p. F108)

producer (prə dü′sər) Any of the plants and algae that produce oxygen and food that animals need. (pp. B7, B20)

product (prod′ukt) A new substance produced by a chemical change. (p. E71)

prop root (prop rüt) One of the roots that grow out of a plant's stemlike main roots and help prop up the plant. (p. A31)

property (prop′ər tē) A characteristic of matter that can be observed, such as mass, volume, weight, or density. (pp. E6, E24)

protective coloration (prə tek′tiv kul′ə rā′shən) A type of camouflage in which the color of an animal blends in with its background, protecting it against predators. (p. A109)

protein (prō′tēn) A substance rich in nitrogen that the body uses for growth and the repair of cells. (p. B54)

protist (prō′tist) A member of a kingdom that contains one-celled and many-celled living things, some that make food and some that hunt for food. (p. A18)

proton (prō′ton) A particle in the nucleus of an atom that carries one unit of positive electric charge. (p. E27)

Q

quality (kwol′i tē) The difference you hear between two sounds of the same loudness and pitch. (p. F72)

R

radar (rā′där) A device for tracking the position and path of a distant moving object. (p. D80)

radiation (rā′dē a′shən) The transfer of heat through electromagnetic rays. (p. E97)

rarefaction (râr′ə fak′shən) The part of a sound wave where molecules are spread apart. (p. F51)

raw material (rô mə tîr′ē əl) Material not yet refined, manufactured, or processed. (p. B58)

reactant (rē ak′tənt) An original substance at the beginning of a chemical reaction. (p. E71)

reaction (rē ak′shən) The force with which an object responds to an action, as in Newton's third law of motion. (p. F24)

reflection (ri flek′shən) The bouncing of a sound wave off a surface. (p. F66)

refraction (ri frak′shən) The bending of light rays as they pass from one substance into another. (p. F98)

relative humidity (rel′ə tiv hū mid′i tē) A comparison between how much water vapor is in the air and how much the air could hold at a given temperature if it were full, or saturated. (p. D39)

renewable resource (ri nü′ə bəl rē′sôrs′) A resource that can be replaced in a short period of time. (pp. B58, C62)

reservoir (rez′ər vwär′) A storage area for fresh water supplies. (p. C75)

resistance arm (ri zis′təns arm) The part of a lever that applies force to the load the machine acts against. (p. F26)

resonance (rez′ə nəns) In an instrument or object, a unique blend of the fundamental frequency and its overtones. (p. F72)

resource (rē′sôrs′) Any material that helps support life on Earth. (p. C26)

respiration (res′pə rā′shən) The release of energy in plants and animals from food (sugar). (p. A37)

response (ri spons′) What a living thing does as a result of a stimulus. (p. A44)

reptile (rep′təl) An egg-laying vertebrate with thick, dry skin. (p. A95)

revolve (ri volv′) To move around, or orbit, another object. (p. D10)

rhizoid (rī′zoid) One of the hairlike fibers that anchor a moss to the soil and take in water from the soil. (p. A58)

rhizome (rī′zōm) The underground stem of a fern. (p. A61)

rock (rok) A naturally formed solid in the crust made up of one or more minerals. (p. C42)

rock cycle (rok sī′kəl) Rocks changing from one into another in a never-ending series of processes. (p. C52)

root cap (rüt kap) A thin covering made up of cells that protect the root tip of a plant as it grows into the soil. (p. A30)

root hair (rüt hâr) Any of the threadlike projections from a plant root that absorb water and dissolved minerals from the soil. (p. A30)

rotate (rō′tāt) To make a complete spin on an axis, causing one day on a planet. A day differs in length from planet to planet. (p. D9)

runoff (run′ôf) Precipitation that flows across the land's surface or falls into rivers and streams. (pp. B51, C20)

S

savanna (sə van′ə) A tropical grassland with some trees and shrubs. (p. B66)

scanning tunneling microscope (scan′ing tun′əl ing mī′krə skōp′) A device that uses electric current flowing through a needle to trace the contours of atoms and magnify them as much as 30 million times. (p. E26)

scavenger (skav′ən jər) A meat-eating animal that feeds on the remains of dead animals. (p. B21)

sea breeze (sē brēz) Wind that blows from sea to land. (p. D56)

sea-floor vent (sē′flôr′ vent) An opening in a mid-ocean ridge where mineral-saturated water boils up from the seafloor crust. (p. C93)

seamount (sē′mount′) A huge underwater volcanic mountain that may emerge from the ocean surface as an island. (p. C90)

PRONUNCIATION KEY

a **at**; ā **ape**; ä **far**; âr **care**; ô **law**; e **end**; ē **me**; i **it**; ī **ice**; îr **pierce**; o **hot**; ō **old**; ôr **fork**; oi **oil**; ou **out**; u **up**; ū **use**; ü **rule**; ů **pull**; ûr **turn**; hw **white**; ng **song**; th **thin**; th **this**; zh **measure**; ə **about**, **taken**, **pencil**, **lemon**, **circus**

secondary succession (sek′ən der′ē sək sesh′ən) The beginning of a new community where an earlier community already exists. (p. B82)

sediment (sed′ə ment) Pieces of material carried and deposited by water or wind (p. C20)

sedimentary rock (sed′ə men′tə rē rok) A rock made of bits of matter joined together. (p. C44)

seed (sēd) An undeveloped plant with stored food sealed in a protective covering. (p. A68)

seed coat (sēd kōt) The outer covering of a seed. (p. A82)

seed dispersal (sēd di spûr′səl) The movement of a seed from the flower to a place where it can sprout. (p. A83)

self-pollination (self′pol′ə nā′shən) The transfer of pollen from an anther to a stigma in the same plant. (p. A80)

sexual reproduction (sek′shü əl rē′prō duk′shən) The production of a new organism from a female sex cell and a male sex cell. (pp. A62, A81)

shear (shîr) A movement of plates that twists, tears, or pushes one part of Earth's crust past another. (p. C8)

short-day plant (shôrt′dā plant) A plant that blooms when there is more darkness and less daylight. (p. A46)

simple machine (sim′pəl mə shēn′) A machine with few moving parts, making it easier to do work. (p. F26)

smog (smog) A mixture of smoke and fog. (p. C64)

solar system (sō′lər sis′təm) The Sun and the objects that are traveling around it. (p. D6)

solid (sol′id) A form of matter that has a definite shape and takes up a definite amount of space. (p. E36)

solubility (sol′yə bil′i tē) The ability of a substance to be dissolved by another substance. (p. E58)

solute (sol′ūt) A substance that is dissolved by another substance to form a solution. (p. E57)

solution (sə lü′shən) A mixture of substances that are blended so completely that the mixture looks the same everywhere. (p. E54)

solvent (sol′vənt) A substance that dissolves one or more other substances to form a solution. (p. E57)

sound wave (sound wāv) A vibration that spreads away from a vibrating object. (p. F51)

spectrum (spek′trəm) A band of colors produced when light goes through a prism. (p. F108)

speed (spēd) How fast an object's position changes with time at any given moment. (p. F11)

spore (spôr) Cells in seedless plants that grow into new organisms. (p. A58)

spring (spring) A place where groundwater seeps out of the ground. (p. C75)

spring tide (spring tīd) The greatest changes from high to low tide that occur when the Sun, the Moon, and Earth are lined up. (p. C89)

state of matter (stāt uv mat′ər) One of the three forms that matter can take—solid, liquid, or gas. (p. E36)

stimulus (stim′yə ləs), *n., pl.* **stimuli (-lī)** Something in the environment that causes a living thing to react. (p. A44)

stomata (stō′mə tə) *pl. n., sing.* **stoma** Pores in the bottom of leaves that open and close to let in air or give off water vapor. (p. A34)

storm surge (stôrm sûrj) A great rise of the sea along a shore caused by low air pressure. (p. D79)

stratus cloud (strā′təs kloud) A cloud that forms in a blanketlike layer. (p. D44)

streak (strēk) The color of the powder left when a mineral is rubbed against a hard, rough surface. (p. C34)

strip farming (strip fär′ming) Trapping runoff by alternating tightly growing grasses with more widely spaced plants. (p. C51)

subscript (sub′skript′) A number in a chemical formula that tells the number of atoms in the compound. (p. E25)

surveyor (sər vā′ər) A specialist who makes accurate measurements of Earth's crust. (p. C6)

suspension (sə spen′shən) A mixture in which suspended particles can easily be seen. (p. E59)

symbiosis (sim′bē ō′sis) A relationship between two kinds of organisms that lasts over time. (p. B24)

T

taiga (tī′gə) A cool forest biome of conifers in the upper Northern Hemisphere. (p. B67)

taproot (tap′rüt′) A root that has few hairy branches and grows deep into the ground. (p. A31)

temperate (tem′pər it) Free from extremes of temperature. (p. B66)

tension (ten′shən) A movement of plates that stretches or pulls apart Earth's crust. (p. C8)

terracing (ter′is ing) Shaping hillsides into steps so that runoff and eroded soil get trapped on the steps. (p. C51)

texture (teks′chər) An identifying quality of a rock based on how coarse, fine, or glassy it is and on how angular or rounded it is. (p. C42)

threatened species (thret′ənd spē′shēz) A species that is in danger of becoming endangered. (p. D36)

thunder (thun′dər) The noise caused by lightning-heated air during a thunderstorm. (p. D76)

thunderhead (thun′dər hed′) A cumulonimbus cloud in which a thunderstorm forms. (p. D76)

thunderstorm (thun′dər stôrm′) The most common severe storm, formed in cumulonimbus clouds. (p. D76)

tissue (tish′ü) A group of similar cells that work together at the same job. (p. A8)

topsoil (top′soil′) The dark, top layer of soil, rich in humus and minerals, in which many tiny organisms live and most plants grow. (p. B9)

tornado (tôr nā′dō) A violent, whirling wind that moves across the ground in a narrow path. (p. D77)

trade wind (trād wind) A belt of winds around Earth moving from high pressure zones toward the low pressure at the equator. (p. D58)

translucent (trans lü′sənt) Letting only some light through, so that objects on the other side appear blurry. (p. F96)

transparent (trans pâr′ənt) Letting all light through, so that objects on the other side can be seen clearly. (p. F96)

transpiration (tran′spə rā′shən) The loss of water through a plant's leaves. (pp. A35, A38, D39)

trench (trench) A deep valley in the sea floor. (p. C91)

tropical rain forest (trop′i kəl rān fôr′ist) A hot biome near the equator, with much rainfall and a wide variety of life. (p. B71)

tropism (trō′piz′əm) A response of a plant toward or away from a stimulus. (p. A44)

PRONUNCIATION KEY

a **a**t; ā **a**pe; ä f**a**r; âr c**are**; ô l**aw**; e **e**nd; ē m**e**; i **i**t; ī **i**ce; îr p**ier**ce; o h**o**t; ō **o**ld; ôr f**or**k; oi **oi**l; ou **ou**t; u **u**p; ū **u**se; ü r**u**le; ů p**u**ll; ûr t**ur**n; hw **wh**ite; ng so**ng**; th **th**in; <u>th</u> **th**is; zh mea**s**ure; ə **a**bout, tak**e**n, penc**i**l, lem**o**n, circ**u**s

troposphere (trop′ə sfîr′) The layer of the atmosphere closest to Earth's surface. (p. D32)

tube worm (tüb wûrm) Large wormlike animals that live near sea-floor vents and obtain their food through bacterial chemosynthesis. (p. C93)

tundra (tun′dra) Large, treeless plain in the arctic regions, where the ground is frozen all year. (p. B68)

U

ultrasonic (ul′trə son′ik) Said of a sound with a frequency too high to be heard by humans. (p. F57)

unbalanced forces (un bal′ənst fôrs′əz) Forces that do not cancel each other out when acting together on a single object. (p. F21)

updraft (up′draft′) An upward rush of heated air during a thunderstorm. (pp. D55, D76)

V

vacuum (vak′ū əm) A space through which sound waves cannot travel because it contains no matter. (p. F116)

valley breeze (val′ē brēz) A cool wind that blows up a mountain slope and replaces the slope's rising Sun-warmed air. (p. D56)

variable (vâr′ē ə bəl) One of the changes in a situation that may affect the outcome of an experiment. (p. A48)

vascular (vas′kyə lər) Containing plant tissue through which water moves up and food moves down. (p. A15)

velocity (və los′i tē) The speed and direction of a moving object. (p. F12)

vertebrate (vûr′tə brit) An animal that has a backbone. (p. A16)

vibration (vī brā′shən) A back-and-forth motion. (p. F50)

volume (vol′ūm) **1.** A measure of how much space an object takes up. (p. E6) **2.** The loudness or softness of a sound. (p. F58)

W

warm front (wôrm frunt) A front where warm air moves in over a cold air mass. (p. D72)

water cycle (wô′tər sī′kəl) The continuous movement of water between Earth's surface and the air, changing from liquid to gas to liquid. (pp. B51, C74)

water table (wô′tər tā′bəl) The top of the water-filled spaces in the ground. (p. C75)

water vapor (wô′tər vā′pər) Water in the form of a gas. (pp. B50, D38)

watershed (wô′tər shed′) Area from which water is drained; region that contributes water to a river or river system. (pp. C20, C68–C69)

weather (weth′ər) What the lower atmosphere is like at any given place and time. (p. D34)

weathering (weth′ər ing) Breaking down rocks into smaller pieces. (p. C10)

weight (wāt) The force of gravity between Earth and an object. (pp. E7, F36)

well (wel) A hole dug below the water table that water seeps into. (p. C75)

wind (wind) Air that moves horizontally. (p. D55)

work (wûrk) The use of force to move an object a certain distance. (p. F26)

X

xylem (zī′ləm) The tissue through which water and minerals move up through a plant. (pp. A30, A32)

Y

year (yîr) The time it takes a planet to orbit the Sun. A *year* is different from planet to planet. (p. D7)

Index

A

* Indicates an activity related to this topic.

*Indicates an activity related to this topic.

D

E

*Indicates an activity related to this topic.

*Indicates an activity related to this topic.

J

K

L

M

*Indicates an activity related to this topic.

N

O

P

*Indicates an activity related to this topic.

*Indicates an activity related to this topic.

T

*Indicates an activity related to this topic.

X

Y

Credits

Cover Photos: Chris Johns/National Geographic Image Collection; bkgd. ThinkStock/SuperStock. Spine: Chris Johns/National Geographic Image Collection Back Cover: bkgd. ThinkStock/SuperStock; t.l. Kelvin Aitken/Peter Arnold, Inc.; t.r. Tim Flach/Stone/Getty Images; c.l. Jules Cowan/Index Stock Imagery; c.r. NOAA, colored by John Wells/Science Photo Library/Photo Researchers Inc; b.l. Roger Ressmeyer/CORBIS; b.r. Comstock, Inc. Endpaper: ThinkStock/SuperStock.

Photography Credits: All photographs are by Macmillan/McGraw-Hill (MMH) and Richard Hutchings for MMH, Ken Karp for MMH, Cesar Llacuna for MMH, and Dan Howell for MMH except as noted below:

i: bkgd. ThinkStock/SuperStock; t.l. Ken Lucas/Visuals Unlimited; b.l. Joe McDonald/Visuals Unlimited. iii: Konrad Wothe/Minden Pictures. iv: bkgd. Taxi/Getty Images; t.r. NASA/CORBIS; b.l., b.r. Courtesy, Sally Ride. v: l. David Sanger Photography/Alamy; r. Roger Ressmeyer/CORBIS. vi: Norbert Wu. vii: Tim Flach/Stone/Getty Images. viii: l. Jules Cowan/Index Stock Imagery; c. Joyce Photographics/Photo Researchers, Inc.; r. A.J. Copley/Visuals Unlimited. ix: l. NOAA, colored by John Wells/Science Photo Library/Photo Researchers, Inc.; r. Runk/Schoenberger/Grant Heilman Photography, Inc. x: l. Roger Ressmeyer/CORBIS; r. Science VU/Visuals Unlimited. xi: Paul J. Sutton/Duomo/CORBIS. xiv: ThinkStock/SuperStock. xvi: b.r. PhotoDisc/Getty Images. SO: Gavriel Jecan/CORBIS. S0-S1: James A. Sugar/CORBIS. S2-S3: David Sanger Photography/Alamy. S4-S5: Roger Ressmeyer/CORBIS. S6-S7: J.D. Griggs/CORBIS. S8-S9: Roger Ressmeyer/CORBIS. S10: Roger Ressmeyer/CORBIS/MAGMA. S10-S11: Roger Ressmeyer/CORBIS. AO: Kelvin Aitken/Peter Arnold, Inc. A0-A1: Norbert Wu. A1: Kelvin Aitken/Peter Arnold, Inc. A2-A3: Gallo Images/CORBIS. A4-A5: Ted Levin/Animals Animals/Earth Scenes. A6: Peter Miller/Photo Researchers, Inc. A7: Dick Thomas/Visuals Unlimited. A9: Rob Hadlow/Bruce Coleman, Inc. A12-A13: Carol Cohen/CORBIS. A17: l. Veronika Burmeister/Visuals Unlimited; c. Doug Sokell/Visuals Unlimited; r. R.M. Meadows/Peter Arnold, Inc. A18: t.l. Patrick W. Grace/Science Source/Photo Researchers, Inc.; t.c. Veronika Burmeister/Visuals Unlimited; t.r. Cabisco/Visuals Unlimited; b.l. Gilbert S. Grant/Photo Researchers, Inc.; b.r. R. Kessel-G. Shih/Visuals Unlimited. A19: l. R. Robinson/Visuals Unlimited; c.l. Telegraph Colour Library/FPG/Getty Images; c.r. A. & F. Michler/Peter Arnold, Inc.; r. Blair Seitz/Photo Researchers, Inc. A20: t.l. John Cancalosi/Peter Arnold, Inc.; t.r. E.R. Degginger/Color-Pic, Inc.; c. Skip Moody/Dembinsky Photo Associates; b.l. Jim Roetzel/Dembinsky Photo Associates; b.r. John Shaw/Bruce Coleman, Inc. A21: t. Manfred Kage/Peter Arnold, Inc. A22: t. Bob Gibbons/ardea.com; b. Bernard Edmaier/Photo Researchers, Inc. A23: t.l. Andrew Syred/Photo Researchers, Inc.; t.r. Brandon D. Cole/CORBIS; b. Tim Davis/Photo Researchers, Inc. A25: Hans Reinhard/Bruce Coleman, Inc. A26-A27: William Waterfall/The Stock Market/CORBIS. A28-A29: Dominique Braud/Dembinsky Photo Associates. A33: t.l. George Bernard/Animals Animals/Earth Scenes; t.r. Robert Maier/Animals Animals/Earth Scenes; b. Willard Clay/Dembinsky Photo Associates. A35: Pixland/Index Stock Imagery. A36: PhotoDisc/Getty Images. A38: t. Gerry Ellis/ENP Images; b.l., b.r. Jack M. Bostrack/Visuals Unlimited. A39: Phil Degginger/Color-Pic, Inc. A41: James R. Holland/National Geographic Society. A42-A43: Kalpana Kartik/Alamy. A44: David Newman/Visuals Unlimited. A45: R. Calentine/Visuals Unlimited. A47: t. Parke H. John, Jr./Visuals Unlimited; b. Bill Beatty/Visuals Unlimited. A49: Royalty-Free/CORBIS. A50-A51: Jim Olive/Pictor/Uniphoto/Image State. A51: t. Prof. K. Banks/Courtesy of Katherine Banks; c. Hans Reinhard/Bruce Coleman, Inc.; b. WHM Bildarchiv/Peter Arnold, Inc. A53: David Newman/Visuals Unlimited. A54-A55: Bob Krist/CORBIS. A56-A57: Michael Fogden/Bruce Coleman, Inc. A58: t.l. Doug Sokell/Visuals Unlimited; b.l. John Trager/Visuals Unlimited; r. David Sieren/Visuals Unlimited. A59: l. Ed Reschke/Peter Arnold, Inc.; c. Mike Perry/Pictor/Uniphoto/Image State; r. E.F. Anderson/Visuals Unlimited. A61: David Dennis/Animals Animals/Earth Scenes. A64: Dick Keen/Visuals Unlimited. A65: E.R. Degginger/Color-Pic, Inc. A66-A67: Michael Gadomski/Animals Animals/Earth Scenes. A68: l. Jim Hughes/Visuals Unlimited; c. W. Ormerod/Visuals Unlimited; r. V.P. Weinland/Photo Researchers, Inc. A69: t.l. Jan Taylor/Bruce Coleman, Inc.; l. inset John N. Trager/Visuals Unlimited; b.c. Gerald & Buff Corsi/Visuals Unlimited; t.r. E.R. Degginger/Bruce Coleman, Inc.; b.r. E. Webber/Visuals Unlimited. A70: Scott T. Smith/CORBIS. A71: t. E.F. Anderson/Visuals Unlimited; b. V. McMillan/Visuals Unlimited. A73: b. Arthur R. Hill/Visuals Unlimited; r. Mark S. Skalny/Visuals Unlimited. A74: SIME s.a.s./eStock Photo. A75: PhotoDisc/Getty Images. A76-A77: Robert P. Carr/Bruce Coleman, Inc. A79: t. Derrick Ditchburn/Visuals Unlimited; c. Doug Sokell/Visuals Unlimited; b. Adam Jones/Photo Researchers, Inc. A82: Henry T. Kaiser/Pictor/Uniphoto/Image State. A83: t.l. Inga Spence/Visuals Unlimited; t.r. Ken Wagner/Visuals Unlimited; b. Stephen J. Lang/Visuals Unlimited. A84: l. John Gerlach/Visuals Unlimited; r. Jerome Wexler/Photo Researchers, Inc. A86: BrandX/RobertStock.com. A87: inset BrandX/RobertStock.com. ; r. Emilio Ereza/Pixtal/AGE Fotostock. A89: t. John McAnulty/CORBIS; b. Hans Reinhard/Bruce Coleman, Inc. A90-A91: R&V Taylor/Bruce Coleman, Inc. A92-A93: Clem Haagner/ABPL/Animals Animals. A94: t. Fred Bavendam/Minden Pictures; b. ZEFA/Rauschenbach/Masterfile. A95: t. Joe McDonald/Bruce Coleman, Inc.; b. BIOS/Klein/Hubert/Peter Arnold, Inc. A96: t.l. Susan Blanchet/Dembinsky Photo Associates; t.c. Jeff Mondragon/Mondragon Photography; t.r., b.r. E.R. Degginger/Color-Pic, Inc.; c.l. Scott Johnson/Animals Animals/Earth Scenes; b.l. Tom E. Adams/Peter Arnold, Inc. A97: t.l. Hans Pfletschinger/Peter Arnold, Inc.; c. Robert Lubeck/Animals Animals/Earth Scenes; t.r., b.r. Fred Bavendam/Peter Arnold, Inc.; c.l. Jeff J. Daly/Stock Boston; c.r. Pictor/Uniphoto/Image State; b.l. Breck P. Kent/Animals Animals/Earth Scenes. A98: t.l. Zig Leszczynski/Animals Animals/Earth Scenes; t.r. UNIPHOTO, Inc./Pictor/Image State; c.l. Norbert Wu/Peter Arnold, Inc.; c.r. Marilyn Kazmers/Dembinsky Photo Associates; b.l. Skip Moody/Dembinsky Photo Associates; b.r. Gary Meszaros/Bruce Coleman, Inc. A99: t.l. Darrell Gulin/CORBIS; t.c. Michael Newman/PhotoEdit; t.r. UNIPHOTO, Inc./Pictor/Image State; c.l. E.R. Degginger/Color-Pic, Inc.; c. Des & Jen Bartlett/Bruce Coleman, Inc.; c.r. Bob Cranston/Animals Animals/Earth Scenes; b.r. Rob Simpson/Pictor/Uniphoto/Image State. A101: Graham Pizzey/Bruce Coleman, Inc. A104: Rolf Kopfle/Bruce Coleman, Inc. A104-A105: John Gerlach/Dembinsky Photo Associates. A106: t., b.r. Stan W. Elems/Visuals Unlimited; b.l. L. West/Bruce Coleman, Inc. A106-A107: Stan W. Elems/Visuals Unlimited. A107: t. Stan W. Elems/Visuals Unlimited; b.l. E.R. Degginger/Color-Pic, Inc.; b.r. Rod Planck/Dembinsky Photo Associates. A108: Steve Kaufman/Peter Arnold, Inc. A109: Kim Taylor/Bruce Coleman, Inc. A110: l., r. E.R. Degginger/Color-Pic, Inc. A110-A111: D. Robert Franz/Bruce Coleman, Inc. A111: t.l. John Snyder/Bruce Coleman, Inc.; t.c. John Shaw/Bruce Coleman, Inc.; t.r. Skip Moody/Dembinsky Photo Associates; b. Erwin & Peggy Bauer/Bruce Coleman, Inc. A112: t. Randa Bishop/Pictor/Uniphoto/Image State; b., r. E.R. Degginger/Color-Pic, Inc. A113: l. The Image Bank/Getty Images; c. G.K. & Vikki Hart/PhotoDisc/Getty Images; r. Shoot Photography/Image State. A114: Stan Osolinski/Dembinsky Photo Associates. A115: Gerard Lacz/Animals Animals/Earth Scenes. A117: Stan W. Elems/Visuals Unlimited. A118: Photo C. Mike Hettwer, courtesy Project Exploration. A119: t. Dutheil Didier/CORBIS; b. Photo C Mike Hettwer, courtesy Project Exploration. BO: Tim Flach/Stone/Getty Images. B0-B1: Art Wolff/Stone/Getty Images. B1: Tim Flach/Stone/Getty Images. B2-B3: Lee Rentz/Bruce Coleman, Inc. B4-B5: Zig Leszczynski/Animals Animals/Earth Scenes. B8-B9: John Shaw/Bruce Coleman, Inc. B10: t. David J. Sams/Stock Boston; b.l. John Giustina/Bruce Coleman, Inc.; b.r. Joe McDonald/CORBIS. B11: Lee Rentz/Bruce Coleman, Inc. B12: t. Laura Riley/Bruce Coleman, Inc.; b. Robert M. Balou/Animals Animals/Earth Scenes. B13: PhotoDisc/Getty Images. B14: James Carmichael/Bruce Coleman, Inc. B15: Jeremy Woodhouse/PhotoDisc/Getty Images. B16-B17: Beverly Joubert/National Geographic Collection/Getty Images. B22: t. Gary Braasch/Stone/Getty Images; c. Larry West/Bruce Coleman, Inc.; b. Joe McDonald/Bruce Coleman, Inc. B22-B23: Scott Smith/Animals Animals. B23: Doug Wechsler/Animals Animals. B24: M.P.L. Fogden/Bruce Coleman, Inc. B24-B25: Mark Newman/Bruce Coleman, Inc. B26: t. David Overcash/Bruce Coleman, Inc.; b.l. Image Club; b.l. inset E.R. Degginger/Animals Animals; b.r. John Shaw/Bruce Coleman, Inc. B27: t. Lawrence Naylor/Photo Researchers, Inc.; b. Patty Murray/Earth Scenes. B30: t. Jeff Foote/Bruce Coleman, Inc.; b. John Pontier/Animals Animals. B32-B33: James Randklev/Stone/Getty Images. B34: l. John Shaw/Bruce Coleman, Inc.; r. B&C Calhoun/Bruce Coleman, Inc. B35: Jeff Foott/Bruce Coleman, Inc. B36: N.E. Swedberg/Bruce Coleman, Inc. B37: Joe McDonald/Animals Animals/Earth Scenes. B38: Buddy Mays/CORBIS. B39: t. Creation Captured/Index Stock Imagery; b. Steve Dunwell/Index Stock Imagery. B40: John H. Hoffman/Bruce Coleman, Inc. B42-B43: bkgd. Joe Sroka/Dembinsky Photo Associates; t. Lynn Funkhouser/Peter Arnold, Inc. B43: l. Kelvin Aitken/Peter Arnold, Inc.; r. Fred Bavendam/Peter Arnold, Inc. B46-B47: Kennan Ward/The Stock Market/CORBIS. B48-B49: John Shaw/Bruce Coleman, Inc. B56: E.R. Degginger/Earth Scenes. B59: Peter Beck/The Stock Market/CORBIS. B60: t. Bill Freeman/PhotoEdit; b.l. Tom Lang/CORBIS; b.c. Photodisc Blue/Getty Images; b.r. Alan L. Detrick/Photo Researchers, Inc. B61: l. Bob Krist/CORBIS; r. James A. Scherer/Mira.com. B62-B63: UNIPHOTO, Inc./Pictor/Image State. B64: t. Breck P. Kent/Earth Scenes; c. Lee Rentz/Rentl/Bruce Coleman, Inc.; b. Nigel J.H. Smith/Earth Scenes. B65: t.l. J.C. Carton/Bruce Coleman, Inc.; t.r. Eastcott/Momatiuk/Earth Scenes; b. M. Timothy O'Keefe/Bruce Coleman, Inc. B66: A. & M. Shah/Animals Animals. B67: Eastcott/Momatiuk/Earth Scenes. B68: Joe McDonald/Bruce Coleman, Inc. B68-B69: Joy Spurr/Bruce Coleman, Inc. B69: Jen & Des Bartlett/Bruce Coleman, Inc. B70: l. Jeff Foott/Bruce

Coleman, Inc.; r. John Shaw/Bruce Coleman, Inc. B71: t. Joe McDonald/CORBIS; b. E. & P. Bauer/Bruce Coleman, Inc. B72: PhotoDisc/Getty Images. B74: M. Newman/Bruce Coleman, Inc. B76: NASA. B76-B77: L. Lefkowitz/Getty Images. B78-B79: Gary Braasch/CORBIS. B79: Danny Lehman/CORBIS. B80: John Elk III/Bruce Coleman, Inc. B82: l. Steve Satushek/The Image Bank/Getty Images; r. David Falconer/Bruce Coleman, Inc. B83: l. John Lemker/Earth Scenes; r. Gibson Stock Photography. B85: l. E.R. Degginger/Earth Scenes; r. PhotoDisc/Getty Images. B86: t. S. Jonasson/Bruce Coleman, Inc.; b. E.R. Degginger/Earth Scenes. B88: Tom Bean/CORBIS. B88-B89: Bob Burch/Bruce Coleman, Inc. B91: b. John Elk III/Bruce Coleman, Inc. B94: t. Catherine Toft/University of California; b.l. Jennifer F. Brown/Sokia Calendar/University of California; b.r. Ken Timm Photography. B95: University of California. CO: Jules Cowan/Index Stock Imagery. C0-C1: Jules Cowan/Index Stock Imagery. C2-C3: Peter French/Bruce Coleman, Inc. C4-C5: AFB/CORBIS. C6: b. John D. Cunningham/Visuals Unlimited; inset Sinclair Stammers/Science Photo Library/Photo Researchers, Inc. C8-C9: Dr. E.R. Degginger/Color-Pic, Inc. C9: Stella Snead/Bruce Coleman, Inc. C10: t. Jeff Greenberg/Index Stock Imagery; b.l. Jerry Schad/Photo Researchers, Inc.; b.r. Jim Steinberg/Photo Researchers, Inc. C11: t. Zandria Muench Beraldo/CORBIS; b. Gilbert Grant/Photo Researchers, Inc. C12: Renee Lynn/Photo Researchers, Inc. C13: Terranova International/Photo Researchers, Inc. C14: t. NASA/PhotoTake; c. John Chumack/Photo Researchers, Inc.; b. Detlev van Ravenswaay/Photo Researchers, Inc. C18-C19: Walter Bibikow/Index Stock Imagery. C20: t. Mick Roessler/Index Stock Imagery; b. Jim Wark/Index Stock Imagery. C21: Yann Arthus-Bertrand/CORBIS. C22: b. Bob Krist/CORBIS; inset Jules Cowan/Index Stock Imagery. C23: Diaphor Agency/Index Stock Imagery. C24: NASA/Goddard Space Flght Center, The SeaWiFs Project and ORBIMAGE, Scientific Visualization Studio. C26: NASA. C27: Randy Faris/CORBIS. C28: Mark Mellett/Stock Boston. C28-C29: Dave Bartruff/Stock Boston. C29: l. Annie Griffiths Belt/CORBIS; r. Morton Beebe/CORBIS. C30-C31: bkgd. George D. Lepp/CORBIS. C32: t.l. E.R. Degginger/Photo Researchers, Inc.; t.c. Joyce Photographics/Photo Researchers, Inc.; b.c. Charles D. Winters/Timeframe Photography Inc./Photo Researchers, Inc.; t.r. George Whiteley/Photo Researchers, Inc.; b.r. Function Thru Form. C33: l. David Lees/CORBIS; c.l. Roberto De Gugliemo/Science Photo Library/Photo Researchers, Inc.; t.c. Kaj R. Svensson/Science Photo Library/Photo Researchers, Inc.; c.r. J.H. Robinson/Photo Researchers, Inc. C34: l. John D. Cunningham/Visuals Unlimited; c. Mark A. Schneider/Visuals Unlimited; r. Tom Pantages/PhotoTake. C35: A.J. Cunningham/Visuals Unlimited. C36: t. A.J. Copley/Visuals Unlimited; c. Joyce Photographics/Photo Researchers, Inc.; b. Ross Frid/Korner Gems, Traverse City, MI/Visuals Unlimited. C36-C37: Charles O'Rear/CORBIS. C37: Peter Aitken/Photo Researchers, Inc. C38: t. Richard T. Nowitz/Photo Researchers, Inc.; c.r. Color Image, Inc./SuperStock; b.l. David Young-Wolff/PhotoEdit/PictureQuest; b. inset A.J. Copley/Visuals Unlimited. C40-C41: Lee Rentz/Bruce Coleman, Inc. C42: l., r. Andrew J. Martinez/Photo Researchers, Inc.; c. Doug Sokell/Visuals Unlimited. C43: l. E.R. Degginger/Photo Researchers, Inc.; r. A.J. Copley/Visuals Unlimited. C44: t., b.l. Andrew J. Martinez/Photo Researchers, Inc.; t.c. Martin G. Miller/Visuals Unlimited; b.c. Joyce Photographics/Photo Researchers, Inc.; b.r. A.J. Copley/Visuals Unlimited. C45: bkgd. John D. Cunningham/Visuals Unlimited; t.l. Kjell B. Sandved/Photo Researchers, Inc.; b.l. Joyce Photographics/Photo Researchers, Inc. C46: t.l. Arthur R. Hill/Visuals Unlimited; t.r. L.S. Stepanowicz/Visuals Unlimited; b.l. E.R. Degginger/Photo Researchers, Inc.; b.r. Charles R. Belinky/Photo Researchers, Inc. C47: Michael P. Gadomski/Photo Researchers, Inc. C48: b.l. PhotoDisc/Getty Images; b.r., inset Joyce Photographics/Photo Researchers, Inc. C50: G. Büttner/Naturbild/OKAPIA/Photo Researchers, Inc. C51: l. Ron Spomer/Visuals Unlimited; r. Hilarie Kavanagh/Stone/Getty Images. C53: John Elk III/Stock Boston. C54: Dr. David Kring/Science Photo Library/Photo Researchers, Inc. C55: David A. Hardy/Science Photo Library/Photo Researchers, Inc. C57: Detlev van Ravenswaay/Photo Researchers, Inc. C58-C59: Paul Steel/The Stock Market/CORBIS. C60-C61: NASA. C62: PhotoDisc/Getty Images. C64: bkgd. Gary Withey/Bruce Coleman, Inc.; l. Phil Degginger/Color-Pic, Inc.; r. Hattie Young/Science Photo Library/Photo Researchers, Inc. C65: Simon Fraser/Science Photo Library/Photo Researchers, Inc. C66: NASA. C67: Chase Swift/CORBIS. C68: Lowell Georgia/CORBIS. C70-C71: IFA/Peter Arnold, Inc. C72: PhotoDisc/Getty Images. C73: Calvin Larsen/Photo Researchers, Inc. C76: Simon Fraser/Science Photo Library/Photo Researchers, Inc. C80: Lester V. Bergman/CORBIS. C82-C83: Dave G. Houser/PICTOR/Image State. C84: L. Lipsky/Bruce Coleman, Inc. C84-C85: VCG/FPG/Getty Images. C85: l. Jan Stromme/Bruce Coleman, Inc. C86: NASA/Tom Pantages. C87: Ira Rubin/Dembinsky Photo Associates. C88: Jeff Greenberg/PhotoEdit. C92: t. R&V Taylor/Bruce Coleman, Inc.; b. Emory Kristof/National Geographic/Getty Images. C93: Norbert Wu/Norbert Wu Productions. C94: t. Chinch Gryniewicz/Ecoscene/CORBIS; b. Fulvio Eccardi/Bruce Coleman, Inc. C95: PhotoLink/PhotoDisc/Getty Images. C96-C97: Royalty-Free/CORBIS. C97: t. Bettmann/CORBIS; b. Time Life Pictures/Getty Images. C98-C99: Ron Sherman/Stock Boston, Inc. C100: l. Phil Degginger/Color-Pic, Inc.; r. Joseph Nettis/Photo Researchers, Inc. C101: Ted Speigel/Bettmann/CORBIS. C104: t. Phil Degginger/Color-Pic, Inc.; b. Simon Fraser/Science Photo Library/Photo Researchers, Inc. C104-C105: Russell D. Curtis/Photo Researchers, Inc. C105: t. John Keating/Photo Researchers, Inc.; b. Kevin Schafer/Peter Arnold, Inc. C106: Patrick Grace/Photo Researchers, Inc. C107: Matt Meadows/Peter Arnold, Inc. C109: t. John Keating/Photo Researchers, Inc. C110: NOAA. C110-111: bkgd. NASA/Roger Ressmeyer/CORBIS. C111: Woods Hole Oceanographic Institution. DO: NOAA, colored by John Wells/Science Photo Library/Photo Researchers, Inc. D0-D1: World Perspectives/Stone/Getty Images. D2-D3: Courtesy NASA/JPL-CalTech. D4-D5: STSI/Photo Researchers, Inc. D10: Science VU/Visuals Unlimited. D11: UCO/Lick Observatory. D12: Pekka Parviainen/Dembinsky Photo Associates. D13: E. Karkoschka (Univ. of Az.)/NASA. D14-D15: Courtesy NASA/JPL-CalTech. D16: l. USGS/Photo Researchers, Inc.; c.l. NASA/Science Source/Photo Researchers, Inc.; c.r. NASA; r. USGS/Photo Researchers, Inc. D18: l. NASA/Photo Researchers, Inc.; r. Comstock Images/Alamy. D19: l. NASA and Erich Karkoschka, University of Arizona; c. JPL/NASA; r. NASA/PhotoTake/Alamy. D20: Ron Russell/Index Stock Imagery. D22: t. NASA/Digital Stock; c.r. NASA; b.l., b.r., c.l. JPL/NASA. D23: l. NASA; r. Photo Researchers, Inc. D25: Ron Russell/Index Stock Imagery. D26-D27: Steve Terrill/The Stock Market/CORBIS. D28: b. Price, R. -Surv. OSF/Animals Animals/Earth Scenes. D28-D29: G.L. Kooyman/Animals Animals/Earth Scenes. D33: Royalty-Free/CORBIS/Digital Stock. D34: l. Runk/Schoenberger/Grant Heilman Photography, Inc.; r. Yoav Levy/PhotoTake. D35: E.R. Degginger/Color-Pic, Inc. D36-D37: Wolfgang Kaehler/CORBIS. D42-D43: Bonnie Kamin/PhotoEdit. D44: t. A.J. Copley/Visuals Unlimited; c. Henry W. Robinson/Visuals Unlimited; b. Mark A. Schneider/Visuals Unlimited. D46: l. D. Cavagnaro/Visuals Unlimited; c.l. W. Banaszewski/Visuals Unlimited; c.r. Mark E. Gibson/Visuals Unlimited; r. Layne Kennedy/CORBIS. D47: t. Jeff J. Daly/Fundamental Photographs; b. Michael P. Gadomski/Dembinsky Photo Associates. D48: Runk/Schoenberger/Grant Heilman Photography, Inc. D50-D51: Royalty-Free/CORBIS/Digital Stock. D51: Sean Sexton/CORBIS. D52-D53: Vince Streano/CORBIS. D55: Superstock. D56: Torleif Svensson/The Stock Market/CORBIS. D58: NASA. D61: l. Paul A. Souders/CORBIS. D62-D63: c. PhotoDisc/Getty Images; inset Bill Frymire/Masterfile. D63: Charles D. Winters/Photo Researchers, Inc. D66-D67: Stephen Ingram/Animals Animals/Earth Scenes. D68-D69: Bertram G. Murray Jr./Animals Animals/Earth Scenes. D73: Charles Palek/Animals Animals/Earth Scenes. D74-D75: Peter Beck/Pictor/Uniphoto/Image State. D79: Science VU/Visuals Unlimited. D80: l. NOAA/Peter Arnold, Inc.; r. Carlos Guerrero for MMH. D82-D83: Arthur Gloor/Animals Animals/Earth Scenes. D87: Benelux Press/Index Stock. D88: Science VU/Visuals Unlimited. D89: Superstock. D90: t. Don Smetzer/Stone/Getty Images; b. Jeff Greenberg/PhotoEdit. D91: Frost Fair on the Thames, 1683-84, Hondius, Abraham Danielsz. (c.1625-95) / Museum of London, UK/www.bridgeman.co.uk. D93: Mark A. Schneider/Dembinsky Photo Associates. D94-D95: bkgd. Allan Davey/Masterfile; c. Tim Samaras, Brad Carter. EO: Roger Ressmeyer/CORBIS. E0-E1: Mark M. Lawrence/CORBIS. E2-E3: Christine Osborne/CORBIS. E4-E5: Michael T. Sedam/CORBIS. E11: t.l. Klaus Guldbrandsen/Science Photo Library/Photo Researchers, Inc.; t.r. George Bernard/Photo Researchers, Inc.; c.l. Chris McElcheran/Masterfile; c.r. Sinclair Stammers/Science Photo Library/Photo Researchers, Inc.; b.l. Buddy Mays/CORBIS; b.r. Wolfgang Kaehler/CORBIS. E13: Carl Purcell/Photo Researchers, Inc. E14: t. Phil Degginger/Color-Pic, Inc.; b.l. Kim Sayer/CORBIS; b.r. Phil Degginger/Color-Pic, Inc. E15: t.l. C Squared Studios/PhotoDisc/Getty Images. E16: t. Lawrence Livermore National Laboratory/Science Photo Library/Photo Researchers, Inc.; c. IBM Research/Peter Arnold, Inc.; b. National Railway of Japan/PhotoTake. E18-E19: Rod Plack/Photo Researchers, Inc. E20-E21: StockTrek/PhotoDisc/Getty Images. E22: t. Lowell Georgia/Photo Researchers, Inc.; b. Rich Treptow/Photo Researchers, Inc. E23: t.l. Science VU/Visuals Unlimited; t.r., b.l., b.c., b.r. Charles D. Winters/Photo Researchers, Inc.; t.c. Russ Lappa/Science Source/Photo Researchers, Inc. E24: t. Charles D. Winters/Photo Researchers, Inc.; b.l. Yoav Levy/PhotoTake; b.c.r. PhotoDisc; b.r. Bill Beatty/Visuals Unlimited. E25: David Taylor/Photo Researchers, Inc. E26: Colin Cuthbert/Photo Researchers, Inc. E28: t.l., t.r., b.c. Dr. E.R. Degginger/Color-Pic, Inc.; c.l. George Bernard/Photo Researchers, Inc.; c., c.r. Klaus Guldbrandsen/Science Photo Library/Photo Researchers, Inc.; b.l. Charles D. Winters/Photo Researchers, Inc.; b.r. Russ Lappa/Photo Researchers, Inc. E32: t.l., b. Christine Coscioni/CO2, Inc.; r. Leonard Lessin/Peter Arnold, Inc. E33: Mitch Hrdlicka/PhotoDisc/Getty Images. E34-E35: W.Wisniewski/Okapia/Photo Researchers, Inc. E36: l. Gordon Wiltsie/Peter Arnold, Inc.; c. Clyde H. Smith/Peter Arnold, Inc.; r. Jeff & Alexa Henry/Peter Arnold, Inc. E40 t.c. Carolina Biological Supply/PhotoTake; c. Christine L. Coscioni/CO2, Inc.; b.c., b. Charles D. Winters/Photo Researchers, Inc. E42: t. Richard Choy/Peter Arnold, Inc.; b.l. Jack Plekan/Fundamental Photographs; b.r. Image Port/Index Stock Imagery. E44: bkgd. Courtesy of SOHO/Extreme Ultraviolet Imaging

Telescope (EIT) consortium; inset Richard Cummins/CORBIS. E44-E45: The Goodyear Tire & Rubber Company. E48-E49: Paul A. Souders/CORBIS. E50-E51: Nathan Benn/CORBIS. E52: l. Charles D. Winters/Photo Researchers, Inc; r. Jacana/Photo Researchers, Inc. E53: t.l., t.r., b.l. Dr. Ed Degginger/Color-Pic, Inc.; c. Becky Luigart-Stayner/CORBIS; b.r. Phil Degginger/Color-Pic, Inc. E54: l., b.r. Phil Degginger/Color-Pic, Inc. E55: t. to b. 1., 2., 5. Phil Degginger/Color-Pic, Inc.; 3. Artville; 4. Jim Corwin/Photo Researchers, Inc.; 6. EyeWire/Getty Images. E56: Charles D. Winters/Photo Researchers, Inc. E56-E57: Phil Degginger/Color-Pic, Inc. E57: l. Richard Megna/Fundamental Photographs. E59: t. Joyce Photographics/Photo Researchers, Inc. E60-E61: S. Strickland/Naturescapes/Visuals Unlimited. E61: l. M.I. Walker/Photo Researchers, Inc. E64: Mark E. Gibson/Visuals Unlimited. E65: John Rizzo/Photodisc/Getty Images. E66: Larry Lefever/Grant Heilman Photography, Inc. E67: l. David R. Frazier/Photo Researchers, Inc.; t. David S. Addison/Visuals Unlimited. E68-E69: Nik Wheeler/CORBIS. E72: l. E.R. Degginger/Color-Pic, Inc. E73: b.l. Richard Megna/Fundamental Photographs; b.r. Lee Snyder/Photo Researchers, Inc. E74: t.l. Science VU/Visuals Unlimited; c.l. Christine L. Coscioni/CO2, Inc.; t.r., c.r. Leonard Lessin/Peter Arnold, Inc.; b. NASA. E76: b. Christine Coscioni/CO2, Inc. E78-E79: Henry Horenstein/Stock Boston. E79: bkgd. LSF OSF/Animals Animals/Earth Scenes; t. Michael Newman/PhotoEdit. E80-E81: Michael P. Gadomski/Photo Researchers, Inc. E82: l. Richard Megna/Fundamental Photographs; c.r. C Squared Studios/PhotoDisc/Getty Images; r. E.R. Degginger/Color-Pic, Inc. E83: Kristen Brochmann/Fundamental Photographs. E84: t. John D. Cunningham/Visuals Unlimited; l. Geoff Bryant/Photo Researchers, Inc. E85: t. Renee Lynn/Photo Researchers, Inc. E87: t. Dr. E.R. Degginger/Color-Pic, Inc. E88: Paul Silverman/Fundamental Photographs. E89: r. Tony Freeman/PhotoEdit. E90-E91: bkgd. Denise Mattia/Denise Mattia Underwater Photography. E96: l. Andrew McClenaghan/Photo Researchers, Inc.; r. Science VU/Visuals Unlimited. E97: Michael Dalton/Fundamental Photographs. E99: Bettmann/CORBIS. E101: Craig Lovell/CORBIS. E102: Jacqueline K. Barton. E102-E103: Nick Koudis/PhotoDisc. FO: Comstock, Inc. F0-F1: Paul J. Sutton/Duomo/CORBIS. F2-F3: Tom Sanders/The Stock Market/CORBIS. F4-F5: Annie Griffiths Belt/CORBIS. F7: Paul Silverman/Fundamental Photographs. F8: b. Neil Rabinowitz/CORBIS; inset NASA/Ed Degginger/Color-Pic, Inc. F9: t. Museum of Flight/CORBIS; c. Chris Trotman/Duomo Photography Inc.; b. Joe McDonald/CORBIS. F10: Bill Aron/Photo Researchers, Inc. F11: Jerry Wachter/Photo Researchers, Inc. F12: Peter Turnley/CORBIS. F13: t. Robert Mathena/Fundamental Photographs; b. George Lepp/CORBIS. F15: Photri/The Stock Market/CORBIS. F16-F17: Ed Kashi/CORBIS. F17: t.l. C Squared Studios/PhotoDisc/Getty Images; t.r. PhotoDisc/Getty Images. F20: t., b.c. Ed Degginger/Color-Pic, Inc.; t.c., b. Tony Freeman/PhotoEdit. F21: t. Ed Degginger/Color-Pic, Inc.; b. Phil Degginger/Color-Pic, Inc. F22: b. LBJ Space Center/NASA. F25: t. Paul A. Souders/CORBIS; c.l. Russ Schleipman/CORBIS; c.r. Peter Turnley/CORBIS; b. Kevin R. Morris/CORBIS. F26: t.l. RDF/Visuals Unlimited; t.c. Larry Mulvehill/Photo Researchers, Inc; t.r. Walley Eberhart/Visuals Unlimited; b.l. Gregg Occo/Visuals Unlimited; b.c. Eric Roth/FlashFocus/Index Stock Imagery; b.r. StockByte. F30: l. Royalty-Free/CORBIS; r. Comstock Images. F30-F31: David Martyn Hughes/images-of-france/Alamy. F32-F33: Philip Gendreau/Bettmann/CORBIS. F34-F35: G. Sauvage/Vandystadt/Photo Researchers, Inc. F36: J-L Charmet/Science Photo Library/Photo Researchers, Inc. F40: t.l. Petrified Collection/The Image Bank/Getty Images; t.r. Davis Barber/PhotoEdit; b. Kevin R. Morris/CORBIS. F41: NASA/Media Dallas. F42-F43: bkgd. JSC/NASA; b. ZERO/JSC/NASA. F45: NASA. F46-F47: Miro Vintoniv/Stock Boston. F48-F49: NASA/Galaxy Contact/Oxford Scientific Film and Photo Library. F50: Artville/PhotoDisc/Getty Images. F52: t. PhotoDisc/Getty Images; b. Ken Fisher/Stone/Getty Images. F54-F55: Ulrike Welsch/Ulrike Welsch Photography. F56: Artville/PhotoDisc/Getty Images. F57: Tim Davis/Photo Researchers, Inc. F58: t. William James Warren/CORBIS; b. Courtesy Alexander Graham Bell National Historic Park. F59: George Hall/CORBIS. F60: C Squared Studios/PhotoDisc/Getty Images. F61: Dr. Jeremy Burgess/Photo Researchers, Inc. F62-F63: Brenda Tharp/Photo Researchers, Inc. F64-F65: Kevin Fleming/CORBIS. F66: l. Ron J. Berard/Duomo/CORBIS; r. Brian Bahr/Allsport/Getty Images. F67: t. Marty Loken/Stone/Getty Images; b. Museum der Stadt, Vienna, Austria/ET Archive, London/SuperStock. F68: b. John M. Roberts/The Stock Market/CORBIS. F69: Wolfgang Kaehler/CORBIS. F72: t. Artville/PhotoDisc/Getty Images; b. Joseph Schuyler/Stock Boston. F73: Luc Novovitch/Liaison/Getty Images. F74: GCa/Science Photo Library/Photo Researchers, Inc. F74-F75: Jeffery Myers/Index Stock Imagery. F77: Artville/PhotoDisc/Getty Images. F78-F79: Steve Bloom/Taxi/Getty Images. F80-F81: Richard Cummins/CORBIS. F82: t. Arthur Morris/Visuals Unlimited; b. Robert Holmgren/Peter Arnold, Inc. F83: bkgd. Barb Gerlach/Visuals Unlimited; l. Rich Treptow/Visuals Unlimited; r. C.P. George/Visuals Unlimited. F85: Image courtesy of Barry Luokkala, Department of Physics, Carnegie Mellon University. F87: t. Paul Silverman/Fundamental Photographs. F88: b.l., inset Roger Ressmeyer/CORBIS. F91: Tony Freeman/PhotoEdit. F92: bkgd. Wolfgang Kaehler/CORBIS; b.l. Science Photo Library/Photo Researchers, Inc.; b.r. North Wind Picture Archives. F93: l. The Queens Borough Public Library, Long Island Division, Latimer Family Papers; r. The Schenectady Museum. F94-F95: Jack Plekan/Fundamental Photographs. F96: t. Science VU/Visuals Unlimited; c. Alfred Pasieka/Science Photo Library/Photo Researchers, Inc. F97: t. Jeff Greenberg/Visuals Unlimited. F98: t. Bill Beatty/Visuals Unlimited. F103: James Webb/PhotoTake. F106-F107: Jeremy Walker/Stone/Getty Images. F113: Ed Degginger/Color-Pic, Inc. F114-F115: NASA. F118: Bettmann/CORBIS. F119: Hewlett Packard/Fundamental Photographs. F120: b. PhotoDisc/Getty Images; inset Science VU/Visuals Unlimited. F121: Carolyn A. McKeone/Photo Researchers, Inc. F122: Science VU/Visuals Unlimited. F126: t. S.J. Gates/2003. The Center for String & Particle Theory; b. Mehau Kulyk/Science Photo Library/Photo Researchers, Inc. F126-F127: Space Telescope Science Institute/NASA. R1: ThinkStock/SuperStock. R10: t.r. Jim Harrison/Stock Boston/PictureQuest. R14: l. bkgd. PhotoDisc/Getty Images; l. inset G.R. Roberts/Photo Researchers, Inc. R15: map Accuweather/NASA. R20: David Madison/Getty Images. R31: Ingram/PictureQuest. R39: Lester V. Bergman/CORBIS.